The Best P

SOUTH AMERICA

Volume I

CHILE, PERU, ECUADOR, COLOMBIA & BOLIVIA

Alex Newton

HUNTER
PUBLISHING INC

Hunter Publishing, Inc.
300 Raritan Center Parkway
Edison NJ 08818
(908) 225 1900

ISBN 1-55650-696-1

Cover photograph:
Keel-billed toucan, Kevin Schafer & Martha Hill
Global Pictures

Black & white sketches throughout book: *Fernando Molina*

About Alex Newton

Alex Newton hails from Madison, Georgia, a small town that, as legend goes, Sherman spared on his famous march to the sea in 1864. Since graduating from Brown University, Duke Law School and the New School for Social Research, and surviving a four-year stint in New York City with one of the major law firms there, he has spent most of his years abroad. Starting as a Peace Corps volunteer in Guatemala, he later worked as a labor representative in Togo and went on to become a development specialist for the US Agency for International Development in Maui, the Ivory Coast and, now, Bangladesh. While in Ecuador, he quickly grew to appreciate the fascinating hotels there, many of which were centuries-old *haciendas* that had been converted into hotels, some astonishingly cheap, whence came the inspiration for this guide. He is married to Betsy Wagenhauser, a professional photographer, writer, adventure travel guide and one of the foremost authorities on travel in South America. They have one child, Nicola, born during the writing of this book.

Acknowledgements

First of all, I would like to thank my wife, Betsy Wagenhauser, of South American Explorers Club fame, for putting up with my having to spend many late-night hours, on both weekdays and weekends, in front of the computer, typing away, searching for the right word or phrase to describe a place or experience. Your patience is as incredible as your wit. I'd also like to thank Fernando Molina, a young professional artist from Quito, for the many wonderful drawings in this guide. There really are certain limits to words, and these drawings are a tremendous help in bringing alive the general ambience of the hotels herein. Finally, I would like to thank Mr. Hunter for recognizing the potential contribution of this book to travelers' overall enjoyment in visiting South America. Perhaps more than is generally acknowledged even by intrepid travelers to this region, hotels themselves in South America can be objects of great interest and sources of joy. So, thank you Mr. Hunter, for allowing me to demonstrate this.

Dedication

To my infant daughter, Nicola.
May your future be as bright and happy as the twinkling of your eyes and the cheeriness of your smile would suggest, and may your life be useful and helpful to others, as I hope this book is.

Contents

BOLIVIA 5

La Paz 7
The South 13
Cochabamba 13
Sucre 18
Potosí 22
The East 24
Santa Cruz 24
Lake Titikaka 31
Copacabana 31
Yungas Valley 34
Chulumani, Coroico & Sorata 34
Northern Amazon Region 37
Rurrenabaque 37

CHILE 41

Santiago 43
Around Santiago 50
Viña Del Mar 50
Portillo 55
Pelequén 57
The North 58
Arica 58
Iquique 61
Antofagasta 66
The South 68
Concepción 68
Temuco 70
Villarrica 73
Pucón 76
Valdivia 80
Osorno 82
Lake Puyehue 85
Puerto Octay, Frutillar & Puerto Varas 86
Ralún, Ensenada, Petrohué & Peulla 91
Puerto Montt 97
Chiloé Island 100
Ancud 100

Castro 102
Easter Island 104

COLOMBIA 107

Bogotá 109
Eastern-Central Region 118
Paipa-Lake Sochagota 118
Villa De Leyva 120
Sogamoso-Duitama 123
Western Central Region 127
Giradot 127
Medellín 130
Cali 134
Buenaventura 139
Popayán 140
San Agustín 144
Southern Region 146
Pasto 146
Coastal Region 151
Cartagena 151
Barranquilla 157
Santa Marta 162
El Rodadero 162
San Andrés Island 166

ECUADOR 173

Quito 175
Northern Highlands Region 183
Otavalo & Cotacachi 183
Ibarra 188
Central Highlands Region 192
Latacunga 192
Baños 195
Riobamba 198
Cuenca 200
Around Cuenca 203
Vilcabamba 203
Coastal Region 205
Guayaquil 205
Salinas & Beaches To The North 209
Esmeraldas & Atacames-Same 213
Santo Domingo 216

Amazon Basin Region 219
Coca & Misahualli 219
The Galapagos Islands 224

PERU 227

Lima 229
The North 240
Trujillo 240
Cajamarca 242
Huaraz 244
The South 248
Paracas 248
Ica 250
Nazca 252
Arequipa 255
The East 258
Cuzco 258
The Sacred Valley Of The Incas 263
Machu Picchu 267
Puno 270
Tambopata Wildlife Reserve & Manu National Park 273
Iquitos 277

Introduction

One of the unnappreciated highlights of traveling around South America is the opportunity to stay at an array of fascinating hotels. They range from friendly and inexpensive bed and breakfasts, with cozy living rooms and knick-knacks adorning the walls, to picturesque *haciendas* and monasteries, some dating back to the 17th century. Many of these have been converted into charming small hotels or rustic trout-fishing lodges nestled in the forests, and some remain as grand majestic beauties with marble floors, high ceilings, huge glass chandeliers and accommodations fit for royalty. Throughout the rest of the world, staying at such places will cost you, relatively speaking, an arm and a leg. In South America, however, prices are frequently so low that you cannot afford to miss staying at one of these glorious establishments. Quito, Ecuador, for example, has been rated as one of the cheapest capital cities in the world to live and you can spend a night in a luxurious 17th-century hotel here for under $30. Lima, Peru and Bogotá, Colombia are also near the top of this list and, again, you can find any number of wonderful places to stay for a night or two without breaking the bank.

South American countries also have a large number of old colonial buildings that now serve as hotels. The result of staying at one of these is that, rather than just finding a place to bed down for the night, you enjoy a more complete experience of being swept away with the history and culture of these lands. In many places the owners are so friendly and knowledgeable about the local area that they'll contribute enormously to your trip, offering tips on how to get around and often sharing their home-cooked dinner with you at the kitchen table! All that for as little as $10 a night.

While many modern establishments are listed herein, I have a penchant for older hotels with character. In some cases what stands out in my mind may be the exceptional service; in other cases it may be the history or architecture; sometimes it's simply the "feel" of the lobby and communal rooms. Other lodgings may be listed for the fact that the owners themselves are the "character." Just meeting Edward of Edward's Inn, a cheap backpackers' haven at the foot of the spectacular Cordillera Blanca in Peru, is reason enough to spend a night there. One of my favorite places is an old *hacienda* in the highlands of Colombia where you can fall asleep to the sound of trickling water as it makes its way around the hotel's grounds. Finding such atmospheric hotels, however, is not so easy. The descriptions of accommodation choices in most guidebooks are often vague and rather neutral in tone, making it difficult to pick one hotel out from another. This guide, on the other hand, is intentionally selective, profiling the best offered. Almost all of these recommendations are followed by alternative selections in case a given hotel is full or there is something about it that makes it unsuitable for you.

Hotels are also listed by class (and, thus, by price range) with one or more recommendations in each category. If you find yourself in Cuzco, Peru, choices range from a deluxe hotel, which was once Pizarro's residence, to a tiny inn just off the main plaza, where the guest rooms feature original Inca walls. The choice is yours and, with the help of this guide, you can pick something that meets your budget and fills your needs. In some towns none of the hotels are particularly noteworthy; even in these cases, however, you will find the best of the lot.

This guide is comprehensive, covering over 60 cities and towns in Peru, Bolivia, Colombia, Peru and Ecuador. Volume 2 of this series covers Venezuela, Brazil, Paraguay, Uruguay, and Argentina.

Since hotels have been categorized by class/quality, some explanation of the division is in order. The four categories used are intended to reflect the *quality*, rather than the prices. Unfortunately, prices do not always serve as an accurate guideline for the class of service offered (you will notice this particularly when comparing urban and rural areas).

- Deluxe – *resorts, grand old establishments and modern hotels (comparable to Inter-Continental).*

- A – *perhaps an old estate with plenty of character or a newer hotel with good amenities (similar to a Holiday Inn).*

- B – *typically a small B&B or a modern low-budget motel/hotel (rather like an Econo-Lodge).*

- C – *cheap places suitable for backpackers (comparable to youth hostels). This category is not covered extensively here, as many other guides deal exclusively with ultra-low-budget options.*

At any hotel you may be given the choice of rooms *de lujo* (deluxe) or *sencilla* (single). Be sure to find out what each offers before making the decision to save a few dollars! You may be surprised.

Prices shown throughout this book are in US dollars. Readers should be aware that rates may fluctuate along with the exchange rate.

A final word. The great majority of hotels listed here have been around for many years and, while other establishments may rise and fall, these will almost certainly be in business for years to come. Five years from now, having stood the test of time, they will still offer the visitor hospitality, history and some of the most exquisite places to stay on this earth. You can still expect them to be the best in their area.

Bolivia

Bolivia is a country of many geographical contrasts and the most rugged country in the Andes. The only major cities that can be driven to from La Paz by paved road are Cochabamba, Copacabana and Santa Cruz. Fortunately, the dirt roads are in good condition, so driving to cities such as Sucre is not a problem – just time consuming. Flying is frequently an option. La Paz, the capital, is located in a huge canyon which starts at 4,018 meters/13,187 feet in the El Alto district. It is here that the airport (the highest commercial one in the world) is situated. The canyon descends through the heart of town and down to around 3,350 meters/11,000 feet, where some of the nicer residential sections can be found. It's a fascinating city, with a wide boulevard through the heart, numerous old colonial buildings, and wonderful markets for shopping.

There are some good weekend-excursion possibilities from the city, including north-west to Lake Titikaka and Copacabana, which are located on the Bolivian altiplano at 14,000 feet, and north to the Yungas Valley, in particular Chulumani, Coroico and Sorata. All three of these towns are in a temperate climatic zone and sit in the traditional coca-growing area of the Aymara and Quechua Indians. Copacabana is the principal town on the Bolivian side of Lake Titikaka. The best time to visit it is during the warm summer months or, if you have the chance, February 1-2, when people come from both Peru and Bolivia to celebrate the Feast Day of the Virgin with dancing and singing. If you haven't made a hotel reservation, however, you'll never find a place to stay during the festival. Taking a reed boat out on the lake is a must, but be prepared for some chilly breezes whipping over the near-freezing water.

Chulumani, Coroico and Sorata are all small towns and are surrounded with mountains and deep valleys. There are all kinds of lodgings here, from classy hotels on the outskirts of town with swimming pools and breathtaking views, to small, family-run B&Bs, typically near the center of town. The areas around these towns, as well as the Inca Trail in the altiplano, are the best in the country for hiking. Further north in the Amazon lowlands are some small, riverside communities such as Rurrenabaque, from where you can take a motorized canoe to nearby jungle camps run by travel agencies in La Paz. Hiking through the rainforests, fishing for pirana, swimming in the warm rivers, bird watching, and looking for crocodiles at night are some of the highlights of trips to these hot and humid areas.

Heading south from La Paz you'll come to Cochabamba, the country's second largest city, with over 1 million inhabitants. It's a pleasant city set in a valley at 2,570 meters/8,435 feet, and offers a noticeably warmer climate than that of La Paz. While there's little of interest to see in the city itself, there are a number of nearby attractions, including Indian villages. If you head about an hour's drive on the paved road towards Santa Cruz, known as the "cocaine highway," you'll come to the Chapare region, where 80% of the coca used for making cocaine is grown. Not the safest area to visit, especially at night.

Further south by dirt road is Sucre, the country's legal capital and its most beautiful city. Unlike Cochabamba, which has few buildings of interest, Sucre is loaded with architectural gems. Yet it's not a museum; the old and the new blend quite well here, producing an interesting and vibrant city. From here you can head off to Tarabuco (40 miles/64km), which every Sunday has one of the most colorful markets in all of South America – not to be missed.

Not far away is Potosí which, at 4,070 meters/13,358 feet, is the highest city of its size in the world. Founded by the Spanish in 1545 as a mining center, it quickly became world-famous for its silver. Along with the mines came appalling working conditions and, over the ages, some eight million people have died mining silver here. Today, Potosí is something of a grim backwater town, but it does have a picturesque central area. If you decide to visit here, you'll definitely want to take a trip out to the mines. Getting to them is easy, and guides are plentiful.

The country's fastest growing city, and now its third largest, is Santa Cruz. This is a typical Wild West town that grew from being little more than a village in 1950, to a substantial town with over 600,000 inhabitants today. The original attraction was the lowland area used for farming and cattle ranching; more recently it has become the country's cocaine trafficking center. So it's now a rich city with relatively high prices, fancy hotels, and little or no unemployment. There's not much to see in this flat, hot and humid city, but for overland travelers it's the starting point for the long trip to Brazil.

La Paz

HOTEL PLAZA
Paseo del Prado 1789
Phone (02) 378317/378311
Fax (02) 343391
Telex 2674
Category: Deluxe
Sleek highrise, 180 rooms, indoor pool, sauna, shops, disco, travel agency, handicraft and sweater shop.
Rates: $91/$106 S/D, incl. tax. All major credit cards.
Directions: In the center on the Prado, which is the main drag and promenade.

For years, this sleek, imposing highrise in the heart of town has been the city's finest hotel. The raw concrete and dark glass create one of the most intriguing facades among the city's modern buildings. The Plaza's hallmark, however, is its service, which is tops in La Paz, plus the staff is totally bilingual. Inside, you'll find a tastefully restrained lobby done in wood, marble, and beige tones, with a huge Indian tapestry behind the reception. The ambience here is vibrant, a key sign that this place retains its leading position. On the ground floor and below are most of the shops, among which is a branch of Millma, which sells some of the finest and most expensive alpaca sweaters in the city, as well as Bolivian handicrafts and weavings. Additional facilities at the hotel include a small indoor heated pool, a sauna, an exercise room, Plaza Tours travel agency, a gift shop, a piano bar, a disco, and a public dry cleaning establishment. Whether or not you stay here, be sure to check out the **Penthouse Bar** which offers fabulous views of Mt. Ilimani, particularly at sunset. There's also a fine international restaurant on the top floor; Lake Titikaka trout is the specialty.

The accommodations here are standard size with twin or king beds, blue carpeting, beige curtains, plain white walls, dressing tables with matching mirrors, breakfast tables, TVs with cable (including all major US networks), walk-in closets, Indian tapestries on the walls, bright fabrics and brass lamps. The tile bathrooms have long, marble counters, combination baths, and telephones and are well stocked with shampoo and other toiletries. The units in the front can be a bit noisy, so ask for one in the back. While the rooms are well designed, the hotel's high standards are beginning to slip ever so slowly; a refurbishing, however, could reverse this trend.

If you're looking for a place to eat outside the hotel and you like Japanese food, try the restaurant at the **Japanese Cultural Center** at Calle Batallones Colorados 172. It caters to its local Japanese members, but is open to the public for lunch and dinner. Leaving the hotel, you'll find it around the corner to your left and at the end of the street on your right. The meals, which include sushi, teriyaki and tempera among other dishes, are terrific and cost under $10. It makes an excellent spot for lunch.

Alternative: **HOTEL LA PAZ**
Avenida Arce, phone/fax (02) 356950, telex 3275
Rates: $88/$111 S/D, incl. tax. All major credit cards.
Directions: On the same street as the Plaza, but further from the center in the Sopocachi district.

Formerly a Sheraton and still known as such, the La Paz, which reopened in 1994 after being refurbished, is trying to win back clients from the more popular Hotel Plaza. This glass and concrete structure, which is typical of the Sheraton style, remains the city's largest, with 345 rooms. The facilities include a pool, an elegant restaurant on top with fine views, a small gym, a sauna, shops and a disco. The rooms are top quality, with large beds, TVs, tile combination baths and, most important, heating.

If you stay here, head to **Prontos** for dinner. This New York-style Italian restaurant is two blocks away on Calle Jauregui 2248 and is very moderately priced; pasta is the specialty. Several other possibilities, all highly recommended and not cheap, are the ever-popular **Charlie's II**, an excellent Italian restaurant facing Plaza Isabel la Católica, **Restaurante Montesano**, which is a more expensive Italian restaurant at Calle Sanchez Lima 2329 near plaza Abaroa, and **El Arriero** at Avenida 6 de Agosto 2535. The latter is an Argentine churrasquería which serves excellent Argentine meat and wines.

HOTEL GLORIA

Calle Potosí 909
Phone (02) 370010/1/2
Fax (02) 324512
Telex 5536
Category: A
Modern highrise, central location, 90 rooms, two restaurants, parking, money exchange.
Rates: $36/$47 S/D incl. tax. AmEx accepted.
Directions: One block off the Prado and 2 blocks from the tourist market area.

The best hotel in the medium price range is unquestionably the Gloria, which is particularly popular with Latin business people because of its moderate prices, location in the heart of the business district, and good service at all levels. Tourists seem to like it as well. The small lobby won't win any design awards but it's functional and has attractive, dark stone floors and a lounge area with sofas and chairs in garish colors, a TV, plants, and interesting wall hangings, including some local weavings. An electronic screen provides information to guests. Business people in particular will appreciate the fact that there are secretarial services, fax and telex facilities, 24-hour room service, same-day laundry service, and money change facilities.

There are two restaurants: the **Naranjos** restaurant which serves a very popular vegetarian lunch buffet for $2; and a more formal dining room near the top which is slightly more expensive but offers spectacular views of the city and Mt. Illimani. The food at the latter is quite good and offers native dishes such as *pejerrey a la criolla* (mackerel), *aji de lengua* (tongue with chili pepper sauce), *picante mixto* (mixed hot spices), and *sajta de pollo* (chicken smothered in onions and tomatoes with a hot sauce). Their special soup, *sopa Illimani*, is delicious and made with lots of vegetables, bits of beef and an egg on top. Among the numerous international selections are coq au vin, canneloni, fettuccini Alfredo with chicken, and eggs with Russian sauce and caviar. Their grilled Titikaka trout, however, is the specialty of the house and quite delicious.

The accommodations are on the small side, but are well maintained and have central heating, thick pile carpets, TVs, comfortable beds with colorful plush bedspreads, good lighting, desks, curtains which keep out all sunlight, and small bathrooms with tile floors, marble-top counters, large mirrors, thick towels, and combination baths. There are also some less expensive singles which are quite small and cramped, with showers only and no mirrors in the rooms.

HOTEL ELDORADO

Avenida Villazón
Phone (02) 363-355/403
USA phone (800) 223-5652 (SRS Reservation Service)
Telex 5531
Category: A
80-room modern highrise, central location, restaurant, bar, laundry.
Rates: $25/$35 S/D incl. breakfast & tax; children under 6 free. AmEx accepted.
Directions: In the heart of town on the main drag, near the Plaza Hotel.

A less expensive alternative to the Gloria is the Eldorado, which is efficient, clean, well maintained and offers very good value for money. As a result, it's fairly popular with European tour groups. Built in the late 1970's, it's a modern, 12-story hotel in the heart of town on the main drag and very presentable, though totally lacking in local color. The small lobby, for example, has a marble floor, vinyl-covered chairs and sofa, fresh flowers, a TV, and music in the background. Similarly, the modest restaurant with its vinyl-covered chairs, plain tablecloths, unadorned white walls, and thin red carpeting, is totally uninspired and offers only views of the street. The food is likewise unimaginative but quite adequate and moderately priced; the four-course menu of the day costs about $5. On the menu, which is fairly extensive, you'll find grilled trout in butter sauce, *pejerrey al vino* (mackerel in wine sauce), chicken with hot sauce, cannelonis, ravioli with parmesan cheese, and broiled Argentine steak.

The best feature of the Eldorado besides its efficient service is the rooms, which are on a par with those of the higher-priced Gloria. They have color TVs, phones, comfortable but narrow twin beds, undecorated but freshly painted walls, thick shag rugs, comfortable reading chairs, breakfast tables, good lighting, central heating, large closets, and decent tile bathrooms with adequate counter space, large towels, and combination baths.

First Alternative: **HOTEL LIBERTADOR**
Calle Obispo Cardenas 1421, phone (02) 343360/362510, telex 2552
Rates: $27/$35 S/D incl. breakfast & tax. AmEx credit card is accepted.
Directions: In the center, 3 blocks north of the Prado and 3 blocks east of the main square, Plaza Murillo.

An equally good, similarly-priced alternative is the Libertador, which is a 12-story, 53-room highrise dating from 1973. It's on a quiet side street near the business district and is well patronized by foreigners, especially Europeans. The lobby is a bit shabby and the restaurant is plainly decorated but, overall, the hotel is in better condition than many of its competitors plus you can eat here cheaply and well. In addition, the management is very helpful and will offer to store luggage. The guest rooms have decent beds, worn carpets, central heating, TVs, ample closet space, and artistically tiled bathrooms, some with combination baths. Many units also have fine views of the city or Mt Illimani.

Second Alternative: **HOTEL CRILLON**
Plaza Isabel la Católica 2478, phone (02) 352121/30, telex 3275
Rates: $23/$30 S/D incl. tax. AmEx is accepted.
Directions: On the main drag, but a good km from the center in a residential area.

This 10-story, apartment-like structure overlooks a small plaza and is one of the city's better mid-range hotels, with a pleasant, tranquil ambience and probably the best restaurant compared to those offered at similarly-priced hotels. However, because of its less central location, it's not a top choice, even though taxis are easy to find and good restaurants are nearby. Amenities include a travel agency, several shops, a beauty parlor, and a baby-sitting service. The rooms are standard size, carpeted and have comfortable queen beds, central heating, decent old furnishings, private baths (some with tubs), and many have views of the plaza.

RESIDENCIAL ROSARIO
Calle Illampu 704
Phone (02) 325348/326531
Fax (02) 375532
Telex 3639
Category: B-C
Colonial style, 48 rooms, restaurant, luggage deposit, travel agency, book exchange, sauna, jacuzzi, laundry.
Rates: $8/$9 S/D with shared baths incl. tax ($16 private bath). No credit cards.
Directions: Near handicraft market, 5 blocks behind San Francisco Cathedral and 1 block from Plaza Eguino.

For the money, ambience and good food, you simply can't beat the Rosario, which is in an old colonial building that has been extensively remodeled. It's by far the most popular lower-end hotel in the city and the one most often suggested by virtually every organization or publication that recommends modestly priced hotels for its members or readers. As a result, the clientele here is almost entirely European and North American. The rooms are fairly small and nothing special although they are definitely adequate – attractive wooden floors, plain white walls, telephones, squeaky beds, overhead light bulbs, plain wooden chairs and tables. There are also eight common baths that are clean and have showers with electric heating elements. The more expensive units have private baths.

What's special about the Rosario is the atmosphere, not the rooms. The quick, cheerful service, and the facilities, are unusually extensive for a cheap hotel: an immensely popular restaurant, a travel agency which gives 10% discount to hotel guests, a good book exchange, next-day laundry service, luggage storage, even a sauna and jacuzzi. The hotel's new restaurant, the **Tambo Colonial**, is excellent but not cheap. It specializes in Titikaka trout, which is relatively expensive, and vegetarian and pasta dishes. It also offers a salad bar, French toast, granola with yogurt and fruit, and some exotic concoctions such as *Vienessa* (ice cream, coffee and whipped cream). Most recently, the restaurant has added a new feature – live music during the evening.

If you come here during the peak tourist season, June through August, you should reserve in advance; otherwise you're likely to find this place full. And ask for a room in the back as those near the foyer are a bit noisy.

First Alternative: **HOSTAL REPUBLICA**
Calle Commercio 1455, phone (02) 357966
Rates: $8/$10 S/D incl. tax ($10/$16 S/D with private bath). Discounts for longer stays. Credit cards not accepted.
Directions: At the corner of Commercio and Bueno, 3 blocks east of the main square, Plaza Murillo, and just back of Hotel Libertador. A 10- to 15-minute walk from the Rosario, which is on the opposite side of the Prado.

If the ever-popular Rosario is full and you're looking for a place with a colonial feel, try the República, formerly the residence of one of the country's presidents. A picturesque colonial house with a central courtyard, it has a friendly staff, a café where breakfast is served, laundry service, stored luggage service, and very clean, similarly-priced rooms with private baths and hot showers. Units with common baths are cheaper.

Second Alternative: **HOTEL SAGARNAGA**
Calle Sagárnaga 326, phone (02) 350252/358757, fax (02) 360831, telex 3605
Rates: $11/$14 S/D incl. tax & very basic breakfast. Credit cards not accepted.
Directions: Between San Francisco Cathedral and Residencial Rosario.

If the Rosario is full and you'd prefer a convenient place in the same area, try the Sagárnaga, which is two blocks away and closer to the center of town. A long-standing hotel with an English-speaking staff, it has 35 decent rooms with phones, carpets, TVs, and private, hot-shower bathrooms as well as some rooms with shared baths for about a third less. There's also a restaurant and bar, a travel agency, a laundry service, and direct-dial, international telephone. Just two blocks away at Calle Sagárnaga 161, across from the cathedral, you'll find Peña Naira, which has one of the best *peña* (bar) shows in town, but is geared to tourists. The nightly shows start around 10:30 p.m. and cost about $5 a person with drink.

The South

Cochabamba

PORTALES HOTEL
Avenida Pando 1271
Phone (042) 48507/48897
Fax (042) 42071
Telex 6370
Category: Deluxe
Modern, 3 stories, 76 rooms, pool, racketball, sauna, jacuzzi, gym, shops.
Rates: $64/$78 S/D incl. tax & breakfast. AmEx & Visa accepted.
Directions: 3 km from the center in a residential area.

The Portales is Cochabamba's finest hotel and the scene of frequent marriage receptions and birthday celebrations of the city's elite families (some of whom are undoubtedly connected with the city's notorious cocaine business). The hotel is named after the incredible, Newport-like mansion next door, which is now a museum called the Centro Cultural de Portales. Whether or not you stay at the Portales, make a point of visiting the museum. As you enter the hotel's elegant lobby, with its chandeliers, black marble floors and walls, and expensive wood trim, you'll appreciate why the locals give this place five stars. Flanking the lobby is the equally impressive main sitting room, which has a two-story ceiling, huge glass chandeliers, large mirrors, black leather sofas, oriental rugs, brass trim and a fireplace.

On weekend evenings, you're likely to hear music coming from out back. A dance band plays then, alongside the popular pool, emitting peppy sounds that flow throughout the hotel. This three-story brick complex is attractive and well designed so that all of the rooms have bay windows facing the pool and the grassy area surrounding it. During the day, this central area is very active; many guests can be seen hanging out around the kidney-shaped pool, swimming and soaking up rays. Guests have other options for exercise aside from swimming: racketball, working out at the gym, relaxing in the sauna or jogging in the surrounding posh, residential district. All three of the hotel's restaurants face the pool. One is fancy in line with the lobby and main reception room. Another, the **Jatata**, is less formal, with a thatched roof, an exposed-beam, A-frame ceiling, wicker furnishings, red tile floors, plus a long bar at one end. Breakfast is served here as well as at the snackbar.

The only problem with the rooms is that they are a bit small and definitely don't rate five stars. Try to get one with a queen-size bed as the twin beds are so narrow you'll think that with one turn, you'd fall off! Otherwise, the accommodations are fine, with comfortable reading chairs, carpets, satellite TVs, minibars, heating and air conditioning, and very nice tile bathrooms with combination baths. The morning hours are particularly nice: when you push back the curtains from the attractive, wood-framed bay window, sunlight will fill your room, welcoming you to a new day.

Alternative: **HOTEL ARANJUEZ**
Avenida Buenos Aires E-0563, phone (042) 41935/80076, fax (042) 40158

Those who prefer small hotels should check the new Aranjuez, which is only two blocks away and slightly less expensive. It's a cozier, colonial-style hotel and, although it has fewer amenities, offers a bar with jazz musicians at night on weekends as well as plush rooms and a good restaurant.

GRAN HOTEL COCHABAMBA
Plaza Ubaldo Anze
Phone (042) 82551/2
Fax (042) 82558
Telex 6314
Category: A
Old style, 50 rooms, pool, tennis, gardens.
Rates: $30/$43 S/D incl. tax & breakfast. AmEx & Visa accepted.
Directions: One block from Hotel Los Portales.

For grand, old-style ambience, the Cochabamba can't be beat in all of Bolivia. It's over 45 years old, but is well maintained and has been recently remodeled. The two-story, white structure has a very plain, unimposing facade. Inside, it's a bit more interesting, with a tiled lobby floor, a number of high quality, modern paintings by local artists and a popular, carpeted card room complete with a fireplace. Further back you'll come to the restaurant, which offers good views of the central patio and pool beyond. The decor here is nothing special, but the silverware has the hotel's initials in the grand old style and, more important, the meals, although somewhat expensive, are quite good – especially the bread, which is excellent. The chicken *a la Española* is one of the specialties of the house and quite tasty, but not outstanding. There are many other choices, however, including chicken with chili pepper *a la Peruana*, trout with black butter sauce, noodles *à la Parisienne*, lobsters Greek style, chateaubriand with mushrooms, Peruvian ceviche, and sea bass.

If you continue further towards the rear, you'll come to the rooms, all of which open onto a walkway or second-floor balcony facing a grassy courtyard with several palm trees, lots of flowers, and a delightful octagonal gazebo in the center; those in the know have their breakfasts and afternoon tea brought to them here. This small gazebo with about eight wicker chairs is also a wonderful place for relaxing, talking or reading. Back of it is the hotel's private rectangular pool, which is long enough for doing laps and popular on weekends. Further back still are two clay tennis courts, which are lighted and well used, plus a picturesque, old-style garden with stone seats at all four corners.

The accommodations are fairly plain, with ordinary furnishings, but are larger than those at the Portales, with higher ceilings too. They come with comfortable beds, industrial carpets, color TVs, telephones, lighted walk-in closets, and large tile bathrooms with combination baths and old facilities in good working condition. None of the standard units have heating or air conditioning, but in this delightful climate at 8,000 feet such amenities aren't really necessary.

If you tire of the hotel's food and you like grilled meat, head for **La Estancia**, which is on a side street just off the same plaza and serves excellent steaks and grilled fish, or, better, **Los Troncos**, which is not far away at Calle Junín 942. Open every day and extremely popular, this *churrasquería* (grill) has a breezy, somewhat rustic atmosphere, with about 10 grilled-meat selections, several choices of fish, and a salad bar. For a place with greater variety, try **La Suiza** at Avenida Ballivían 820; it has many international dishes and is also good value.

***Alternative:* GRAN HOTEL AMBASSADOR**
Calle España 349, phone (042) 48777/48781, fax 28778
Rates: $25/$35 S/D incl. tax. AmEx is accepted.
Directions: In the center, 3 blocks north of the main drag, Avenida Heroinas.

If you prefer to be in the center, your best bet is the Ambassador, which is far less inviting than the Cochabamba, but as good as you'll find downtown. The seven-story, 105-room structure has a dirty, aged facade but is modern and well maintained inside. The lobby is spacious and functional, with a tile floor flanked by a comfortable sitting area and a restaurant with a continental menu. The rooms come with modest furnishings, carpets, telephones, color TVs with video channels, closets, and modern tile baths with showers.

HOTEL BOSTON
Calle 25 de Mayo 167
Phone (042) 28530/24421
Category: B
Modern-looking, 32 rooms, 4 stories, central location, restaurant, laundry.
Rates: $14/$23 S/D incl. tax. No credit cards.
Directions: In the center of town, 1 block off the main drag.

The remodeled Hotel Boston is a very well-maintained older hotel in the heart of town with a friendly staff that looks after guests well. It's quite popular and often fully booked. Outside, the hotel's plain exterior is hardly inviting; inside, the ambience is not bad at all. The lobby is carpeted and just big enough for a small reception counter, a TV, and four comfortable chairs. The main drawback is that there is no place to sit other than this somewhat cramped reception area and the restaurant. At the latter you can get a full breakfast for about $1.50 and other meals as well.

The accommodations are small but quite passable, with industrial carpeting, freshly painted walls, narrow twin beds, radios, telephones, bureaus, and private tile bathrooms with modern fixtures in good working order.

***Alternative:* HOTEL CAPITOL**
Calle Colombia 415, phone (042) 24510/23421
Rates: $13/$21 S/D incl. tax. No credit cards are accepted.
Directions: Half a block from Hotel Boston.

If the Boston's rooms are too small or having a TV is important, check out the nearby, 24-room Capitol. Don't let the hotel's shabby old exterior deter you from poking your head inside. It's reasonably well maintained. The lobby is large and inviting, with comfortable seating, carpeting and plants, and the guest rooms are standard size with TVs, telephones, carpets, and decent tile baths with old fixtures that do the trick.

HOTEL DORIA
Calle Junín 765
Phone (042) 45386
Category: B-C
Old house, 17 rooms, restaurant, bar.
Rates: $12/$16 S/D incl. tax. No credit cards
Directions: 7 blocks north of the main drag, Ave. Heroinas.

Run by a very friendly, elderly European couple, Marieta de Tomsich and her husband, the Doria is popular with Europeans, including expatriates living in Bolivia. Over 50 years old and formerly a home, this two-story, corner-block structure has an attractive, if not well maintained, facade and a pleasant, relaxed feel to it. In the back you'll find some tables and chairs for reading under the shade of trees – not very atmospheric but functional. There's also a small dining room where breakfast is served and a *wisqueria* (bar) for drinks.

The rooms do not have telephones and are a bit spartan – rugless tile floors and minimal furnishings. They do have tiny private baths with simple fixtures, including showers with electric heating elements. Moreover, the beds are reasonably comfortable and the rooms are well lighted by wrought iron overhead lamps and smaller bedside lamps.

First Alternative: **HOTEL COLONIAL**
Calle Junín 134, phone (042) 21791
Rates: $7/$14 S/D incl. tax. Visa is accepted.
Directions: On the same street as the Doria, but much closer to the center, just half a block north of the main drag.

An equally good alternative to the Doria is the more centrally located, homey and peaceful Colonial. The rooms may be slightly inferior to those at the Doria, but in other respects this place is as good or better. Formerly called La Coruna, it has operated as a hotel since the mid-1960's; before that it was a clinic. Popular with gringos and often full, it has two very attractive features: a lovely garden onto which all 13 rooms face; and a large, second-floor balcony onto which many rooms open. The accommmodations are nothing to write home about as the beds are a bit lumpy, but there is hot water all day in the private baths. And in the morning you can have an excellent breakfast on the shaded terrace in the gardens for less than $1.

Second Alternative: **HOSTAL FLORIDA**
Calle 25 de Mayo 583, phone (042) 27787
Rates: $5/$9 S/D incl. tax. Credit cards are not accepted.
Directions: On the same street as Hotel Boston, which is 4 blocks away.

For a central location and cheaper rooms, try the Florida, which is popular with Peace Corps volunteers and other gringos. The staff is quite friendly and the rooms are clean, with hot water and shared baths. The hotel serves a decent breakfast and offers a 24-hour laundry service and safe deposit boxes for valuables.

Sucre

HOSTAL LIBERTAD
Calle Aniceto Arce 99
Phone (064) 23101/2
Category: A-B
Modern, 24 rooms, restaurant.
Rates: $17/$22 S/D incl. tax. No credit cards accepted.
Directions: 1 block north of the main plaza.

If having a central location and a modern room are important, the recommended hotel is the Libertad. It's definitely not attractive from the outside as it occupies two stories above a small, fairly ugly shopping center, but it's a friendly and efficient operation. So don't let the uninviting entrance through this center deter you; the hotel is much better inside than its outward appearance would seem to indicate. The accommodations have a rather ordinary, uninspired appearance because of the plain furnishings, but they are reasonably spacious and have minibars, TVs, thin industrial carpeting, and tiny tile baths with showers. In addition, each room on the top floor shares an unusual, glassed-in sitting area with the adjoinging unit. All 24 units open onto a spacious central lobby, which has reasonably comfortable sofas, thin industrial carpeting, a TV, plants, and a small restaurant that serves good breakfasts.

First Alternative: **HOSTAL COLONIAL**
Plaza 25 de Mayo 3, phone (064) 24709/25487
Rates: $22/$28 S/D incl. tax. AmEx and Visa are accepted.
Directions: Faces the main plaza.

The 30-room Colonial, which faces the main plaza, is the top choice of tour groups because of its central location, modern accommodations and attractive appearance. As a result, it's also slightly overpriced. The century-old facade is lovely, but this is deceptive. Inside, the hotel has been entirely remodeled and has lost most of its charm in the process. However, the four-story, central atrium, onto which all rooms face, is impressive and remains intact. There's a fireplace on the ground level that should add a bit of warmth but doesn't as it's rarely used. The rooms have modern furnishings, comfortable beds, TVs, closets, and modern tile baths with showers. There's no restaurant, but you can order an excellent breakfast to be brought in your room or in the atrium. For other meals, there are many possibilities nearby, including the popular **Plaza Restaurant** on the opposite side of the plaza. It features live music on Friday nights. Better, but more expensive, **El Solar** is four blocks away at Calle Bolívar 800.

Second Alternative: **HOTEL MUNICIPAL**
Avenida Venezuela 1052, phone (064) 21074/25508, telex 2409
Rates: $21/$26 S/D incl. tax. AmEx and Visa cards are accepted.
Directions: 7 blocks from the main plaza, bordering Bolívar Park.

The modern, 39-room Municipal, which was built in 1963 with US foreign aid, is still rated as the city's top hotel and is one of only several hotels with a fully-operational restaurant. However, it's definitely showing its age, especially in the public areas. And the location, a good walk from the center, is a major drawback for those without wheels. The single-floor, red brick structure, which has an attractive, modern facade and spreads out over several acres, raises expectations which, upon entering, you are likely to find quickly dashed. The lobby is rather plain and disappointing, with only a few seats. As there is no sitting room, the only place to hang out is outside on the spacious terrace which flanks the lobby. It's a pleasant area, with shade trees and potted plants. The numerous tables here frequently draw large weekend crowds. Few people other than the hotel's guests, however, patronize the adjoining restaurant, which has worn carpets, plain walls, a cold feel to it, and bland meals.

The rooms, while fairly small, are in reasonably good condition, with plain furnishings, thin carpeting, narrow but comfortable twin beds, ample closet space, TVs, and medium-size tile bathrooms with showers and simple fixtures. The best units face the shady patio; others face a small grassy area.

HOSTAL CRUZ DE POPAYAN

Calle Loa 881 y Colon
Phone (064) 25156/31706
Cables: Hostacruz
Category: B
Colonial house, 11 rooms, TV-reading room, patio, breakfast.
Rates: $17/$22 S/D incl. tax. AmExp & Visa are accepted.
Directions: 4 blocks from the central plaza.

The Cruz de Popayán is not rated as the city's top hotel, but it's the best in Sucre and one of only a handful in the country that have an authentic colonial ambience. Also, the city's higher-rated hotels are all a bit disappointing; in contrast, this place is marvelous and highly recommended. The entrance to this 17th-century former residence, which has a traditional tile roof, is through an ornate old doorway. It leads over a stone walkway to the central courtyard, which has a wonderful old shade tree in the middle, a fountain, and a porch to one side lined with white columns and potted plants. There are ample garden chairs and tables in this area, making it the perfect place to hang out during the day and soak up some rays, or read a book in the shade.

During the day or evening, guests can wander over to the reception room, which has a fireplace, comfortably cushioned sofas and chairs, two wrought iron chandeliers, windows with wood panelled shutters, throw rugs on the red tile floor, a wonderful collection of some 30 old keys over the fireplace, a TV, plus a large number of magazines, many in English. Like most hotels here, the guest rooms have no heating and, consequently, can get quite chilly. During the colder months this reception area is an especially good place to relax and chat with the friendly manager, Gaston Querejazu.

There are only eleven rooms, so an advance booking is wise. The rooms have tile floors, tall ceilings, old-style lighting fixtures, throw rugs, straight-back chairs, and simple narrow beds with firm but comfortable mattresses. They are both attractive and rustic and maintain the colonial ambience. Each one has some modern conveniences, including telephones, large built-in closets, color TVs available upon request, and private baths with large towels, showers, and a reliable supply of hot water. Breakfast is served in your room or on the patio. In short, it's no wonder this place gets high ratings.

HOSTAL SUCRE
Calle Bustillos 113
Phone (064) 21411/31928
Category: B-C
Colonial building, restaurant.
Rates: $16/$20 S/D incl. tax. AmEx & Visa are accepted.
Directions: 1 block southwest of the main plaza.

The Sucre is a former colonial mansion near the center that has been converted into a very attractive hotel. Some travelers may prefer it because of the slightly lower price and its location. Many of the rooms overlook the original central courtyard which has a fountain; some fairly plain, modern rooms have been added in the back. The main problem with the rooms is that they are quite small. Otherwise they're not too bad, with reasonably comfortable beds and private baths with hot-water showers. The Sucre also has a good restaurant, and it's one of the few in town which is open all day, so you can get a drink or snack anytime you wish.

HOSTAL LOS PINOS
Calle Colón 502
Phone (064) 24403/32212
Cables: Los Pinos
Category: B-C
10 rooms
Rates: $16/$20 S/D incl. breakfast & tax. Visa card is accepted.
Directions: 2 blocks west of the Cruz de Popayán.

Travelers who enjoy the feel of B&Bs are likely to prefer Los Pinos, which is an ordinary, two-story house that has been converted into a hostel. It's peaceful, clean, comfortable, and also very well maintained, as you'll be able to tell from the neatly-cut hedge surrounding the well-kept front yard. A big plus is the friendly family, the Pinos, who run this establishment. They welcome guests into their living room and allow them to use the house telephone. The rooms are medium size and have bare wooden floors, freshly painted walls, TVs, and comfortable beds. The tile baths have showers with electric heater heads. Finally, Carmen Pinos provides each day a good breakfast which is included in the price.

Potosí

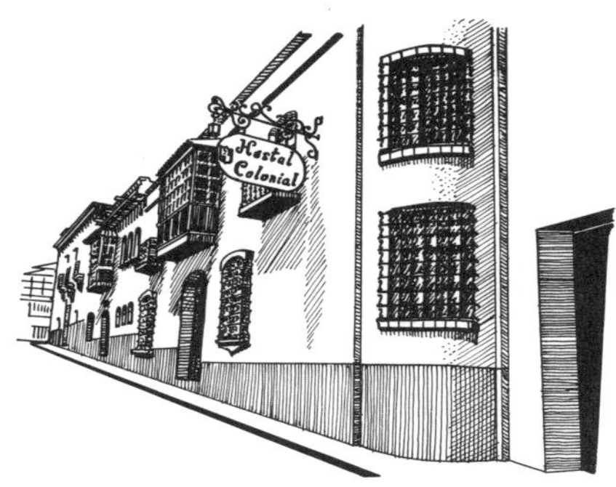

HOSTAL COLONIAL

Calle Hoyos 8
Phone (062) 24265/24809
Category: A-B
Colonial building, central, 20 rooms, breakfast served.
Rates: $19/$23 S/D incl. tax. AmEx & Visa are accepted.
Directions: ½ block from the main square, Plaza 6 de Agosto.

This has been the best place to stay in Potosí since about 1980 when it was converted into a hotel. Like many former colonial residences, it has a large, ornate doorway, white walls inside and out, a red tile roof, and a central courtyard with a stone floor and a fountain in the middle. Many of the rooms face this area.

The guest rooms, which are standard size and, most important, are heated, have TVs, telephones, comfortable twin beds, carpets, breakfast tables and wooden-back chairs, closets, and modern tile bathrooms and showers with a reliable supply of hot water. There's no restaurant, but breakfast is served in the rooms and there are some good places to eat within easy walking distance. The best is probably **Restaurante El Maison**, which is three blocks away on the opposite side of the park at the corner of Calles Tarija and Linares.

Finally, the staff is very friendly and helpful and, whether or not you're staying here, will provide you with names and telephone numbers of professional guides for the Potosí area.

Alternative: HOSTAL LIBERTADOR
Calle Millares 58, phone (062) 27877/24629
Rates: $17/$21 S/D incl. tax.
Directions: Near the Colonial on Calle Millares, which runs southward starting half a block east of Hostal Colonial.

The owner of the Casa Real de Moneda, a former mint and now the city's main museum, has started a new *hostal*, the Libertador, which is an excellent alternative and nearby, around the corner from the Colonial and to the south. This comfortable, quiet place likewise has clean rooms with heaters and hot water, private baths, plus parking and good views.

HOTEL GLORIA
Avenida Universitaria
Phone (062) 26406/27215
Telex 7412
Category: B
Modern, 15 rooms, restaurant
Rates: $9/$12 S/D incl. tax. No credit cards accepted.
Directions: On city's northern outskirsts at the end of Ave. Universitaria, 2 km from the center, facing the bus station.

Formerly called the Gran, the Gloria is a relatively new, four-story establishment with a boring feel to it. However, it does have modern rooms and a sleek, white facade and is convenient for those arriving by bus. In addition it features a restaurant, private parking and radio taxi service. The units are a bit small, but not cramped, and vary considerably, from singles to triples and junior suites. The standard double has two narrow beds, thin dark green carpeting and matching bedspreads, reading lights over the beds, closets, telephones, and small, tile bathrooms with new fixtures including hot-water showers. There's also a restaurant which serves local and international dishes; at Sunday lunch time, it sometimes becomes a *peña* (bar) with local music as well as food and drinks.

HOSTAL SANTA MARIA
Avenida Serrudo 244
Phone (062) 23255
Category: B-C
House-like B&B
Rates: $8/$12 S/D incl. tax. No credit cards accepted.
Directions: On a side street leading east off Ave. Bustillos, 1 km north of the main plaza towards the bus station.

If you'd prefer a more homey, family-run B&B, try the Santa María, which is half-way between the central plaza and the bus station, about a 12-minute walk from the center. It's a single-story house that has been converted into a B&B and is located on a well-known side street with a number of other cheap hostels. Better than the competition, it has a pleasant lounge with TV, plus clean, decent rooms with comfortable beds and hot water all day. You can get a good, inexpensive breakfast here, too.

First Alternative: **HOSTAL CARLOS V**
Calle Lanza 19, phone (062) 25121
Rates: $7/$10 S/D incl. tax. Credit cards are not accepted.
Directions: On Calle Lanza, a block behind Hostal Colonial and 20 meters from the southeastern corner of Plaza 6 de Agosto.

If you'd prefer to be in the center of town, a good choice would be the Carlos V, which is just off the main plaza. The rooms have no heating, but are quite comfortable, and the shared baths have showers with hot water all day. There's also a pleasant sitting area. In addition, you can get an excellent breakfast here for just $1 and useful information from the owner, who is friendly, helpful and will allow you to store luggage.

Second Alternative: **HOSTAL EL TURISTA**
Calle Lanza 19, phone (062) 22492/22341
Rates: $6/$9 S/D incl. tax. Credit cards are not accepted.
Directions: 2 blocks due south of Plaza 10 de Noviembre.

If the Carlos V is full, try the Turista, four blocks away and similar in virtually all respects. It's easy to find as the Lloyd Aereo Boliviano office is here.

The East

Santa Cruz

LOS TAJIBOS HOTEL
Avenida San Martín 455
Phone (033) 30022/51000
La Paz phone (02) 325974
Fax (033) 33915
Telex 4241
Category: Deluxe
Modern, sprawling complex, 170 rooms, pool, hot tub, jogging track, Turkish bath, sauna, gym, racketball, shops, travel agency.
Rates: $98/$105 S/D incl. breakfast & tax. AmEx & Visa cards accepted.
Directions: On the edge of town, 5 km from the center.

Most expatriates living in Bolivia would rate the Tajibos as the country's nicest hotel. Certainly this modern, sprawling, three-story complex, with its beautiful garden setting and plush appointments, is the pride of Santa Cruz. The lobby, with its red marble floors, stylish cane furnishings, huge brass lamps and oriental rugs, is quite impressive and inviting. Entering further, you'll pass by a number of fancy shops with expensive foreign goods. Further back you'll come to an extensive, grassy area with palm trees and numerous tropical plants. The focal point here is a large, kidney-shaped pool with a fountain in the center. Surrounding it are 60 or so sunning chairs, and to one side you'll find an open-air hot tub which is well-used throughout the day. The health club has another hot tub as well as a Turkish bath, sauna, racketball courts, and a jogging track.

One of the more popular places to hang out is the **Terraza Bar**, which overlooks the pool. It's a breezy, open-air area with hanging ferns and walls in bold, green and white stripes. A second bar, called the **Tucan**, is inside, air conditioned, and more intimate. Adjoining the Terraza Bar is the hotel's main restaurant, the **Papagayo**, which is an elegant dining room with white wicker chairs, fancy place settings, flowers, carpets, and superb international cuisine.

The accommodations are spacious and provide all that you would expect, including plush wall-to-wall carpeting, sofas and matching chairs, king-size beds, brass lamps, satellite TVs, minibars, balconies, large glass-door closets, breakfast tables, and modern, tile bathrooms with telephones, wide mirrors, long counters, and combination baths.

Alternative: **HOTEL CAPARUCH**

Avenida San Martín 1717, phone (033) 33303, fax (033) 51735, telex 4377

Rates: $40/$50 S/D incl. tax & buffet-style continental breakfast. Major credit cards.

Directions: 3 blocks beyond Los Tajibos Hotel.

An excellent, much less expensive alternative to the Tajibos is the new Caparuch, which is a deluxe, 41-room hotel on the same street. A modern, three-story structure in pale pink and white trim, it has an elegant, marble floor in the lobby with walls of mirror, attractive sofas in pastel colors and thick carpeting. The color scheme is carried over into the stylish adjoining restaurant, which has similar carpeting and modern paintings and features a buffet breakfast and good continental cuisine. The hotel's numerous amenities include a pool, exercise room, sauna, a Turkish bath and whirlpool. The pool, however, is more like an oversized bathtub than a real pool as it's too tiny for anything other than cooling off. Accommodations here are fairly small but have satellite TVs, plush carpets, minibars, queen-size beds, breakfast tables, natural wood closets, and modern tile bathrooms with wide basins and combination baths.

LAS PALMAS HOTEL

Ave. Trompillo, 2nd Anillo Sud, phone (033) 30366, telex 4429
Category: A. Modern, tropical ambiance, 40 rooms, small pool, restaurant, bar.
Rates: $55/$66 S/D incl. breakfast & tax. AmEx and Visa accepted.
Directions: 2 km from center on the 2nd Anillo Sud.

Those looking for a less expensive alternative to the Tajibos should definitely check the Palmas, which is a very popular hotel and is often fully booked. It's an attractive, Spanish-looking tile-roof structure and is well maintained, with a breezy, tropical feel to it in the public areas. The active, inviting lobby, for example, has tile flooring, wicker furnishings, plush sofas, and glass walls facing a busy street. The tropical theme is carried over into the adjoining **Bar Sumuque**, which has wicker furnishings and ceiling fans, as well as the coffee shop and the main restaurant, **Las Palmas**.

Further back you'll come to a triangular area onto which rooms on all three floors face. The tall palm trees as well as the numerous shrubs and ferns add to the tropical feel. In the center is a pool, which is too small for anything other than cooling off; still, it's well used and guests seem to enjoy it. There are also a few chairs here for sunning and some garden furniture for drinks and cards. It's an inviting and relaxing area, but be warned – more than about 10 people here make things a little cramped!

The rooms are medium size and well appointed but not plush, with attractive modern furnishings, comfortable large beds, breakfast tables, balconies with glass sliding doors, industrial carpets, ample closet space, many with color TVs, and modern combination baths with marble basins.

HOTEL LA QUINTA

Barrio Urbari, 2nd Anillo
Phone (033) 42244
Fax (033) 42667
Telex 4319
Category: A
Modern apartment-hotel, weekly rates, 74 rooms, pool, restaurant.
Rates: $245/$294 S/D per week incl. tax ($50/$60 S/D day if available). AmEx card accepted.
Directions: Near Hotel Las Palmas, 2 km from the center.

Those staying a week or more, especially families, should check La Quinta, which is nearby. Better and more deluxe than Las Palmas, La Quinta is a pleasant, Spanish-style hotel with a laid-back ambience. It's usually booked solidly by long-term guests because of its heavily discounted weekly and monthly rates, which are comparable to those of Hotel Cortez on a daily basis. Daily rates are offered only on a space-available basis, and reservations for such are not accepted; consequently, for the great majority of travelers, staying here isn't feasible.

As you enter the main lobby, you'll be struck by the impressive, exposed-beam, cathedral ceilings. Red marble floors, thick carpets, plush leather sofas and recorded classical music playing in the background all contribute to create a tranquil, sophisticated atmosphere. The hotel's restaurant flanks the lobby to one side, while further back and outside you'll come to the pool area, which is surrounded by various two-story, apartment-like buildings with red tile roofs. There are chairs around the pool for sunning and, for those who wish to get out of the sun, there's a terrace to one side that is attractive and shaded by vines. All units consist of a living room, kitchenette, and one or two bedrooms. The ground-level living areas have comfortable sofas and chairs, carpets, TVs, breakfast tables, and fully-equipped kitchenettes with stoves and refrigerators, while the upstairs bedrooms are sunny, with large beds, carpets and tile combination baths.

GRAN HOTEL CORTEZ
Ave. Cristóbal de Mendoza 280
Phone (033) 31234
Telex 4333
Category: A
Long-standing hotel, good service, 85 rooms, pool, small zoo, kiddy pool and play area, beauty salon.
Rates: $30/$40 S/D incl. breakfast & tax. All major credit cards accepted.
Directions: 2 km from center, on the 2nd Anillo.

Most of the better hotels in Santa Cruz are quite new. One that isn't but remains well regarded is the family-run Gran Cortez, which is on the same street as Las Palmas and La Quinta. Martin Cortez, the well-known owner/manager, and his five sons and daughters keep this family-oriented place impeccably clean and ensure that the hotel's greatest asset, its reputation for top notch, award-winning service, remains untarnished. The exterior is modern but nothing special. Upon entering the lobby, however, you'll see very quickly that this place still has style despite its age. The attractive wicker chairs with plush, brightly colored cushions, the tile floors, and the judicious use of numerous plants combine to give this area an inviting, tropical atmosphere.

Further back you'll come to a large, shady area with lots of mango and avocado trees, shrubs, bushes and chirping birds, plus a long, rectangular pool, which is the only one among those of the city's top hotels that is good for swimming laps. In addition, there's a kiddy pool plus a children's play area with a slide, see-saw and swings. A tiny zoo with tropical birds, including several scarlet macaws and a gorgeous white crane, is an added atrraction.

About half of the accommodations face this shady area in back; the remainder face the street. All the rooms are spacious and reasonably attractive. They have air conditioning, thin industrial carpets, queen-size beds, reading chairs, small color TVs, minibars, walk-in closets, and tile bathrooms with old facilities in good working order, including combination baths. The main restaurant faces the pool. It has a relaxed, breezy atmosphere with overhead fans and tile flooring; guests can also sit out on the terrace alongside the pool to eat. The food is good, but not extraordinary. The menu is not extensive, but it does offer chicken with mushrooms, *surubí a la vasca* (fish with cream sauce), grilled pork chops, chateaubriand, noodles with chicken, and various desserts, including apple pie, flan, and fruit salad.

GRAN HOTEL SANTA CRUZ

Calle Pari 59, phone (033) 348811/348997, telex 4419
Category: A-B. Old-style hotel, 32 rooms, pool, restaurant, laundry.
Rates: \$20-\$23/\$30-\$32 S/D incl. breakfast & tax. Visa & AmEx accepted.
Directions: 3 blocks south of the main plaza.

An excellent, less expensive, and more centrally located alternative to the Cortez is the old-style Santa Cruz. It's now over 35 years old but continues to attract economy-minded foreign travelers looking for a pool and a place with a relaxing atmosphere. The drab, four-story exterior needs a paint job and attention, as does the lobby, with its frayed 1950's furnishings. In back, however, the hotel's character changes dramatically – a long, clean pool surrounded by palm trees, flowers, plants and lots of grass, plus an attractive, thatched-roof restaurant with soft music playing in the background. There's also a covered area near the pool with comfortable, padded chairs for cocktail hour or reading. It offers protection from the sun. Not surprisingly, this backyard area and especially the restaurant are where most guests spend their time.

As for the rooms, be sure to ask for one of the newer units as they are standard size and by far the best. All of these have carpets, TVs, air conditioning, breakfast tables, large closets, and private baths with marble-top basins, good lighting, and new fixtures, including showers. The older, less expensive units, which are not recommended, have rugless tile floors, plain furnishings, and old bathroom fixtures. If only the latter are available, try to get one with a balcony overlooking the pool.

***First Alternative:* HOTEL ASTURIAS**
Calle Moldes 154, phone (033) 39611, fax (033) 50897, telex 4380
Rates: $20/$28 S/D incl. tax. AmEx & Visa accepted.
Directions: 7 blocks from the central plaza.

If the Santa Cruz is full and having access to a pool is important, try the friendly, 60-room Asturias. It has extensive grounds, a clean, medium-size pool, a baby pool and private parking. On weekends, however, the pool is usually so full of locals who come here to cool off that's it's virtually impossible to squeeze in among them. Facing the pool is the hotel's restaurant, which has a fairly extensive menu and four-course specials for just $3. The rooms, which are nothing special, have air conditioning, tile floors, color TVs, closets, reading chairs, telephones, and baths with old fixtures in good working order, including hot-water showers.

***Second Alternative:* HOTEL FELIMAR**
Calle Ayacucho 445, phone (033) 25942/28502
Rates: $18/$24 S/D incl. breakfast & tax. Credit cards are not accepted.
Directions: 3 blocks from the central plaza.

If all you care about is a decent room, try the four-story, 60-room Felimar, a relatively new budget hotel which is very clean but totally lacking in character. The mirror-walled, tile-floor lobby is quiet and presentable, and the adjoining cafeteria-bar is spotless and functional but seldom used except for breakfast. The rooms, which are slightly less than standard size, are quite nice and offer excellent value, with relatively new furnishings, air conditioning, dark green carpets, single or queen-size beds, telephones, TVs, ample closet space, and tile baths with modern fixtures.

HOTEL VIRU-VIRU
Calle Junín 338
Phone (033) 22687/35298
Category: B-C
26 rooms, courtyard, breakfast served.
Rates: $11/$17 S/D incl. tax & breakfast; $13/$19 S/D with air conditioning. No credit cards accepted.
Directions: 2 blocks west of the main plaza.

One of the more popular lower-end hotels in the center of town is the Viru-Viru. The colonial-looking, single-story exterior suggests that this place is small and old. Inside, however, you'll find a fairly new two-story, red brick structure, with 26 rooms overlooking a spacious courtyard and with plants all around. The reception area is just big enough for a reception desk, several chairs and a TV. Between the reception and the rooms in back is a patio with tile flooring, shade trees, potted plants, several round tables, and numerous chairs with cushions – a perfect place to relax. This is where drinks are served and it's also the best place to hang out during the day or night. An inviting, carpeted breakfast area is just beyond, followed by a larger courtyard onto which all the rooms face.

The accommodations are standard size and decent. There are narrow twin beds or queen-size beds with fairly thin foam mattresses, tile floors, unadorned white walls, wooden closets, telephones, rental TVs ($2), piped-in music, fans, and small private baths with hot-water showers. The more expensive units have air conditioning.

First Alternative: **HOTEL COLONIAL**
Calle Buenos Aires 57, phone (033) 23568/33156
Rates: $12/$16 S/D incl. tax. AmEx & Visa cards accepted.
Directions: 2 blocks from the main plaza.

An equally good if not better alternative is the Colonial, and those with a penchant for old hotels are almost certain to prefer it. The exterior of this old, two-story building is inviting, as is the appealing central patio inside. The patio is fairly small, but full of ferns and plants and has an old bell hanging over it. Garden chairs and tables are set at one end of the room. All of the hotel's 20 rooms face this area. The rooms are tiny but have air conditioning, telephones, freshly painted walls, carpets, double beds, closets and tile baths with hot-water showers. There's also a cafeteria and a small lobby with attractive cane furnishings and a TV that is often, unfortunately, blasting away.

Second Alternative: **HOTEL COPACABANA**
Calle Junín 217, phone (033) 30257
Rates: $5/$8 S/D with shared baths incl. tax ($9/$14 S/D with private bath). No credit cards.
Directions: 1½ blocks west of the main plaza.

If you're looking for a cheap, category C hotel in the center, try the long-standing, ever-popular Copacabana, which is very near the main square. It has four floors with lots of rooms, so reservations are not usually necessary. The rooms are quite good, as are the shared baths; slightly more expensive units offer private baths. The hotel has no restaurant, but there are good places to eat nearby, including **La Plaza** and the **La Pascana**, both of which face the main square. The latter is a popular meeting place for both locals and travelers and is especially good for drinks, snacks, and ice cream.

Lake Titikaka

Copacabana

HOTEL TITIKAKA
Km 64 Carretera Copacabana
No phone on property
La Paz phone (02) 374877/343172
La Paz fax (02) 374877
Telex 2304
Category: A
Lakefront, 24 rooms, heated pool, sunning area, game room, excursions, sauna, racketball, play area.
Rates: $27 per person incl. tax. No credit cards accepted.
Directions: About half-way between La Paz and Copacabana at Km 64 on the paved road northwest to Tiguina and Copacabana, between the villages of Huarina and Huatajata.

Only an hour's drive north-west of La Paz across the high, flat altiplano will bring you to Hotel Titikaka, which is by far the best hotel on the Bolivian side of Lake Titikaka and a good place from which to start excursions on the lake. This complex, which has a somewhat neglected exterior, is definitely not deluxe, but it has some features that only deluxe hotels might have. Indeed, it's hard to grasp that this unlikely place, in a somewhat frigid environment at 14,000 feet and seemingly in the middle of nowhere, has so many facilities. The most surprising is the indoor glass-covered pool, which has pale blue-green water and is long enough for swimming laps. Well warmed by the bright sun, this area is great for sunning, which explains why the pool is encircled with 60 or more cushioned deck chairs. It has a bar to one side and a banana tree growing on the other.

Adjoining the pool area are two racketball courts in excellent condition and a well-maintained sauna. Downstairs you'll find a large game room, with a ping-pong table, video games, and hand-operated soccer tables. Outside are more sunning chairs, a soccer field, a pen with several llamas, plus a children's play area with two spaceship-design slides, swings, and see-saws. Just beyond the playground is a pier where guests can hire a traditional reed boat for a trip out on the lake. They can also make arrangements at the reception desk for an excursion on one of the hotel's large sightseeing boats to nearby islands, such as Suriqui and Pako, as well as an overland tour to the famous Tiahuancu ruins.

The spacious second floor lobby affords breathtaking views of the lake. It's a warm area with a fireplace, carpeting, potted plants, a large-screen TV, and numerous brightly colored leather sofas. On the walls are two three-meter-long replicas of the reed boats for which this area is famous. One of them was made by Paulino Esteban, who constructed the famous *Ra-II* reed boat in 1973. *Ra-II* was used to sail from Anarruecos to Barbados to prove the boat's worth as a sea-going vessel in ancient times. Adjoining the lobby is the restaurant, the **Suma Uru**. Trout is the house specialty, and it's prepared with four different sauces – lemon, tomato, tartar, and onions with garlic. A typical meal with wine runs about $10.

The rooms here are standard size and more than adequate, with golden brown carpets, small color TVs, comfortable beds, ample closet space, sofas, desks, central heating, and tile bathrooms with modern fixtures, including showers with electric heating elements.

HOTEL PREFECTURAL
Copacabana
No phone on property
La Paz phone (02) 362041
Category: C
Dilapidated, 3 stories, lakefront, restaurant, bar, game room.
Rates: $8/$16 S/D incl. tax; No credit cards.
Directions: Located in Copacabana on the edge of Lake Titikaka, 4 blocks from the central plaza.

There's no way that the Prefectural could be recommended as a place to stay except for the fact that the competition in Copacabana is worse or at least equally miserable! The only advantage of staying here is that you get good views of the lake, which is only 100 meters away. The hotel's restaurant overlooks the water and offers food of quality equal to surrounding eateries, which isn't saying much.

Badly in need of repair, it's a decaying three-story building with an untidy yard leading down to the lake. Inside, you'll find a cold, wooden-floor bar, where room-temperature beers and continental breakfasts are served only when the staff can be found. An adjoining double-room restaurant offers lunch and dinner. It has lots of atmosphere, with creaky wooden floors, an upright piano, several hanging ferns, a few posters on the walls, wooden tables with plain tablecloths, and plastic light fixtures. Only the front room has good views of the lake. A typical meal here costs about $5. The public areas also include a large game room where, for about $1.25 an hour, guests can rent equipment to play either billiards or ping-pong. There are some reasonably comfortable sofas and chairs here and in the adjoining room overlooking the lake, but these rooms are usually too cold to enjoy.

The rooms are small, chilly and pretty sad, with bare lightbulbs hanging from the ceilings, beds with sagging mattresses, hard pillows, plain wooden floors, old furnishings, and private bathrooms with poorly-maintained facilities. The showers only have electric heater elements and water for a few hours a day. The Prefectural provides, of course, no heating in any of the rooms, but neither do any of its competitors. If you come here during the relatively warm December-February period, however, this place can be much more tolerable. Even then, don't expect the service to be good.

Alternative: **HOTEL PLAZA AZUL**
Calle 6 de Agosto, Copacabana. No phone on property. La Paz phone (02) 320068
Rates: $8/$16 S/D incl. tax ($13/$21 with full board). Credit cards not accepted.
Directions: In the heart of town, two blocks from the main plaza in the direction of the lake.

If having a view of the lake is not so important, check the nearby Plaza Azul because you may find this place more to your liking; the ambience is a bit livelier, the service is better, and the restaurant, while not great, is one of the more popular ones in town. Many tour groups stop here. Consequently, the restaurant is large and presentable, with attractive wooden floors and checkered tablecloths. It is well lighted and slightly heated by the sunlight which filters through the glass ceiling panels. You can get a standard, four-course meal of the day for as little as $2, but the more expensive à la carte selections, which include grilled trout, are much better.

Aside from the restaurant, this hotel has little to recommend it. An unattractive, three-story building, it has 50 rooms facing a plain central courtyard with no plants or adornment of any kind. The accommodations have attractive wooden floors and clean painted walls, but the rooms are unheated and are so tiny that there's space for only a single or twin bed plus a chair and a small closet. The private baths are likewise tiny and have showers with heating elements, but water is available only for a short time in the mornings and occasionally at night.

Yungas Valley

Chulumani, Coroico & Sorata

MOTEL SAN BARTOLOME
Chulumani
No phone on property
La Paz phone (02) 377499/378322
(Plaza Tours)
Fax (02) 343391
Telex 2674
Category: A
Modern hotel, 10 rooms and 10 bungalows, restaurant, pool, billards, ping-pong, volleyball.
Rates: $35 per room, $67-$78 per bungalow, incl. tax ($17 per extra person full board). Visa card accepted.
Directions: On the western outskirts of Chulumani (113 km from La Paz), 2 km from the center. Take a left at the gas station as you enter town and continue down that road for 1½ km.

For a relaxing place in the Yungas Valley, it's hard to beat the San Bartolomé. The main attraction here is the swimming pool. It's oddly shaped, making it hard to swim laps, but the water is reasonably clean and the surrounding, mountainous scenery is magnificent. During the day, most guests hang out around the pool; there are numerous sunning chairs for this purpose. Those more athletically inclined go off hiking in the hills. When you tire of the pool or hiking, you can try your luck at their cement miniature golf course, provided you remember to bring your own clubs and balls along. There's also a well-used volleyball court and a game room with three billiard tables and a ping-pong table. Alternatively, head for the bar; it has comfortable leather chairs, tile flooring, high ceilings, and excellent views of the mountains.

The hotel's dining room serves excellent food; a typical meal runs between $8 and $10. Their fish dishes, mainly *surubí* (a freshwater fish) and *pejerrey* (mackerel), are best and are prepared in several different ways including *à la meuniere* and *à la romana* (with egg, crust and tomatoes). And don't miss trying their fruit drinks; they're non-alcoholic and terrific. For dessert, you can have fresh strawberries or crèpes.

The rooms are quite attractive, with red brick floors, exposed-beam ceilings, wrought iron light fixtures, breakfast tables, comfortable beds, closets, and private baths with electric heating elements on the showers. The rooms and bungalows both have balconies with chairs, affording wonderful views of the mountains and valleys below. The bungalows, which can sleep six people, have two bedrooms instead of one, plus sofas that pull out into beds.

Similar Class Hotel in Coroico: **HOTEL SAN CARLO**
Phone 813266, La Paz phone (02) 372380
Rates: $38 per room incl. tax. Credit cards are not accepted.
Directions: On the outskirts of Coroico (96 km from La Paz), 1 km from the center.

In Coroico, a place with similar quality facilities is the San Carlo. Like the San Bartolomé, it has decent rooms, a good restaurant, a pool, sports facilities, and good views of the surrounding area.

Similar Class Hotel in Sorata: **HOTEL PREFECTURAL**
No phone on premises, La Paz phone (02) 362041 or through any travel agency
Rates: $12/$18 S/D incl. tax. Credit cards are not accepted.
Directions: At the southern entrance to Sorata, which is a 4-hour ride to the north-west of La Paz (105 km) via the road to Copacabana. The turn-off for Sorata is at Huarina, a few km before Hotel Titikaka.

The Prefectural in Sorata is the town's best hotel. It's a reasonably attractive place that offers a pool (open to non-guests for $1), decent rooms with hot-water showers, a bar, and a restaurant with good, although relatively expensive, meals. Situated at 2,695 meters (8,845 feet) in a scenic valley at the foot of Mt. Illampu, Sorata is an ideal place for hiking or just relaxing and enjoying the scenery. Consequently, it is often fully booked on weekends with expatriates and Bolivians from La Paz. If you plan to come here on a weekend, make a reservation.

RESIDENCIAL EL MILAGRO
Chulumani
No phone on property
Category: C
B&B, 4 rooms, hot-water showers, drinks available.
Rates: $6 per person. No credit cards.
Directions: At the western entrance to Chulumani on the main drag. 100 meters from the gas station on the left

The nicest thing about this small B&B is the delightful elderly woman who runs it. The lovely grassy garden that she maintains here makes this "miracle" place truly special; guests can sit out on the grass, soak up rays and enjoy the mountain views. All kinds of flowers and plants color the gardens, which are illuminated at night and make pleasant strolling spots. She has set out three tables and chairs for guests to use; those who bring their own food can prepare it on the outdoor grill. She doesn't serve food, but cold drinks are available and good restaurants are as close as two blocks away towards town. The center of town is only a 10-minute walk away.

There are only four rooms, two of which have private baths. The mattresses sag a bit, but the rooms are clean, with tile floors, attractive curtains, hangers, mirrors, and very clean bathrooms with electric heating elements on the showers and a fairly reliable supply of water. She provides toilet paper and towels on request; guests must bring their own soap.

Similar Class Hotel in Coroico: **RESIDENTIAL KORY**
Plaza Principal, Coroico, no phone
Rates: $6/$13 S/D incl. tax; credit cards are not accepted.
Directions: In the heart of Coroico (96 km from La Paz) at the top of the steps leading down from the main square.

A great inexpensive place to stay in Coroico is the Kory, which is in the very heart of town and features a pool (open to non-guests too) and a terrace with stunning views. It's a quiet, family-run B&B with decent, clean accommodations that vary considerably in configuration and price, some with private baths and cheaper ones with shared baths. Rooms on the top floor are best. The owners are very hospitable and run a great, popular restaurant. Although the food is not cheap, the restaurant is open all day and serves as a meeting place of sorts for the locals; don't miss trying their fantastic vegetable omelettes in the morning – they're superb! And only a block or two away is another excellent place to eat, **La Casa**. This restaurant affords wonderful views of the surrounding area and is run by a German lady who, for $4 a plate, serves a huge, outstanding Swiss fondue with meat and five sauces. Raclette, vegetarian dishes, and five excellent salad selections are also on the menu, but order in advance to be sure of getting what you want!

Similar Class Hotel in Sorata: **RESIDENCIAL SORATA**
Plaza Principal, no phone
Rates: $3/$6 S/D incl. tax; credit cards are not accepted.
Directions: In the heart of Sorata, just off the main square.

Residencial Sorata, also known as Hostal Casa Gunther, is in an old mansion and comes highly recommended for those who like places with some history behind them. It was the former residence of a German merchant who became wealthy selling goods to nouveau-riche gold miners passing through Sorata en route to La Paz. Ask the friendly caretaker, Louis from Quebec, to elaborate on the house's history – he'll be more than happy to share it with you! Although the building has been recently renovated, the rooms, which are large and clean, are still quite basic. The hot-water supply in the communal bathrooms, which are clean and have showers, is unreliable. The minuses, however, are outweighed by the hotel's pluses, which include a large reading room, a ping-pong table, and a lovely garden of flowers and palm trees. Moreover, the meals are good and hearty and include homemade jams with breakfast.

Northern Amazon Region

Rurrenabaque

HOSTAL TACUARA

Plaza 2 de Febrero, Rurrenabaque. No phone on property. Through Plaza Tours in La Paz; phone (02) 377499/378322, fax (02) 343391, telex 2674
Category: A
Rates: $21/$39 S/D incl. tax; $20 extra for full board. No credit cards.
Directions: In Rurrenabaque (1 hour's flight north-east of La Paz) in the heart of town facing the main plaza, one block off the Beni River.

Rurrenabaque is located alongside the Beni River at an elevation of 240 meters and is frequently used as a starting point for adventures along the Beni and into the rainforests. The Tacuara, which is well maintained and the only first-class hotel in the area, is a beautiful old building in the center of town facing the main plaza. When you see it, you'll think the pilot must have dropped you off on the Mississippi River, not the Beni, as it's surrounded by tall, white columns and very closely resembles a Civil War-era mansion from the Deep South. Every Sunday evening after mass, the plaza becomes a festive place as a military band plays tunes for an hour while the citizens promenade around the square. Guests can view it all from the hotel's second-story balcony.

Upon entering the main building, you'll find a small, attractive lobby but probably no guests, as they usually hang out at the thatched-roof restaurant and around the small pool, which is about a meter deep and only good for cooling off. What's most entertaining are all the animals from the jungle that the owners have tamed and allow to wander about freely. You are likely to encounter, for example, several monkeys, a friendly anteater-like tejon that likes to crawl on people, and a very interesting, pig-like tapir. The hotel manager, who loves animals, delights in teaching guests about the hotel's variety of unusual pets. Indeed, the staff here is simply great and they, above all else, make this a wonderful place to stay. The cook, for example, aims to please and will make you anything you request, provided he can find the ingredients. As a general rule, however, there's not much variety in the menu.

The hotel's rooms are breezy and pleasant, with comfortable beds, throw rugs, screen doors, windows, fans, and decent private baths with showers that have electric heater elements. And, since the hotel has it's own generator, hot water is guaranteed 24 hours a day. All in all, this is an enjoyable place to stay. If you come during the December-February period, you'll probably encounter rain, so try to pick another season for visiting here. Regardless, even during the coolest months, June through August, not many travelers venture this way, so you may find yourself the only guest here.

Alternative: **HOSTAL SANTA ANA**

All alternatives to the Tacuara are much less expensive but pretty sad. Your best bet is the Santa Ana, which is just a block or two away and very near the river. It has clean, basic rooms, cold-water showers, and washing facilities. Just opposite the hotel is a nameless restaurant.

TAWA TOURS JUNGLE CAMP

Upriver from Rurrenabaque
No phone on property
La Paz address:
Tawa Tours, Calle Sagárnaga 161
Phone: (02) 325796
Category: B
Jungle Lodge
Rates: About $400/person for a 4-day excursion incl. roundtrip air fare from La Paz. AmEx & Visa.

Directions: On the banks of a tributary of the Beni, 4 hours upriver by boat from Rurrenabaque.

Tawa Tours Jungle Camp, upriver from Rurrenabaque, is probably the best jungle lodge in Bolivia. It's well located on a bluff above the river, but views thereof are somewhat blocked by the surrounding vegetation. The lodge consists of various thatched-roof bungalows where guests stay and a central lodge where they eat. The beds are simple but comfortable, and the cabin windows and doors are screened so bugs are not a major problem. The bungalows also have porches with hammocks, which guests tend to make good use of. There's no generator, so all night light is provided by candles and kerosene lanterns. The meals are good and varied, grilled pirana being one of the specialties. Besides swimming in the river and canoe trips up and down it, two of the more popular activities here are fishing for pirana in a nearby lake and, at night, paddling around the lake looking for crocodiles.

Most guests arrive here by taking a regularly scheduled LAB flight from La Paz to Rurrenabaque and then a motorized boat upriver to the camp. An alternative, possibly more expensive, is chartering a five-seater plane; there's a small airstrip at the camp for this purpose. In case of emergencies the lodge has a two-way radio system with Tawa Tours in La Paz to bring assistance, including evacuation by air.

The longest country in South America, Chile, which is the size of France but never more than 112 miles/180 km wide, also has the most varied climate – from the hottest deserts on the continent in the north to the continent's coldest regions, Patagonia and the Magellanes, in the far south. Between these two extremes are some of the Andes' highest summits and snow-capped volcanoes, countless lakes and beaches, fjords and glaciers. And far out in the Pacific Ocean are two more of the country's treasures – tiny Juan Fernández Archipelago where the Scotsman Alexander Selkirk, made famous as Robinson Crusoe by Daniel Defoe, was marooned in 1704 and, further out, the mysterious Easter Island.

Because of the country's great length, 2,672 miles/4,300 km long, few travelers see the country from one end to the other. The area least visited by foreigners is the far north, the Atacama Desert region, which has the distinction of having sections where rain has never been recorded. The major towns in this area are all along the coast – the year-round resort town of Arica in the far north, followed to the south by Iquique and Antofagasta. From Arica, when you tire of the beach you can head east upward to Lauca National Park, a magnificent, high-altitude park with snow-capped volcanoes and herds of the elusive vicuna. Iquique and Antofagasta owe their existence to copper, silver, gold and iron ore. The world's largest open-cast copper mine near Calama attracts quite a few passers-by. Iquique is also a beach resort while Antofagasta is not, so the latter, which is the country's major port city in the north, is mainly used by travelers as a jumping-off point for visits inland to the heart of the Atacama Desert, especially San Pedro de Atacama and the nearby famous "Valley of the Moon," so called because of its strange natural sculptures of eroded salt.

Further south is the Central Valley, where you'll find the capital, Santiago, the country's premier beach resort, Viña del Mar, the country's major port, Valparaiso, and Concepción. Bordering this valley to the east in the high Andes are Chile's numerous ski resorts, including world-famous Portillo. This heartland region is also home to many renowned vineyards such as Cancha de Toro vineyard, which is an easy drive from Santiago and welcomes visitors. Santiago is a modern metropolis, with an excellent underground metro system, some fine examples of Spanish colonial architecture, numerous beautifully landscaped parks, and impressive views of the nearby snow-capped peaks when the weather – and smog – permit.

Viña del Mar, which is less than an hour's drive away, is the Chilean equivalent of Cannes. During the summer months it really hops. The southern boundary of the Central Valley is the Bio-Bio, a world-class rafting and kayaking river, Chile's equivalent of the Grand Canyon section of the Colorado River. Unfortunately, it's being dammed and ruined.

Further south still is the incredibly beautiful Lake District, which stretches all the way from Temuco, the northern gateway, to Puerto Montt, the southern gateway. This area, which includes the resort towns of Pucón, Villarrica, Entre Lagos, Puerto Octay, Frutillar, Puerto Varas, and Ensenada, as well as the larger commercial cities of Valdivia and Osorno, is simply incomparable in all of Latin America. Not only are there hundreds of lakes here, most notably Villarrica, Calafquen, Panguipulli, Ranco, Puyhue and Llanquihue, but also near-perfect snow-capped volcanoes, the most famous of which are Villarrica and Osorno. Both of these can easily be climbed by novices with the help of a guide. During the summer months people from Santiago flock to the lakes in droves, some families staying for the entire three-month school recess.

The Lake District is also a freshwater fisherman's paradise. Some of the classiest hotels in all of South America are located here, catering mostly to rich American trout-fishing enthusiasts, but the majority of lodgings are rustic, charming and inexpensive. This hilly, mountainous area is also great for swimming and trekking. Those less sports-inclined shouldn't worry – during the wonderful summer weather the festive ambience is everywhere and gorgeous views, plus music concerts (most notably in Frutillar) are more than enough to please anyone.

From the port city of Puerto Montt, travelers can ride down to Chiloé Island or Coyhaique, hop a steamer, plane or long-haul bus further south to the Magellanes, or cross over to Bariloche, Argentina via Petrohué, Todos Santos Lake and Peulla. Chiloé is an easily accessible, picturesque island with a cool climate and numerous quaint fishing villages, the largest or which are Ancud and Castro. Much further south, and far more frigid, is southern Patagonia and Magellanes. It is accessible from Puerto Montt by boat (three days to Puerto Natales), by bus via Río Gallelgos, Argentina or, most easily, by air. The largest city is Puerto Arenas on the Straits of Magellan, but the much smaller port of Puerto Natales is more popular with trekkers as it's the gateway to the spectacular Torres del Paine National Park. The park is one of the highlights of Chile and is quite remarkable, with its huge, windswept granite pillars of black rock erupting from the plains, and the impressive Balmaceda Glacier.

Finally, over 2,000 miles to the west of mainland Chile is the tiny and isolated Easter Island, a fascinating place with mysterious giant stone statues dotting the landscape. Flying here, while expensive, would be a great way to end a trip to this country of unusually varied landscapes and friendly people.

Santiago

HOTEL CARRERA
Avenida Teatinos 180
Phone (2) 698-2011
Fax (2) 721-083
Telex 340222
USA phone (800) 223-5652
Category: Deluxe
Grand dame, central, 321 rooms, member of SRS, pool, sun deck, squash, sauna, shops, Citibank, travel agencies.
Rates: $93-$116/$105-$127 S/D incl. 16% tax. Children up to 12 free. All major credit cards accepted.
Directions: In the heart of Santiago overlooking Plaza de la Constitución.

Dating from 1940 this grand hotel, which has an understated granite exterior with a row of ruffling flags, is clearly the place to stay in Santiago if you like imposing hotels which evoke the spirit of a more elegant age. The location, in the heart of town facing the presidential palace and one of the city's two main plazas, couldn't be more convenient or appropriate to its status. Most important for an older establishment, this 17-story structure, which is about a third less expensive than its modern competitors, is very well maintained and the service remains as good as ever.

Upon entering and taking the red-carpeted, brass-railed stairs to the second-floor lobby, you will surely be struck by the unusual and impressive murals on black glass walls; one depicts the arrival of the Spanish conquistadors with their galleons in the background. This huge public area, perhaps 120 feet long, has Italian marble floors and walls, 12 massive marble columns, 20-foot ceilings, two-story windows with draperies to the floor, floor-to-ceiling mirrors, art-deco glass chandeliers and well positioned large plants. What better place to relax – in comfortable leather armchairs, of course – and watch the world go by. There's also a bar here for drinks as well as an adjoining restaurant.

If you take the elevator to the 17th floor, you'll find a medium-size pool, a snackbar and a sun deck with 20 or so reclining chairs. During the day this is clearly the best place to hang out, and every night (except Monday) you can take in a folkloric show, too. One floor below you'll find the hotel's other sporting facilities, which include a sauna.

One of the nicest features of the rooms, all of which have high ceilings, is their spaciousness. You are unlikely to feel cramped here, especially if you ask for a front room. They are the largest and afford good views of the palace and its guards. Other comforts are the soft, extra-thick carpets, the floor-to-ceiling tan draperies, and the matching thick bedspreads. The rooms also come with satellite TVs, minibars, walk-in closets, safety boxes, brass lamps, full-length mirrors, piped-in music, air conditioning and heat. The bathrooms are relatively large, with long mirrors over marble-top basins, combination baths, thick towels and phones. All in all, this granddaddy of Santiago hotels continues to deserve its high reputation.

First Alternative: HYATT REGENCY SANTIAGO

Avenida Kennedy N 4601, phone (2) 218-1234, fax (2) 218-3155

The new, 332-room Hyatt Regency opened in 1992 and is beautifully decorated throughout. It has gradually edged out the longer-standing San Cristóbal Sheraton (phone 2 233-5000, fax 2 223-6656) for top spot among the city's modern luxury hotels. Like the Sheraton, it's in the Las

Condes district, a 10-minute drive north of the center. It's also next to a major shopping center and at least one-third more expensive than the Carrera.

Second Alternative: **HOSTAL DEL PARQUE**
Calle Merced 294, phone (2) 639-2694

In the downtown area just six blocks east of the Plaza de Armas and nicely located across from Parque Forestal, this smaller, 30-room apartment hotel next to the US Consulate has been around for a number of years and is an excellent alternative if you're looking for one which is slightly less expensive than the Carrera or has rooms with kitchenettes.

HOTEL FORESTA
Ave. Victoria Subercaseaux 353
Phone (2) 639-6262
Category: A
Old European-style, 36 rooms, reading room, TV room, piano, bar, panoramic views from the restaurant.
Rates: $37/$45 S/D incl. tax. All major credit cards accepted.
Directions: Near the center, 6 blocks east of the Plaza de Armas.

Overlooking a verdant park, Cerro Santa Lucía, this seven-story jewel, which was formerly an apartment building, has for years been a favorite of frequent travelers to Santiago. With its green canopy extending to the street and 16-pane windows, the Foresta has the aura, but not the quality, of an old, exclusive European or New York hotel. The understated regal theme extends into the lobby, which has royal red carpeting, small brass and glass chandeliers, antique high-back chairs with gold trim, and a museum-quality coat of armor with matching helmet.

Adjoining it is a small TV room with an antique French look – ornately carved sofas and matching chairs with gold trim, an oriental carpet, original art with gilt-frames, elegant marble-top tables, and flowery wall-paper. To the rear is an equally small, similarly inspired reading room with blue carpeting and blue chairs, oil paintings, a tiny glass chandelier, and a table in the center with numerous Spanish magazines spread around a glass-encased replica of a schooner. There are also conference rooms decorated with some pre-Columbian artifacts, toy soldiers and antique pistols as well as a piano bar.

In reserving a room, ask for one facing the front, as they have large French windows and overlook the park; those in back have uninspiring views. The decor of the rooms, which are fairly small with low ceilings, varies slightly but most of them have tasteful antique furnishings, comfortable chairs, thick carpets, satin curtains and bedspreads, brass beds and mirrors, wallpaper, telephones, radios and, in some rooms, TVs. The bathrooms are in tile and have modern fixtures, including bidets and large mirrors.

On the top floor you'll find the restaurant, which is a great place to relax with a drink and a good book. The front section has huge glass windows affording superb views of the park, various large plant arrangements, carpeting, a silver-colored ceiling that is particularly attractive at night when it is lit up and an unusual horse-drawn cart for kids. The inside section is much more formal with royal blue carpeting, red high-back chairs, original art, two more antique coats of armor and, most thoughtful, two plush sofas in case you have to wait to get a seat. The menu's *entradas* include lots of seafood selections – *langostinos al pil-pil* (crayfish with chilly peppers), *caldillo de congrio* (eel soup), and *ostinos con salsa* (oysters in sauce) – while the 10 *platos de fondo* (main dishes) are mostly meat dishes such as entrecote and *pavo asado* (roasted chicken). There are also over 15 wines to choose from, including half-bottles. Unfortunately, the coffee is instant and the meals are a bit pricey. In comparison, the set three-course menu, which is okay but nothing special, seems like a steal at about $5.

Alternative: **HOTEL ORLY**
Avenida Pedro de Valdivia 27, phone (2) 232-8225
Rates: $27/$46 S/D incl. tax. AmEx is accepted.
Directions: In Providencia, conveniently located 2 blocks from the Pedro de Valdivia metro stop, about 30 blocks from the heart of the city and less than 1 km from the San Cristóbal Sheraton hotel.

Reserve in advance for the Foresta because, if it's full, you'll be forced to look at alternatives, none of which are nearly as good. If you're a sucker for small hotels and don't mind being a good ways from the center, check out the Orly. It's a 15-room, homey place in Providencia, which is one of the better residential areas, near the embassies of Ecuador, Peru and the UK. The attractive three-story exterior, with long French-style windows, makes this establishment seem better than it actually is. The rooms are small, with ordinary furnishings and the attached bathrooms are tiny, with old fixtures. The units are carpeted and heated, however, and the doubles have TVs. The latter are over-priced but the singles are not, and if you're lucky enough to get one of the three cheaper-category single rooms, you'll definitely be getting your money's worth. There's also a small, three-table restaurant, best used for breakfast, and a sitting room overlooking a small garden in back.

If you're going to be in Santiago for a number of days or you're with your family or companions, ask the hotel management about their apartments, which are four blocks to the south and just off Pedro de Valdivia (the same street that the Orly is on) on Calle Juana de Arco. They cost $70 but reductions are sometimes offered. If the Orly is full or, more likely, the rooms are too cramped or frayed for your liking, try the small, friendly **HOTEL SANTA MARIA** (phone 232-3376), which is four blocks north of the Orly on the same street, two blocks beyond Río Mapocho at the intersection with Avenida de los Conquistadores. It's similarly priced and has a restaurant that serves excellent breakfasts, plus lunch and dinner.

HOTEL MONTE CARLO
Ave. Victoria Subercaseaux 209
Phone (2) 633-9905
Fax (2) 335-577
Category: A-B
Modern, 64 rooms, near town center, restaurant, bar.
Rates: $21/$25 S/D incl. tax. AmEx & Diners cards are accepted.
Directions: One block south of Hotel Foresta.

If the Foresta is full or too expensive for your budget, try the Monte Carlo, which is just a block away and likewise faces Santa Lucía Hill. This relatively dark eight-story, undulating structure without corners, dating from around 1980, has one of the most interesting modern facades of any building in Santiago. Plants drip over the edge from the top and partially surround the building at street level, adding a nice touch.

In general the hotel's extremely intriguing design gives it the appearance of being far more expensive than it is, so don't hesitate to check it out. Upon entering, you'll quickly realize this. The public areas and rooms are all attractively arranged, but with the furnishings the accent is clearly functional and little more. The lobby is fairly small, with tile flooring, a built-in sofa, two mirrors, a single framed photo and, as is the case throughout the hotel, roughly plastered white walls. The adjoining restaurant is wonderfully designed, with two-story ceilings, curving walls, floor-to-ceiling windows, and tile flooring. It has about 15 tables, modern chairs of stainless steel, several plants and, for meals, a set menu of the day with several choices plus dessert. There's also a kidney-shaped bar with a shell-like ceiling, modern built-in sofas, glass-top tables, and a TV.

Many of the guest rooms, which occupy the remaining seven floors, have great views of the lovely park across the street. Slightly smaller than standard, they are equipped with simple but comfortable beds, breakfast tables with metal chairs, desks with mirrors, sliding closets, industrial carpeting, TVs, fans, telephones, good lighting, piped-in music and heating. The bathrooms have brown tile floors, combination baths, and modern facilities, including bidets. In sum, the Monte Carlo is an excellent buy and clearly a top choice in its price range.

***Alternative:* HOTEL RIVIERA**
Avenida Miraflores 106, phone (2) 331-176
Rates: $19/$22 S/D incl. tax. All major credit cards are accepted.
Directions: The hotel is at the corner of Miraflores and Moneda, 6 blocks east of the Plaza de la Constitución and 6 blocks southeast of the Plaza de Armas.

If the Monte Carlo is full and location is more critical than quality, try the Riviera, which is somewhat closer to the center and slightly less expensive but far inferior. It's definitely nothing special but then neither are its competitors in the downtown area. The rooms (and private baths), all 46 of them, are about as tiny and cramped as they come, but they do have the basics – carpeting, TVs, phones and closets – plus there's a bar and restaurant. Request a unit on one of the higher levels of this seven-story establishment. They may be a bit quieter.

RESIDENCIAL RODRIGO MATHIAS
Calle Nicasio Retamales 122
Phone (2) 792-273
Category: C
B&B, 13 rooms and cabins.
Rates: $10/$12 S/D incl. breakfast & tax; $18 per cabin. No credit cards accepted.
Directions: 2 blocks from Univ. de Santiago metro stop, 4 stops from the central station, Estación los Heroes.

Santiago has lots of small, family-run B&Bs from which to choose and the quality of most of them is similar. However, finding one that has a friendly staff, a convenient location and is outside the high-crime districts, is not so easy. A *residencial* with all three attributes is Rodrigo's. Something many travelers rave about – and use – is the city's modern underground metro, so the hostel's location near a subway stop is a big plus. This B&B is also in a quiet residential neighborhood and within walking distance of the city's main bus terminal. The hostel's biggest asset, however, is its warm, friendly staff, which is exceedingly helpful and delightfully interested in making sure your stay is enjoyable.

The building itself is 40's kitsch. It is bright pink on the outside and houses an amusing but tacky decor inside; halloween masks on the walls and an old treasure chest are two of the more notable decorating accents. The rooms sleep two to four people; one room has a queen-size bed and the other, decorated for kids, has two single beds. As in all of the hostel's units, the mattresses are firm and comfortable, and TVs, which cost extra, are available on request. Three common baths serve the seven rooms in this section. Hot water is always available and towels and soap are provided, which is not always the case in inexpensive *residencials* in Chile.

The best rooms are the six more expensive wooden cabañas in back. These are relatively new and, despite their small size, are perfectly comfortable for two people. They have private baths and open onto a common corridor which, in turn, opens onto a courtyard where breakfast is served under a grape arbor. For entertainment, check out the family pets in the garden separating the cabins from the main building. They include a tiny turtle in a bowl!

***First Alternative:* RESIDENCIAL LONDRES**
Calle Londres 54, phone (2) 638-2215
Rates: $10/$18 S/D incl. tax. No credit cards are accepted.
Directions: Some 6 blocks south of the Plaza de Armas, it's on Calle Londres, which is a short side street running north-south and starts just west of the landmark Iglesia San Francisco on Avenida O'Higgins and one block east of Calle Serrano. It may appear to be closed, but if you ring the bell on the side of the door, someone will let you in.

Not to be confused with the much inferior Hotel Londres nearby, this *residencial*, a former 19th century Victorian mansion, has been a favorite for years among travelers on the cheap and has the advantage of being closer to the center. The rooms of this once-grand place are spacious, secure, spotlessly clean and are on a par with those at Rodrigo Mathias' place. Guests have a choice between units with shared baths and doubles with private baths; in both, copious hot water is available all day. There's also a sitting room for watching TV or exchanging information with fellow travelers. The Londres has some disadvantages – one being that it has become a gringo hangout; getting a room after 9 a.m. is now very difficult. More important, the downtown location is not the safest.

Second Alternative: **AMIGOS DE TODO EL MUNDO**
Avenida Bulnes 285, phone (2) 672-6525, fax (2) 698-1474

For other guesthouses similar in quality and price to Residencial Rodrigo Mathias, contact this family tourism organisation on Avenida Bulnes, which is 12 blocks west of the Plaza de Armas and near the Metro Moneda stop.

Around Santiago

Viña Del Mar

HOTEL O'HIGGINS
Plaza Francisco Vergara
Phone (32) 882-016
Telex 630479
Santiago phone (2) 696-6826
Santiago fax (2) 696-5599
Category: Deluxe
Grand dame, 262 rooms, in town center away from beach, pool, baby pool, disco, beauty parlor, barber shop.
Rates: $49-$56/$62-$69 S/D incl. tax & breakfast. Children under 10 stay free. All major credit cards are accepted.
Directions: In the heart of town facing the main plaza.

Built around 1940, this wonderful old landmark hotel in the heart of Viña del Mar retains its stately charm. It continues to attract a sedate clientele more interested in the nice weather during the summer than the beach, which is just a five-minute drive away. People with business in nearby Valparaiso, which is six miles away and the country's second largest city, often stay here because the hotels in Valparaiso are atrocious in comparison. This mammoth structure has two entrances; the one to the side facing the city's main square, Plaza Vergara, is the most utilized. With its royal red carpets and high ceilings, it is quite impressive inside. The carpet leads towards a large public area which has four square columns, elevators and is crowned with a huge glass chandelier.

The main front entrance, which is lined with 35 or so flags of various countries, has a more newly constructed, glass-covered bar and restaurant all along the outside which you must pass through in order to enter the main building. This place has a delightfully casual ambience and is the best area to hang out and people watch. Everybody seems to stop here at one time or another. Inside is the original entrance hall – a huge, two-story room with a marvelous, impressive ceiling covered with Tiffany-like, colored glass. The large plush bar adjoining this area is also a good place to have a drink. In back there's a kidney-shaped pool as well as a baby pool. There are lots of lounging chairs for sunning and, during the summer, guests can take lunch here as well. The area is surrounded by trees and flowers, but you can't see the nearby river and the location (overlooking the hotel parking lot) is not the best.

On Saturday nights there is a *cena bailable* (dinner dance) with a special three-course set menu for just $8 a person, including wine and coffee. It's no surprise that this place is usually packed with locals as well as a dance band which plays while the guests dine. With its square columns, French-cafe-style chairs, wallpapered walls, and carpeted floors, the rooms are also reasonably attractive. You won't find the younger set here, however, as they prefer the **Tatoo**, the hotel's modern disco, which is quite lively on weekends and plays hard rock.

The tourist-class rooms are quite large and have bright blue industrial carpets, TVs, minibars, comfortable reading chairs, large closets, and decent bathrooms. The fixtures, which include combination baths and bidets, are somewhat dated but they are still in good working order. The more expensive *de lujo* rooms are similarly sized but have an attractive pastel theme, elegant furnishings including modern Chippendale-like chairs, much thicker carpeting, floor-to-ceiling curtains, breakfast tables, TVs, minibars, bowls of fruit and bouquets of flowers to greet the guests, and bathrooms with more modern fixtures. The best and most expensive units of this class face the plaza and the ocean off in the distance, while the others have dull interior views.

HOTEL MIRAMAR

Caleta Abarca, phone (32) 664-077, telex 234552. Santiago phone (2) 696-6826, fax (2) 696-5599
Category: Deluxe
Rates: $85/$106 S/D incl. breakfast & tax (15% less March-Nov). Major credit cards.
Directions: Overlooking the ocean, 2 km from the center.

Those looking for a beach hotel will almost certainly prefer the Miramar, which has a spectacular location on a rocky point jutting into the Pacific and is flanked on one side by a sandy public beach – one of the hotel's major attractions. From its mirrored glass exterior you'd never guess that this four-story structure dates from the 60's; extensive remodeling around 1980 completely transformed it into a modern hotel. Because of its desirable location and extra amenities such as a health club, sauna and pool, this sporty place with an informal atmosphere commands the highest prices in town and remains the city's best beach resort.

The lobby, which has seven massive columns and is crowned by an enormous brass chandelier, is lavishly appointed with thick carpeting, plush sofas in pleasing soft colors, marble-top coffee tables with brass bowls on top, and huge cushions on the floor that serve as seats. Most unusual, there are some high-quality masks and baskets from West Africa adorning the walls. Further inward you'll come to a large terrace bar with floor-to-ceiling windows; it's a good place for a drink day or night as the views of the sea from here are wonderful. It's fairly informal, with cane furnishings and green carpeting, and you can get light meals here as well. Adjoining this bar is the hotel's more formal main restaurant which has a fountain, a cloud-painted ceiling, a large mural, tables with chairs and cushy sofas, plus a dance floor. On Friday nights there's a popular American buffet here and music filling the air. Just outside the bar is a long winding deck which has green astro-turf flooring and lots of lawn furniture. You can hear the sea just below – the sound of breaking waves is heavenly. This is where most guests spend time during the day.

The guest rooms, which seem slightly larger than standard and are all identical, have glass walls on the sea side and, because of the hotel's semi-circular design, most of them have ocean views. They are also fairly plush, with carpeting, thick bedspreads and matching draperies, comfortable reading chairs, breakfast tables, TVs, and minibars. The bathrooms in turn are very modern with combination baths. In sum, the Miramar is Chile's top ocean resort, and the constant pounding of the waves heard throughout most of the hotel is just icing on the cake.

HOTEL ESPANOL
Plaza Vergara 191
Phone (32) 685-146
Category: A
Former mansion, 24 rooms, in town center away from beach, restaurant, free laundry.
Rates: $16/$25-$30 S/D incl. breakfast & tax. Children under 8 free. All major credit cards.
Directions: One block from the O'Higgins, facing the plaza.

If looks and friendly, personal service count, stay at this gorgeous former mansion, which dates from 1916 and overlooks the city's main square. In operation as a hotel since the mid-1930's, the building is truly an impressive and fancy three-story structure. A pale yellow stone facade with white trim is highlighted by a second-story balcony and a third-story tower topped with an ornate roof. Outside, during the summer months, you're sure to find antique carriages waiting to take you on a slow ride around town.

Inside you'll find a lobby with high ceilings, ornate molding, a new glass chandelier, papered walls, several globed lamps, Victorian furnishings, basic carpeting, a TV, and a wooden staircase winding up to the second floor. The hotel's small breakfast room, in pale yellow like the exterior, flanks the entrance. Surrounded by windows, it's bright and cheery but, otherwise, fairly ordinary.

One of the hotel's best features is its restaurant, the **Cabeza de Buey**, which overlooks the central plaza. It attracts people from all over, so even if you don't stay here, consider coming to dine. The floor is carpeted, the ceiling has ornate molding, and the walls have brass and glass lights. But what gives it a special air are the fresh flowers and candles on the tables and a huge palm-like plant that acts as a canopy over the sideboard, where the day's special (the *Mesón Mariscos)* consisting of 10 different cold fish dishes is served. Hot seafood dishes, such as *machas parmesana* (mussels with parmesan sauce), *gambas al pil-pil* (jumbo shrimp with hot sauce), and *corvina margarita* (sea bass in a margarita-based sauce), must be ordered à la carte.

On weekends during the summer, guests are often entertained by a local musician. Prices are higher than average, but the superb service and excellent food make it all worthwhile.

When reserving a room, ask for one on the second floor (rooms 6, 7, 8, 9, 11, 12, 14, or 15). The units there are all part of the original building and no two are alike. The best ones have high ceilings, old brass chandeliers, wooden shutters, built-in closets, papered walls, industrial carpeting, and antique furnishings, including dressing bureaus with long mirrors. The bathrooms are on the small side and have simple facilities as well as showers. Rooms on the third floor, which are slightly smaller, have lower ceilings and smaller windows and lack the ornate ceiling molding found on the first two floors. Even on this floor, there's still a bit of the hotel's charming ambience. What's really special, however, is the service. At night when you return to your room, don't be surprised to find the bed covers turned down – excellent service is the Español's hallmark.

HOTEL VON SCHROEDERS/ JOSE FRANCISCO VERGARA

Calle Von Schroeders 392
Phone (32) 664-022/664-122
Telex 432001
Category: A
Former mansion, 55 rooms, between town center and beach, restaurant, bar, garden.

Rates: $21/$26 S/D incl. tax & breakfast. All major credit cards.
Directions: Between the city center and the beach, 1 km from each.

Hotel von Schroeders, also known as Hotel José Francisco Vergara, is another old mansion that has been converted to an inn and has the advantage of being within walking distance of the beach, which is only one km away. From the outside this pale yellow structure may appear rather new but, upon entering and passing through the tiny modern lobby, you'll see that the older section retains much of its former charm. The main sitting room is of grand dimensions, with 14-foot, wood-beam ceilings, wainscoting, parquet floors, antique glass chandeliers, a fireplace, an old grandfather's clock, and a huge, gilt-framed oil painting. Most spectacular, perhaps, is the ornately carved Victorian mirror which hangs just above a golden, French-style side table with a marble top. During the day, as light passes through the room's huge stained-glass window, the comfortable sofas and chairs make this a particularly nice place to spend time. Bouquets of flowers just below the window and soft classical music playing in the background add a nice touch and suggest why guests feel so at home here. If you walk into the small adjoining room, which is cozier and simply lovely, you'll see some fine oil paintings and family portraits, including one of Gabriela Mistral after whom this "salon" is named.

The hotel attracts an older crowd, so don't expect to find a lively ambience. Quiet gentility rules here. By 8 p.m. or so, most guests retire, leaving the sitting room and bar deserted. Others linger for up to an hour longer in the restaurant, which is quite spacious with three rooms and over 40 tables. This section was added later and does not appear old except for the parquet floors. One long side is almost entirely glass, affording guests good views of the hotel's central garden. The many plants in the dining area help give it an appealing ambience. Meals here are excellent. Among the selections are *sopa marinera* (seafood soup), *machas parmesana* (mussels with parmesan cheese), and *lomo champignones* (sirloin steak with mushrooms). Guests also have a wide selection of wines from at least six Chilean vineyards to choose from.

The hotel's older rooms are upstairs. They are standard size and have rather simple furnishings – wood flooring, papered walls, old bureaus, ordinary chairs, plain beds, and telephones on the walls. The bathrooms have old fixtures in good working order, including bidets and old-style tubs with showers. Rooms in the newer annex across the street lack the ambience of the older rooms, but in many ways they are superior. Most of them have balconies with rocking chairs, as well as large closets, carpets, and tile bathrooms with more modern fixtures and combination baths.

First Alternative: **HOTEL RONDO**
Calle Errazuriz 690, phone (32) 685-073

For a somewhat cheaper category B hotel, try the Rondo. The staff is very friendly and the hotel has some nice gardens to boot.

Second Alternative: **RESIDENCIAL BLANCHAIT**
Calle Valparaiso 82, phone (32) 974-949

For a much cheaper category C *residencial*, check out the Blanchait. It's a family-run B&B and is clean, friendly, offers good service and hot-water showers; breakfast is included in the price.

Portillo

HOTEL PORTILLO
Carretera Internationale, Km 61. Santiago phone (2) 243-3007/231-3411; telex 440370/440372; USA phone (212) 582-3250 (Lan Chile)
Category: Deluxe, A & B
Rates: From $30 & up for bunk rooms with shared baths to $111-$131/$197-$220 S/D full board, about 25% less during off-season starting in October. Reductions also possible in the early part of high season (June). All major credit cards.
Directions: A 3-hour drive from Santiago on the Santiago-Mendoza road, 145 km northeast of Santiago via Los Andes (77 km to the north) and 7 km before the Argentine border.

There are six principal ski resorts within shooting distance of Santiago; of these, Portillo, the summer home for ski teams from the United States, is by far the most famous. It's also the furthest from Santiago (90 miles), but still close enough that two-day weekend excursions are quite feasible. Mid-June to mid-October is the normal skiing season here. The slopes are in sight of South America's highest peak, Mt. Aconcagua (6,960 meters), and are quite hair-raising. The most famous of them is 2,405-foot Roca

Jack, half of which is vertical. While Portillo is best for experts, beginner and intermediate skiers can rest content, knowing that there are trails for them too, including one that stretches from the imposing Christ of the Andes monument to the Argentine border nine miles away. There are 12 lifts in all, and lift fees are about half those charged by North American and European ski resorts. A few travelers show up during the warm summer months to fish and hike up to the glaciers, an option that may seem paltry in comparison to a challenging downhill run.

On the shore of Laguna de Inca, the huge, sprawling Hotel Portillo is clearly *the* place to stay in this resort. Getting a room, however, is quite difficult during the peak ski season without an advance reservation. The facilities are impressive and include everything from a steamy, heated outdoor pool to a health club, a movie theater and a first-aid/medical unit. And within a few feet of the lodge's front door, ski trails spread in all directions: left and right, up and even down! During the peak winter season, guests can take time off from the slopes to go ice skating on the nearby lake. This establishment is a bit fancy and coats and ties are required in the main dining room. Fortunately, guests also have the option of eating in the more informal grill room. Prices are a bit high for Chile; a full, self-service lunch costs $12 and, even if you come here just for a meal, you'll be charged for parking. For cheaper fare, just walk across the street to **Restaurant Yuly**.

Because of the high price of the rooms, the hotel's clientele is largely foreign skiers. There are, however, some relatively inexpensive bunk rooms catering to skiers on a budget, so don't rule this place out automatically if you're travelling on a shoestring. The cheapest units have bunk beds and shared baths; those with private baths are somewhat more expensive. Further up the price scale are family apartments which are quite comfortable and sleep four. Most expensive of all are the large, new chalets, which face the lake and accommodate more people. Because they are better value and have fabulous views, the chalets are very popular and extremely difficult to book during the high season unless you reserve many months ahead. Even if you end up staying elsewhere, the Portillo is a good place to head after dinner, as much of the action in this resort gravitates towards the bar, nightclub, and game room.

Alternative in Portillo: **HOSTERIA ALBORADA**

Portillo, Santiago reservations c/o Agencia Tour Avión, Avenida Agustínas (in the heart of Santiago near Plaza de la Constitución), phone (2) 72-6148

The Alborada is very comfortable and definitely not cheap, but prices here are nevertheless a bit lower. Give this place a try if the Portillo is full or beyond your budget.

***Alternative in Farellones Ski Area:* HOTEL FARELLONES**
In Farellones, Santiago phone (2) 246-334 (Centro de Ski El Colorado-Farellones, Avenida Apoquindo 4900 Edificio Omnium, Locales 47-48, Santiago
Rates: At the 120-bed Hotel Farallones, a one-week ski package (lodging, breakfast and dinner, plus lift tickets) costs $275 during September and a bit more during July and August.
Directions: 50 km east of Santiago.

Some of Chile's best slopes lie closer to Santiago. El Colorado-Farellones, which is 50 km east of Santiago, is really two skiing areas next to one another. This huge expanse sweeps across mile upon mile of an open, treeless mountain peak, with spectacular vistas. There are a total of 16 lifts and a nearly 1,000-meter vertical drop. Farellones has the best beginner terrain of any of the ski resorts, while El Colorado is intermediate heaven with long, wide cruising runs, but also some truly challenging courses for advanced skiers.

Pelequén

HACIENDA LOS LINGUES
Pelequén. No phone on property. Santiago phone (2) 235-2548; fax (2) 235-7604; telex 346060
Category: Deluxe
Rates: $96 per person incl. tax & breakfast; $189 per person incl. tax with full board. All major credit cards accepted.
Directions: 125 km south of Santiago via the Pan-American Highway then 3 km off the highway, near Pelequén.

If an elegant ranch sounds appealing, this *hacienda*, located 78 miles south of Santiago, is your best bet in South America, not just Chile. The original *hacienda* here dates from 1710. It was originally a gift from the King of Spain; today, some of the finest horses are bred here. In the 1950's an aristocratic European family converted it into a ranch and it is now a hideaway resort. Set within 9,000 wooded acres, it's perfect for horseback riding and hunting, which are the main attractions; fishing and sailboarding are also popular. Some people come primarily to attend small conferences, taking advantage of the outdoor activities on the side. Others come just for the day to dine and witness the equestrian exhibitions.

The main building is a red, colonial-style structure, and the guest rooms therein have been restored very professionally. With their high ceilings, original furnishings, antiques, parquet floors, and Persian rugs, they look almost like museum exhibits. They also have private baths and, upon request, TVs. There are no phones on the premises, however, so guests should come expecting to leave their worldly concerns behind. Antique furnishings, parquet floors and Persian rugs likewise grace the public areas, which also have large period paintings. For lunch and dinner guests eat in the main dining room, which is graciously fitted with crystal and silver settings. Those coming just for the day are directed to the cellar, which has attractive exposed beams and has been reconfigured for dining.

The North

Arica

HOSTERIA ARICA
Avenida San Martín 599
Phone (80) 23-1201
Fax (80) 23-1133
Telex 221089
Santiago phone (2) 696-5599
Category: Deluxe
90 rooms/cabins, modern, beachside, pool, tennis, volleyball, video room, beauty salon.
Rates: $58/$66 S/D incl. tax; $66/$75 S/D bungalows (lower in off-season). Major credit cards are accepted.

Directions: On the main drag along the ocean on the southern outskirts of town, 2 km from the center. Take bus No. 7 or 8.

For almost three decades the Arica has been one of the most popular beach resort hotels in northern Chile, especially around Christmas and Easter when you must reserve months in advance. The Arica is modern in design and well maintained, with rows of palm trees and flowers lining the entrance way. Taxis are always waiting there to take you downtown. On entering the building you'll find a large, modern reception area with comfortable sofas and carpets. You will often see children running about. The ambience here is always very active, especially during the summer.

The sports facilities here are quite adequate – a large angular pool plus a wading pool for toddlers, a volleyball net on the beach, and two lighted tennis courts which are well maintained but a bit breezy. If you're into jogging, you're certain to enjoy running along the ocean on the wide sidewalk paralleling the beach road. One of the city's best beaches, Playa El Laucho, starts just beyond the pool and is partly sandy and protected. Except during the hottest months (December through February) when temperatures soar well past 100°F, you may find the water a bit too chilly for bathing. Hence, the pool here is very popular and while the salt water isn't heated, it's usually warmer than that of the ocean, which is cooled by the Humbolt Current from Antarctica. Palm trees and 30 or so padded sunning chairs surround the pool; not surprisingly, during the day this is where most guests spend their time.

The best feature of the rooms is that most of them face the sea and have balconies; every day you'll awaken to the sound of crashing waves. The standard unit is fairly plain, with linoleum floors, two single beds with firm mattresses, a writing table but poor lighting for reading, a telephone, and a simple tile bath with shower. The more deluxe rooms have TVs, minibars, larger balconies with chairs, and wider beds. Families often prefer the newer and larger bungalows, of which there are 20. They are better value and have sliding glass doors opening on to private, sheltered patios overlooking the ocean.

My favorite place to relax is unquestionably the unusual octagonal bar upstairs, which affords fantastic views of the ocean and the desert-like hills behind the hotel. It's also very breezy here because it's open, except for its woven cane roof. The quiet atmosphere and the numerous plush sofas make this an excellent place for reading, talking or having drinks. For a cozier place, guests can try the bar on the main floor overlooking the pool and near the main restaurant.

The restaurant is quite adequate, but at dinner you'll do better going out. For good seafood, you might try **El Acuario** (phone 23-2686) two blocks from the center at the harbor (Terminal de Pescadores). It has a pleasant atmosphere and great food. Try the *chupe de mariscos* (seafood soup). Alternatively, head for **El Rey de Mariscos** (phone 23-2767) in the center at the corner of Colón and Maipu, which also has excellent food, but is cheaper and more informal. Try the *corvina en mantequilla negra* (sea bass in black butter sauce).

HOTEL EL PASO

Ave. Gral. Velásquez 1109, phone (80) 23-2651/25-2373, fax (80) 23-1965, telex 321003, Santiago phone (2) 251-7350.
Category: A
Rates: $43/$47 S/D incl. breakfast & tax, lower April-November. Major credit cards.
Directions: Half a km from the center of town in the direction of the port.

If having a view of the ocean is not important, you may prefer the less expensive El Paso, which is only a 10-minute walk from the central shopping district. Set in a breezy garden with palm trees, flowers, bushes and birds chirping away, this establishment, part of the Cristóbal Inn hotel chain, has a much more tranquil ambience than the bustling Hostería Arica. The furnishings are quite modern and attractive. The large lobby has pastel-colored walls, beige carpets, modern paintings, plush seating arrangements, and a few plants scattered here and there.

In back you'll find a kidney-shaped pool and four clay tennis courts that are all well maintained. Surrounding the pool is a large sunny lawn which is liberally peppered with wooden sunning chairs perfect for sun bathing. For those sensitive to the sun, the hotel has placed a large green and white striped canopy to one side of the pool, covering the tables and chairs there. Altogether, this makes for an attractive, relaxing area, and even at night it's a nice place to hang out as the yard is well lighted. Kids will like it, too. There is a baby pool and a play area with swings, slides, and see-saws. Standard rooms have queen-size beds, fluffy bed covers, pastel-colored walls, thick carpets, TVs, writing tables, built-in closets and modern tile baths. There are also some *lujo* units, which are about 20% more expensive. These face the pool and have their own private terraces with chairs. In the same area you'll find a small, pleasant bar. The outside section has attractive white cane furnishings and tile floors, while the interior is more formal and modern with carpeting and, most unusual, a huge wooden panel with lots of cubes in various hues of blue that create the illusion of a beach scene. There's also a more than adequate restaurant, but at night you'll do better trying one of the local seafood restaurants, most of which are within easy walking distance.

HOTEL TACORA
Sotomayor 540
Phone (80) 23-2864/25-1240
Telex 221098
Category: B
Modern, single story.
Rates: $10/$12 S/D incl. tax. All major credit cards.
Directions: In the center of town, 6 blocks off the ocean road and 1 block off the main commercial street.

Most of the cheaper establishments have a very sterile, plastic ambience. One that doesn't is the Tacora. What's unusual about it is the central area, which is entirely covered by a huge reed mat above. Sunlight filters through this, spraying small spots of light over everything, including the clients sitting there. During the day this is indeed a pleasant place to relax. Informality reigns here – enormous life-size murals, comfortable chairs with fancy designs, rugs and plants everywhere.

All the rooms face the central courtyard. They are quite small and unadorned but have the essentials – comfortable beds, fans, tiny private baths with showers and, for $1 extra, TVs. There's no restaurant, but breakfast is served and costs only about $1.

Alternative: HOTEL DIEGO DE ALMAGRO
Sotomayor 490, phone (80) 23-2927/22-4444, telex 221107
Rates: $13/$16 S/D incl. tax (25% lower in the off-season). Major credit cards.
Directions: one block west of Hotel Tacora on the same street.

If you find the rooms at the Tacora simply too cramped for comfort, try the two-story, 30-room Diego de Almagro, which is just a block away and has a very friendly staff. The rooms, which are slightly more expensive and not air conditioned, have queen-size beds, minibars, color TVs, telephones, adequate overhead lighting for reading, built-in closets, tile floors, and small private baths with showers. The reception area is uninviting, but the restaurant and bar, which were upgraded in 1990, are okay. The Tacora offers private parking.

Iquique

HOSTERIA CAVANCHA
Avenida Los Rieles 250
Phone (81) 42-1158
Fax (81) 22-5230
Telex 323057
Santiago phone (2) 229-8745
Category: Deluxe
53 rooms, modern, oceanfront, pool, sailboarding, water skiing, beach, tennis, travelagency, jacuzzi, car rentals.

Rates: $58/$70 S/D incl. tax (25% less in off-season). All major credit cards.
Directions: 1½ miles south of downtown, along the beach.

The modern, two-story Cavancha is one of only several hotels in Iquique which face the ocean. It also has its own private beach, so not surprisingly it's the top choice for beach lovers and families. After arriving, you'll want to head for the back brick terrace which is lined with comfortable cane chairs and is a great place to have a drink and listen to the pounding of the waves breaking just 30 yards away. From here you can see the entire length of Playa Cavancha beach and much of the city. There's a good section of the beach right at the hotel and just a few yards away there are rental facilities for water skiing and sailboarding. During the day most guests can be found on the beach, but a few prefer the six-foot-deep, kidney-shaped pool, which is surrounded by grass and is a bit more tranquil. There's a baby pool here, plus a hard-surface tennis court which is lighted and in moderately good condition.

Virtually all the public areas afford excellent views of the ocean and, because the hotel is so close to the water, the pounding of the waves can be heard from virtually any corner. The airy, marble-floor sitting area just beyond the reception is all glass on the ocean side, so guests can enjoy the views and sounds while relaxing in one of the many comfortable sofas and chairs in this spacious area. When the sun goes down the adjoining Bar Neptune, which has identical views, livens up. The dark curtains and numerous potted plants give it a warmer ambience and there are lots of wooden armchairs and tables for the guests. You can also get very good meals at the hotel's bright, marble-floor restaurant, which offers both inside and outside dining. Among the some 20 seafood selections are shrimp flambé, *chupe de mariscos* (an excellent seafood soup), and *almejas machas a la parmesana* (mussels cooked in almonds and parmesan cheese).

Guest rooms at the Cavancha are medium size and dazzlingly bright, with air conditioning, TVs, minibars, built-in closets, and modern tile baths. All of them have terraces and ocean views, so guests are sure to be pleased. The high degree of professionalism among the staff is the icing on the cake.

Alternative: HOTEL CHUCUMATA

Avenida Balmaceda 850, phone (81) 22-3655, telex 223176, Santiago phone (2) 71-3112

Rates: $46/$52 S/D incl. tax. All major credit cards are accepted.

Directions: One block from the Cavancha and one block from the ocean.

The Mediterranean-style Chucumata is an excellent alternative, especially if having a view of the sea is not critical. This single-story hotel is also the choice of General Pinochet during his trips north. The restaurant here is renowned for its seafood and the hotel's facilities, which include 42 brightly colored guest rooms (with air conditioning, minibars, TVs, phones), a pool, volleyball court, miniature golf and a car rental agency, are comparable to the Cavancha's. Moreover, the beach is only a block away. The hotel's best feature is the two-acre grassy area onto which all of the terraces face. It's a relaxing place for sun bathing, volleyball, or even frisbee, without having to contend with the crowds at the beach.

HOTEL ARTURO PRAT
Avenida Anibal Pinto 695
Phone (81) 42-1414
Fax (81) 42-5414
Telex 323105
Santiago phone (2) 251-7350
Category: A
51 rooms, central location, restaurant, bar, Hertz car rentals.
Rates: $28/$31 incl. tax & breakfast. All major credit cards.
Directions: In the heart of town facing the main plaza.

Over 45 years old and showing its age, the three-story Arturo Prat, which faces Plaza Prat, is nothing special. But, among the city's mid-range hotels, it's about as good as they come. It's an attractive building with lots of potential, but the interior is disappointing as the rooms and furnishings are totally unimaginative. The large reception area has comfortable but worn sofas in orange material, worn reddish carpeting, a few plants, and a single painting on the wall. The adjoining breakfast area is no better, plus the carpet is worn and the breakfast served here is quite skimpy. There is one saving grace, however, and that's the bar, which is by far the best place to spend time. It has attractive, wood panelled walls, a ceiling with exposed beams, elaborate full-length curtains, brown carpets, comfortable wooden armchairs, and a bar with interesting barrel-like stools.

The hotel's guest rooms, like the rest of the hotel, are showing their age and have no air conditioning. They do, however, have some good features including TVs, well-stocked minibars, phones, built-in closets, carpets, and renovated bathrooms with modern fixtures.

Alternative: **HOTEL PLAYA BRAVA**
Avenida Playa Brava 3115, phone (81) 42-2705
Rates: $27 per room incl. tax. All major credit cards.
Directions: On the southern outskirts of town, about 3 miles from the central area.

Before settling on the Arturo Prat, you may want to take a look at Hotel Playa Brava on the beach at the southern end of town. It's similar in size to the Arturo Prat and rated higher by some travelers. Three advantages are that it's near the water, has slightly lower prices, and serves superior breakfasts.

HOTEL CAMINO DEL MAR
Calle Orella 340
Phone (81) 42-0465
Category: B
14 rooms, old house, restaurant.
Rates: $13/$19 S/D incl. tax. No credit cards.
Directions: 1 km south of the main plaza and 2 blocks off the main beach.

Well located between the center of town and the beginning of Cavancha beach, the Camino del Mar is a beautifully restored house that is well over 100 years old and has been converted into a hotel. It's in the old section of town at the intersection of Orella and Bacquedano and fits in perfectly with many of the area's lovely old buildings. The hotel's exterior is especially attractive – navy blue with white trim, a veranda on the second floor, and windows and doorways with gray awnings. Entering, you'll find a sitting room with 14-foot ceilings, comfortable wicker furnishings, an overhead lamp, a TV, light gray wall-to-wall carpeting that continues throughout the hotel, and a winding stairway.

The hotel's management is very friendly and, even if no rooms are available, they might invite you to have a family meal in their small dining room. That area is also a good place for a drink and offers views of the central courtyard. As for the guest rooms, they are medium size with high ceilings and tall wooden doorways and have comfortable beds, modern commercial carpeting, telephones, and clean tile baths. In short, it's no wonder that the old Camino del Mar is often full, usually with 100% Chilean clients. To be sure of getting a room you should call in advance.

HOTEL PHOENIX
Ave. Anibal Pinto 451
Phone (81) 42-1315
Category: B
15 rooms, 2 stories, very old hotel, restaurant.
Rates: $14/$19 S/D incl. tax & breakfast. $11 per room with shared bath (less during the off-season). All major credit cards.
Directions: In the heart of town, 1 block north of the main plaza.

If you love old hotels with lots of character and don't care too much about the quality of the rooms, you may love the Phoenix. As you walk up to the second floor where the reception and guest rooms are located, the stairs are sure to creak with every step. At the top you'll find a large open area with an 18-foot skylight of colored glass, along with a few sofas and chairs for relaxing. The walls, which are entirely wooden, are another sign of the hotel's age, which well exceeds 100 years.

The rooms have high ceilings and wooden floors, but are small, with no furniture to speak of other than the beds, which are fairly narrow and have sagging mattresses. The fixtures in the private baths seem as old as the hotel, but the baths are clean enough and if you want to really save money you can take a double with shared bath. There's also a fairly plain restaurant on the main floor, and breakfast comes with the room.

First Alternative: **HOTEL DE LA PLAZA**
Plaza Prat 302, phone (81) 42-8394
Rates: $13/$19 S/D incl. tax & breakfast. No credit cards are accepted.
Directions: Faces the northern side of the city's main plaza.

If you're mainly concerned with the quality of the rooms, you may prefer the friendly Plaza. It is a tiny and inconspicuous four-story, eight-room hotel just one block away, overlooking Plaza Prat. It has much better and larger rooms than the Phoenix; the units are very clean, carpeted and have decent tile baths with modern fixtures. The noise from the plaza, however, can be a problem at times.

Second Alternative: **HOTEL BARROS ARANA**
Calle Barro Arana 1330, phone (81) 41-2840/42-4420
Rates: $12/$18 S/D incl. tax. No credit cards are accepted.
Directions: Between the main plaza and Cavancha beach.

A category B hotel with good rooms (all carpeted, with modern tile baths) is the Barros Arana, a 30-room, three-story hotel seven blocks from the beach and 10 from the main plaza. It has a restaurant and, if you pay a little extra, you can have a TV and a minibar in your room. While this modern, sterile place rates a zero in terms of ambience, it is very clean and, in terms of facilities, the best for the price.

Antofagasta

HOTEL ANTOFAGASTA
Avenida Balmaceda 2575
Phone (83) 22-4710
Fax (83) 22-4710
Telex 325066
Santiago phone (2) 33-3001
Category: Deluxe/A
168 rooms, old style, pool, travel agency, beauty salon, tiny beach, Hertz.
Rates: $32-$44/$35-$49 S/D superior incl. tax & breakfast; $16/$18 S/D standard. All major credit cards are accepted.
Directions: Very near the town center and overlooking the sea.

Dating from the 1940's, the massive, five-story Antofagasta, which is part of the Cristóbal Inn hotel chain, is a wonderful beach-front property near the heart of town and still the city's leading hotel despite its slightly aging facilities. The setting overlooking the ocean seems ideal, but beach lovers are likely to be disappointed, as the beach here is rocky except for a tiny sandy section, which is protected and without waves, just south of the hotel. Those looking for a hotel with a graceful atmosphere, however, will probably be thrilled because this place maintains much of its original charm.

Upon entering, you'll see a huge, two-story reception area with 12 massive columns. This is a good place to pass the time day or night as the atmosphere is both grand and inviting. There is a variety of intimate sitting areas with wicker furnishings that are both attractive and comfortable. They have carpets, numerous plants, and modern pastel water colors on the walls, plus huge cushions that are puffed up daily. Outside and one floor below you'll see the salt water pool. It's not always well maintained, which is probably why most guests prefer the tiny beach.

Many of the hotel's public areas have sides facing the sea. The main reception area, for example, has a two-story glass wall facing the ocean, so you're assured of good views of both the ocean and the pool. For an even better overlook you can walk out on to the breezy terrace, which is lined with tables, or into the adjoining, partially open bar. The latter is surrounded by plants and is quite inviting. For those seeking protection from the sun or rain, there's a section that's covered. Likewise, the large formal dining room, which is dominated by 18 large fluted columns and a big, semi-circular wall of glass with see-through curtains, has good views of the ocean and the crashing waves. When taking breakfast at the slightly less formal cafeteria, you'll again have the pleasure of this sight.

Most of the rooms here are "superiors," facing either town or, more expensive, the sea. Their furnishings are fairly ordinary but adequate – TVs, minibars, telephones, double beds, comfortable reading chairs, bureaus, built-in closets, and old style baths with combination showers. Those facing the ocean have private terraces and carpeting while those facing the city do not; neither has air conditioning. The "standard" rooms, which are smaller and without TVs or minibars, are cheaper and an excellent buy, but they're also in great demand. Book in advance as getting one of these can be difficult.

***Alternative:* PLAZA HOTEL**
Ave Baquedano 461, phone (83) 22-2058, telex 325082, Santiago phone (2) 74-2509
Rates: $26/$40 S/D incl. tax. All major credit cards are accepted.
Directions: One block south of the main plaza.

The very ordinary cement exterior and the plain, functional lobby of the Plaza, a 67-room, three-story structure in the heart of town, are hardly inviting. Nevertheless, this 50-year-old-plus structure is well maintained and has all the facilities (pool, squash court, jacuzzi, travel agency, beauty salon) of a first-class hotel. As a result, business remains brisk despite the hotel's age. The pool, which is in back and surrounded by grass, is too small and shallow for swimming, but for cooling off it's fine. Overlooking it is a cozy bar with carpeting and comfortable seating. The nearby restaurant offers a $4 menu of the day. Rooms at the Plaza are tiny and cramped, but have carpets, TVs, built-in closets, small windows and tile baths.

HOTEL DIEGO DE ALMAGRO
Avenida Condell 2624, phone (83) 25-1721
Category: B
Rates: $18/$24 S/D incl. tax. Visa, AmEx and Diners.
Directions: Two blocks southeast of the main plaza.

Dating from the late 70's, the Diego de Almagro is a five-story, gray cement structure just off the city's main commercial street, Avenida Prat. Stores occupy most of the hotel's first floor. Well maintained and popular with Chilean business people, it has a small dark reception area with sofas and several antique, high-back armchairs. The rooms are fairly small and, with their simple beds, hard wooden chairs, and unadorned walls, have an 18th-century feel about them. Nevertheless, they are immaculately clean and have a few good features, such as carpeting, built-in closets and combination tile baths with fixtures in good working order.

First Alternative: **HOTEL SAN MARCOS**
Calle Latorre 2946, phone (83) 25-1763/22-1492
Rates: $15/$19 S/D incl. tax. All major credit cards are accepted.
Directions: 4 blocks east of the main plaza.

This three-story, 56-room hotel near the center is an excellent alternative and less expensive as well. The units here are so tiny that the beds leave precious little space for walking around and the ones in back tend to be noisy. Also, the windows are small, without curtains, and the walls are bare. Still, the rooms do offer wall-to-wall carpets, TVs, built-in closets, telephones, and combination tile baths that are very clean. Indeed, the hotel's best feature is its spotlessness. A restaurant here serves breakfast.

Second Alternative: **SIETE CABANAS**
Phone (83) 22-1988
Directions: Some 17 km south of the city on the road to Cososo.

If a cabin (with cold showers) along a remote beach sounds appealing, try this beach-side camping spot or **RUCAMOVIL** (phone 22-6734), a similar place nearby. Both are open year round and have cabins for $15.

The South

Concepción

HOTEL ARAUCANO
Avenida Caupolicán 521
Phone (41) 230-606
Telex 260012
Santiago phone (2) 696-6826
Santiago fax (2) 696-5599
Category: A
Modern, 168 rooms, central. Indoor pool, shops, disco.
Rates: $35/$53 S/D incl. tax. All major credit cards.
Directions: In the heart of town, just off the main plaza.

The city's top hotel since the early 1970's when it was constructed, the Araucano is thoroughly modern and set in the heart of town across from the Plaza de Armas. It's quite a large establishment, with a total of 11 floors. Despite being Chile's third largest city and a major port, Concepción has little to offer tourists. Consequently, the hotel caters mainly to business travelers. Located on a pedestrian mall, the hotel's ground level consists almost entirely of shops.

The main lobby is duly impressive, with large brass chandeliers, black marble walls, Chippendale-style chairs, and modern carpeting. To one side is a small, comfortable and attractive waiting area with more antique-style chairs, two plush sofas, carpeting, large porcelain-based lamps, paintings on the wall, and a TV. Guests have a choice of eating at an inexpensive cafeteria or in a more formal dining room. The latter, including the kitchen, occupies the entire third floor and is quite regal, with 14-foot ceilings, fine red carpeting, native tapestries on the walls, and floor-to-ceiling windows surrounding most of the room. Several large square columns help to break up this expansive space into smaller, cozier areas. Because of the city's proximity to the sea, it's no surprise that seafood selections, including *congrio* (eel), *crevettes* (shrimp), *machas* (mussels), and *corvina* (sea bass), dominate the menu. Price-wise, the best deal is the three-course menu of the day which costs $4. Breakfast, which is copious and excellent, is also served here.

The hotel's accommodations are standard size and decent enough, with carpets, TVs, minibars, comfortable leather reading chairs, modern desks, built-in closets, and heating. The bathrooms in turn have tile floors, combination baths and bidets. However, many units, with frayed carpeting and leaky bath fixtures, are beginning to show their age. You may want to check your room and bathroom facilities before accepting. You could also check the newer alternative below, the Alborada, but remember – the Araucano does have a pool.

Alternative: **HOTEL ALBORADA**
Avenida Barros Arana 457, phone (41) 242-144

If the Araucano is full, your best bet is this slightly less expensive, modern establishment on the city's main drag. It's just four blocks from the main plaza and has 40 recently-renovated rooms.

HOTEL EL DORADO
Avenida Barros Arana 348, phone (41) 229-400, telex 260031.
Category: B
Rates: $20/$26 S/D incl. tax. All major credit cards accepted.
Directions: On the main drag, 3 blocks from the central plaza.

For a less expensive establishment, you might try the El Dorado. It's definitely nothing special, but the competition isn't either. Located just three blocks off the Plaza de Armas, this modern, four-story structure is in a good location and has a small, presentable lobby with brown carpeting, several comfortable armchairs, modern recessed lighting and glass walls which give it a fairly new look.

Rooms here are on the small side, but are in reasonably good condition, with freshly painted walls, good carpets, attractive bedspreads, desks, TVs, telephones, heating, and ample closet space. The combination baths have tile floors and walls, plus thick towels and, although the fixtures are a bit old, they do the trick. As long as the El Dorado remains well maintained, it will be a good refuge from pricey establishments and, while you can't get meals here other than breakfast, nearby restaurants can fulfill that need.

Alternative: HOTEL TABANCURA
Avenida Barros Arana 790, phone (41) 226-927

You might also check out this small hotel, which has clean, similarly-priced rooms with private baths. It's on the same street as the El Dorado, four blocks further from the center, on the eighth floor of a modern highrise.

Temuco

NUEVO HOTEL DE LA FRONTERA

Calle Mañuel Bulnes 726, phone (45) 236-190, fax (45) 710-317, telex 367013, Santiago phone (2) 232-6008
Category: A
Rates: $53/$67 S/D incl. tax & breakfast (25% less in off-season). Major credit cards.
Directions: In the center, ½ block off the Plaza de Armas.

This modern, "nuevo" establishment, which has an older and cheaper sister hotel across the street, is conveniently located in the heart of town and is the city's leading hotel. The facade is predominantly glass and unexciting, but the interior is another story altogether. The modern lobby, for example, has an impressive, two-story ceiling, tall plants, and comfortable, interesting furnishings, including several huge, glass-top coffee tables supported by large rocks, ceramic and brass lamps, carpets, and five extremely cushy sofas with pillows that are fluffed up every few hours. Those interested in local art may appreciate the carvings of a deer, a duck and a guinea hen on the walls and, more unusual still, the collection on one of the entrance tables of seven silver animals made with hundreds of tiny strips of metal.

Continuing further inside you'll find the hotel's indoor pool, which is round and covered by a pointed wood and glass ceiling and has plants everywhere, including one extending two stories high. Swimmers may feel a little conspicuous as the hotel's main restaurant, which begins about 10 feet from the water's edge, looks directly onto the pool, with some pool-side tables closer still. This semi-circular restaurant is ultra modern with steel and leather chairs and walls, carpeting and napkins in deep brown. The *trucha grille con mantequilla negra* (grilled trout) is highly recommended; other selections include *ajiaco a la criolla* (a local soup), *machas al horno con queso* (mussels with cheese), and *filete principe Humberto* (steak with mushrooms). Adjoining this area is a tavern-like bar with a dance floor and entertainment on weekends.

The guest rooms here are standard size and quite nice, with windows extending the entire length of the outside wall, curtains, lamp shades and the breakfast table all covered in matching material, industrial carpeting, TVs, desks, minibars, papered walls, built-in closets, and good lighting. The bathrooms are in tile with lots of counter space, thick towels, excellent lighting, and combination baths.

***Alternative:* CLASICO HOTEL DE LA FRONTERA**
Call Mañuel Bulnes 733, phone (45) 236-190
Rates: $16-$21/$22-$28 S/D incl. tax & breakfast. All major credit cards.
Directions: Across the street from the newer sister Frontera hotel.

For rooms at half the price, check out the older, five-story Hotel de la Frontera across the street, which has the same phone. One major advantage is that guests here can use the facilities of the newer sister hotel, including the pool and sauna. There are two categories of rooms; the less expensive ones are a particularly good buy. They are standard size with linoleum floors, telephones, TVs, desks, wide windows, good lighting, and decent bathrooms with older fixtures including combination baths. The more expensive units are slightly larger and have carpeting, but are otherwise virtually identical. Overall, the facilities of this 55-room hotel are well maintained and include a very presentable lobby and a large, high-ceiling restaurant overlooking a garden.

HOTEL CONTINENTAL
Avenida Varas 708
Phone (45) 211-395/231-166
Category: B & C
Old "Wild West" hotel, restaurant, TV room.
Rates: $7-$13/$12-$18 S/D incl. tax. All major credit cards.
Directions: 1 block west of the Plaza de Armas.

If there were one hotel in South America where even those traveling 1st class should consider "downgrading" for a night, the Continental would be it. This wooden, two-story establishment, which is over 100 years old, may well be the oldest continuously-operated hotel in South America. Since it was built in the late 19th century it has had only three owners; the present ones took over around 1934. This marvelous place is truly in a class by itself. Staying here, you'll feel as though you're back in the American Wild West. The construction is entirely of wood, including the walls, floors, ceiling and exterior. While there's virtually nothing new, don't expect this place to be decrepit. Even the local Rotary Club finds it a suitable meeting place for their monthly meetings, when coats and ties are de rigueur!

The bar here is indeed a classic – virtually every aspect of the room is original including, most notably, the long wooden bar itself and the fine paneling behind it. The floor and tables are likewise made of wood and bear the scars of years of use. Two large windows face the street and are partially covered with white curtains to keep people in the street from peaking in. At any moment, someone like Billy the Kid seems likely to enter.

There are two sitting rooms. The TV salon has the same natural-color, wide-board flooring and painted, narrow-board walls with wainscoting as found in most of the rooms. The 15-foot ceiling here is adorned with an antique glass chandelier, while the furnishings include an old, upright piano, a fine sideboard and cabinet, comfortable chairs, throw rugs, three beautifully framed oil paintings, plus a large tapestry. The other sitting area, which is equally homey, has a red tile floor and throw rugs, an old oil heater with pipes to the ceiling, lots of comfortable sofas and chairs and, most unusual, a ceiling with a large skylight.

Adjoining it is the main dining room, which has the same skylights that brighten up the interior during the day. This effect is accentuated by the construction of the wall surrounding the central dining room, which is entirely glass from the midpoint upwards. If you have a meal here, chances are you won't be disappointed, especially if you order the three-course meal of the day which costs only $2.50. There are also interesting à la carte selections, including *choritos bordalesa* (sausages), *salmón del río* (river salmon), *souffle de queso* (cheese soufflé), and 12 desserts, including *tortillas al rhon* (tortillas in a rum syrup).

The service here is so good that the staff even turn down your bed covers at night. Rooms are large, with wooden walls and creaky floors, cheap throw rugs, old mattresses with firm springs, basins lighted by bare light bulbs, original overhead lighting fixtures, wonderful antique bureaus with mirrors, windows with interior shutters and, most important, heaters. Many units have tiny adjoining baths, but if you take one of the cheaper ones you'll have to use a communal bath down the hall. You'll really feel like you're back in the 19th century when you hop into the antique tub. Fortunately, there's lots of hot water – just be sure to let it run a bit before inserting the plug because the first few squirts are sure to be rusty.

Alternative: **HOTEL CASABLANCA**
Avenida Montt 1306 y Zenteno, phone (45) 212-740

Nothing can compete with the Continental, but if it's full you might try the Casablanca, which is nothing special but does have cheap clean rooms. A little further from the center, it's six blocks northeast of the Plaza de Armas.

Villarrica

HOTEL YACHTING CLUB
Avenida General San Martín 802
Phone (45) 411-191
Temuco fax (45) 710-317
Temuco telex 367013
Santiago phone (2) 232-6008
Category: A
Lakefront lodge, 16 rooms and cabins, open year round, fishing, tennis, sauna, pool, access to Hotel Pucó n facilities.
Rates: $42/$63 S/D incl. breakfast & tax, about 50% off 3/15-12/14. All major credit cards are accepted here.
Directions: Overlooking the lake, 5 blocks north of center.

If having a great view is important, you can't beat the Yachting Club. It's one of the few places where you can get great views of both Lago Villarrica and the area's near-perfect volcano, Volcán Villarrica. The latter has hardly been benign to the region. If you look on the walls inside the hotel you'll see some fascinating newspaper articles on the recent eruptions. The volcano erupted once in 1948, killing some 60 people, again in 1971 when six people died and, most recently, in 1984, when the volcano's ski facilities were destroyed.

The lodge has good facilities, including a pool, sauna and tennis court. Guests here can also use the more extensive facilities of the Hotel Pucón, which is 30 minutes away. The principal attraction, however, is fishing, which is why the main lounge looks so "fishy." On the walls are paddles, life preservers, a schooner model, a large brass lantern from an old ship, as well as skis and a moose head. It's a comfortable room, with a stone fireplace, cushy sofas, game tables, a TV, wood-beam ceilings, and fantastic views of the lake and volcano. For a drink, you need only step over to the tiny adjoining bar.

The hotel's restaurant has the same views, which is its best feature. The linoleum floors and vinyl-seat chairs don't exactly add charm, but the ambience is enhanced by a few plants, an old ship's wheel used for overhead lighting, and a prize-winning, glass-encased trout. There's a long wine list, with no fewer than nine Chilean vineyards represented. Unless you like dishes with heavy, almost suffocating sauces, stick to their fish selections such as *corvina con almendras al tomate* (sea bass with almonds and tomato sauce) or *congrio a la plancha* (baked eel), and top it off with their superb *panqueques con miel* (honey pancakes) dessert. The full three-course menu of the day costs around $5.

The best feature of the rooms on the upper level is that they have lakefront decks with chairs. The units are standard size, with linoleum floors, throw rugs, dressing mirrors, exposed-beam ceilings, breakfast tables, ample closets, and reading lights over the beds, which are two singles side by side. The bathrooms are small, with tile combination baths, bidets and, most important, heating. If you want a unit with slightly nicer furnishings, full carpeting, and more modern bathrooms, ask for one on the ground level. There is a trade-off however – those units have no porches.

HOTEL EL CIERVO

Avenida General Koerner 241, phone (45) 411-215.
Category: A
Rates: $38/$45 S/D incl. breakfast & tax (40% off 3/15-12/14). Major credit cards.
Directions: Overlooking the lake, 5 blocks north of center.

If you prefer places with a homey atmosphere, chances are you'll like the Ciervo. Run for years by Fritz Specht, a very friendly German, it's a delightful inn and just a block away from the Yachting Club, with the same great views of the lake and volcano. An added attraction during the peak summer months is the front patio, where guests enjoy cocktails while admiring the views and soaking up the rays. Fishing is the main attraction for most people and is one reason why the crowd here is definitely on the older side.

Built around 1935 as a house, El Ciervo was expanded during the late 70's to include six new rooms; the remaining nine are all in the main building. Fritz makes sure guests feel at home and offers drinks at any time, most often in the three-room living area. The decor here is no different from that of a normal residence – comfortable sofas and chairs, carpets, beige papered walls, a few plants here and there, paintings on the walls, and a good supply of books. During the summer, guests will usually find flowers on their dining tables in the restaurant, which has a knotty-pine ambience because of the wooden walls. Meals are served family style and change daily. A fan helps to cool things off during the hot summers.

All of the rooms benefit from central heating and, in the main section, no two rooms are alike. The best and most expensive room, called the "Colonial," is huge, with a brick fireplace, carpeting, flowery papered walls, a TV, a wonderful old bureau, a three-mirror vanity table, comfortable chairs and antique side tables. The bathroom is also large and has the same carpeting and some fine old fixtures, including a combination bath in good working order. Other rooms in the main house are smaller and those in the front have lake views. Rooms in the newer, motel-like section in back don't have the views and are fairly small, with new industrial carpeting, modern antique-style furnishings, TVs, ample closet space, and modern bathrooms with showers.

***Alternative:* HOSTERIA LA COLINA**
Calle JA 1177, phone (45) 411-503

For a less expensive category B hotel with rooms for half the price, head for La Colina, which is a relatively new hostel run by some delightful Americans. It is located on a hill (*colina*) above town, affording wonderful views of Villarrica and the lake, and there are some very attractive gardens to boot. In addition, the rooms here are decent and the restaurant serves delicious meals. The warm and friendly service on which this place stakes its reputation is without parallel.

Pucón

HOTEL ANTUMALAL
Carretera de Villarrica, Km 3.5
Box 84, Pucón
Phone (45) 441-011
Category: Deluxe
Secluded elite retreat catering to wealthy North Americans, 18 rooms, open year round, lakefront, sailing, water skiing, rowing, tennis, English spoken.
Rates: $160/$230 S/D including tax and full board. $110/$160 S/D in off-season (3/1-12/14). All major credit cards are accepted.
Directions: 2 km west of Pucón on the highway to Villarrica.

The Antumalal is one of the two or three most exclusive hotels on the continent and the clientele – mostly well-heeled North Americans, including many celebrities and top executives – is clear proof thereof. It would be rare for a guest to just pop in here, at least during the summer season. For starters, there are only 18 rooms and prices are particularly high, up to $320 or more for a suite. This Polish-owned, family-run retreat was designed to attract only the crème de la crème; in 1968, even Queen Elizabeth and Prince Phillip graced this secluded, tranquil establishment with their presence!

The Antumalal dates from the mid-1950's, but you'd never guess this from its modern appearance. The exterior, which is somewhat reminiscent of a Frank Lloyd Wright structure, is enveloped in a forest with tiny manicured gardens throughout the grounds. It's impossible to get good views of this meandering, predominantly one-story structure that seems to jut out of the hills. The location, about 100 feet above Lake Villarrica on a cliff, is incomparable. Flowers, small spots of grass, and stone walks are on the grounds leading down to the shore.

Guests can sit out on the wooden patio with a drink and book and enjoy the views while soaking up some rays and listening to the soothing sounds of a nearby stream. Those more inclined towards athletics can enjoy tennis, fishing, sailing, water skiing, rowing and, during the winter months, skiing, which is becoming an increasingly popular sport here. Indeed, you name it and the owner/manager, Pedro Pollak, will make all the necessary arrangements – for a fee of course!

The interior is an intriguing mixture of stone, wood, and glass windows. The main sitting room, for example, has one wall in stone, another entirely in glass, and two more in wood. A long string of plants to one side makes the room seem to extend outside. Two of the lighting fixtures are, in fact, logs with lights on the branches. Of course there are lots of comfortable sofas and chairs for relaxing. Another more intimate and slightly rustic sitting area, also with great views of the lake, has marble floors and animal skins for rugs, a huge fireplace, wooden tables and chairs, cushy sofas and more tree-like lamps.

For such an expensive establishment, the rooms seem rather simple. They are standard size with dark floors, throw rugs, wooden walls, comfortable reading chairs, stone fireplaces, and modern tile bathrooms with combination baths. The three suites are similar, but include an additional room with tile floors, animal-skin throw rugs, a fireplace, breakfast table, and 50 or so English-language paperbacks. All rooms overlook the lake, but the trees slightly impede the views from some of them. The hotel's hallmark is its service, and the fabulous meals at the restaurant are just one of the many reminders of this.

GRAN HOTEL PUCON
Calle Holzapfel 190
Phone (45) 441-001
Telex 367013
Temuco fax (45) 710-317
Santiago phone (2) 232-6008
Category: Deluxe

Stately grand hotel, 153 rooms, lakefront, open year round, private beach, fishing, disco, sailboards, sailboats, sauna, tennis, squash, barber shop, pool, water skiing, horseback riding, access to golf, game room, beauty salon, gym, bank.
Rates: $50-$72/$64-$94 S/D incl. tax & breakfast (35% off 3/1-12/14). All major credit cards are accepted.
Directions: On the northern edge of town facing the lake.

If a grand hotel resembling an Austrian castle is to your liking, take a room at this stately, five-story establishment set on the shore of Lake Villarrica. The entrance side is graced with flowers and a huge lawn, while the back side has a private beach. You'll think you're in Europe at some elegant ski resort like St. Moritz. The old-world ambience definitely predominates here. Public areas are generally large and impressive, while the sporting facilities are about as extensive as you'll find anywhere in South America. There's even an outdoor expedition company that offers same-day trips to the top of Villarrica Volcano (equipment provided) as well as rafting on local rivers.

The main sitting room, which has 15-foot ceilings and measures some 60 feet in length, is dominated by four massive columns and a large antique glass chandelier hanging in the center. The old-world look is accentuated by the wooden wainscoting, exposed beams in the ceiling, and large, gilt-framed paintings on three of the walls. If you're looking for a place to hang out, try this impressive room. The plush, modern sofas and matching armchairs are very comfortable indeed. Adjoining this area is the hotel's main restaurant. It is similarly massive with huge arched windows facing the lake, stylish modern carpeting, elegant wooden chairs, and flowers on all the tables. Meal plans here are optional.

Even the TV room in this old-world establishment is grand – an antique chandelier, oriental carpets, parquet floors, paintings, and leather chairs. For a little action, head for the game room, which is filled with card tables. Alternatively, try one of the hotel's two bars, one of which has a disco. The main bar is a large room with a magnificent long bar, a grand piano, various old-style lighting fixtures on the walls, carpets, paned windows with floor-to-ceiling drapes, and great views of the lake.

There are several classes of accommodations. Even the standard ones are large and well maintained, with floor-to-ceiling draperies, carpeting, leather reading chairs, breakfast tables, desks, and ample closet space. In the adjoining tile combination bathrooms you'll find lots of thick towels, bidets and fairly old fixtures in excellent working order. In the late 80's rooms on the fourth floor were renovated and are now the best and most expensive. These *lujo* rooms are quite large, with modern furnishings in designer fabrics, double beds, minibars, TVs, piped-in music, breakfast tables, thick carpets, ample closet space, comfortable reading chairs, and ultra-modern bathrooms. During the off-season when prices take a nose dive, even these more expensive rooms are very reasonable.

HOSTERIA GUDENSCHWAGER
Ave. Pedro de Valdivia 12
Phone (45) 441-156
Category: B
Rustic Bavarian-type hostel, 21 rooms, open 12/15-3/15, B&B, bar, English spoken.
Rates: $15-$19/$22-$32 S/D incl. tax. All major credit cards.
Directions: On the northwest edge of town near the lake, 6 blocks from the center.

In operation as a hotel since its construction in 1934, this rustic lodge with, as the charming owners advertise, an "ambiente Europeo," is a lively place with great atmosphere. It's also very popular with the younger crowd, so getting a room during the busy summer months can be difficult. On the outside it's an aesthetically pleasing gray shingle structure with windows in white trim and a rusty red tin roof. A dirt road passes directly in front, but there's enough room for five or so large bushes.

The harsh winters take their toll on this wooden, three-story lodge, but inside it's in clearly good condition. The decor is fairly spartan as the wooden floors and walls are, respectively, bare and largely without adornment except for some antlers. To the right as you enter is a long bar with six or so plain wooden tables and a number of chairs; this and the patio out back are where most guests gather. Fortunately, the bar has several sofas and wooden armchairs with cushioned seats and backs that add a bit of badly needed warmth and comfort. Adjoining the bar is a large dining room that looks out onto the lake and serves excellent food, but for a change you can always eat out. The center of town is only a few blocks away. Just outside the restaurant you'll find the patio; it has built-in wooden seats for sunning and viewing the lake.

The best accommodations are doubles, which are not cramped like the triples. They have only the bare essentials – firm foam mattresses, plain curtains, two tables, a single chair, a dangling light bulb, and small attached baths with old fixtures and water heated by a central, wood-burning stove below. Less expensive doubles and triples have similar shared baths. Rooms on the third floor offer bunk beds and are cheaper still; even they are quite acceptable if all you need is a comfortable bed and a guaranteed hot shower.

***First Alternative:* PENSION SALZBURG**
Avenida O'Higgins 311 y Fresia, phone (45) 441-907
Rates: $10-$15 per room with breakfast. Credit cards are not accepted.
Directions: It's in the heart of Pucón on the main drag, across from Almacenes Eltit and near the bus stations.

If the Gudenschwager is full or sounds too rustic, try the Salzburg – a homely, wood-frame inn in the center of town. Open 11/1-3/31, this small B&B, which has been operated as a hostel since 1959, has friendly German-speaking owners who do their best to make you feel at home. The best place to spend time is the small sitting room. It has a TV, a stone fireplace with a mantel lined with knick-knacks, and comfortable chairs and sofas. Next to it is a small breakfast area that has four tables, posters and paintings everywhere, and a tiny bar.

The guest rooms are all configured differently and several have views of Villarrica Volcano; three have private tile baths and the remaining three (all cheaper) have shared baths. The former units are medium size and home-like, with comfortable beds, throw rugs, flowery curtains, sofas and relaxing armchairs. The cheaper rooms upstairs are smaller with fewer furnishings.

Second Alternative: **HOTEL LA POSADA**
Calle Pedro de Valdivia 191, phone (45) 441-088

Pucón can get very crowded during the summer, so if you arrive then and haven't made reservations in advance, don't be surprised if both the Gudenschwager and Salzburg are full. In that case, try the Posada, which has similarly-priced rooms and is three blocks north of the main drag (O'Higgins) and near Lake Villarrica. There are rooms with private baths and cheaper rooms with shared baths, plus cabins and a restaurant.

Valdivia

HOTEL PEDRO DE VALDIVIA
Avenida Caranpangue 190
Phone (63) 21-2931
Telex 271021
Category: A
85 rooms, 6 stories, old style, restaurant, bar, laundry.
Rates: $25-$37/$31-$43 S/D incl. tax & breakfast. Children free. All major credit cards.
Directions: In the center of town, 3 blocks from the main plaza, overlooking Río Calle Calle.

Since 1935, this massive six-story establishment has been the leading hotel in Valdivia, and while there is some serious competition these days from newer hotels, the Pedro de Valdivia's old-style charm still makes it a winner. The location on the banks of the Calle Calle River is unbeatable. From the front this pink structure is imposing, but in back towards the river the ambience is relaxing, with a lawn the size of a football field surrounded by trees, flowers and shrubs.

If you pass through the lobby you'll come to the main sitting room. It's a large, high-ceiling area with a huge, well-used fireplace near the center.

This grand room is divided into several sitting sections, each with comfortable sofas, Chippendale-style chairs, coffee tables and rugs. Unfortunately, despite the glass wall along the back side, the river is barely visible from here. For a better view guests can walk out on the terrace just beyond, but they may have to stand as there are generally no chairs here. For a drink, you can step into the **Bar Doña Ines** which faces the front. The original wooden bar, with brass foot-rails and leather-seated stools, is still here. It's a comfortable and attractive room with wood-panelled walls, huge paned windows, carpeting, round wooden tables with old-style wooden chairs. If you want a cup of coffee, have it here as opposed to the dining room because you'll get superb French-style coffee instead of powdered instant. And if you're here on a Wednesday, which is bridge night, you can play some cards.

Head downstairs to the main restaurant, **Don Pedro**, for dinner. It's a 70-foot-long, two-story-high room with a huge mural at one end depicting the arrival of the Spaniard, Pedro de Valdivia, who founded this city in 1552. On the room's back side is a wall of paned glass which affords superb views of the rear lawn, if not the river. This is an impressive area with several large fluted columns, Old Masters reproductions on the walls, brass and glass lighting fixtures, parquet floors, and brass railings. Vines dangling down the wall from the lobby above add a nice touch. The menu includes *congrio* (eel) cordon bleu, *paella Valenciana*, and *pavo al cognac* (turkey with cognac). A better option might be to walk 200 yards towards the river to reach the **Camino de Luna**, an attractive riverboat restaurant where you can get all kinds of well-prepared seafood that is no more expensive.

The tourist-class rooms are medium size with slightly frayed carpets, reading chairs, TVs, dressing tables, matching curtains and bedspreads, large closets, and combination bathrooms with thick towels and old-style fixtures in good working order. The Type B suites, which are 50% dearer but still not expensive, are larger and in better condition, with more furnishings, including several comfortable reading chairs. The bathrooms are the same no matter which room you choose.

First Alternative: **HOTEL VILLA DEL RIO**
Avenida España 1025, phone (63) 21-6292, telex 271001

If the quality of the rooms is more important than location or ambience, try this similarly-priced hotel, which is also on the banks of the Calle Calle River. It is located near the central area and rents apartments with kitchenettes and TVs. There's also a yacht basin, gardens, free parking, and an excellent, but expensive restaurant.

Second Alternative: **VILLA PAULINA**
Calle Yerbas Buenas 389, phone (63) 21-6372/21-2445

For a less expensive category B hotel, try Paulina's friendly B&B, which is also outside the downtown area and has a pool, free parking, spotlessly clean rooms, and decent bathrooms with hot showers.

Third Alternative: **HOTEL SCHUSTER**
Calle Maipu 60, phone (63) 21-3272
Rates: $13/$15 S/D incl. tax. No credit cards are accepted.
Directions: In the center, 2 blocks off the Plaza de la República toward the river.

For a category C hotel in the center, try this friendly establishment, which dates from 1910 and is full of character. You'll feel as though you're taking a journey back in time. An entirely wood construction, the Schuster looks run-down on the outside, but inside it's still in good condition. There are 34 sizeable guest rooms with heating, fine wooden floors, beds with slightly lumpy mattresses, telephones, and original brass overhead lamps. They also have en suite baths with hot water all day and ancient fixtures in fairly good working order. You'll find a sitting area with comfortable armchairs, a marvelous old bar with most of the original furnishings, and a restaurant that serves only breakfast.

Osorno

HOTEL DEL PRADO
Calle Cochrane 1162 y Bilbao
Phone (64) 23-2203/23-5020
Telex 273156
Santiago phone (2) 251-7350
Category: A
Small, one story, modern, 20 rooms, pool, garden, parking.
Rates: $34/$46 S/D incl. tax. Children under 10 free. All major credit cards.
Directions: 6 blocks off the main plaza.

Part of the Hoteles Estratégicos de Chile chain, the Prado is the city's best hotel and a good choice for those who appreciate small, refined establishments. It offers good service, modern facilities, and a tranquil atmosphere that is perfect for relaxing. The Prado is a small single-story hotel with free parking and very modern facilities including a small, kidney-shaped pool surrounded by grass. It is well located just six blocks off the main plaza. The modern rooms are of standard size and include TVs, minibars, attractive furnishings, carpets, reading chairs, ample closet space, and modern tile bathrooms with combination baths. The management prides itself on offering professional personalized service and if you stay for five days, they'll give you a sixth day for free!

You'll be hard pressed to find better meals anywhere else in town and the chef will offer suggestions if you ask. As in most restaurants, the fish selections, including *congrio* (eel), *machas* (mussels), and *lenguada* (sole), are usually the best. For a change you could also try the **Club Alemán** (phone 23-2784) at Calle O'Higgins 563, just off the Plaza de Armas. It's a popular club-like place with attractive wood-panelled walls. Another possibility is **Peter Kneipe** at Calle M. Rodriguez 1039; the fare there is also German and delicious, although expensive by Osorno standards.

Alternative: HOTEL WAEGER

Calle Cochrane 816, phone (64) 23-3721/2, fax (64) 23-7080, telex 273156, Santiago phone (2) 251-7350
Rates: $17-$24/$32 S/D incl. tax. Children under 10 free. All major credit cards.
Directions: 2 blocks off the main plaza.

If the Prado is full, your best bet is the larger, four-story sister hotel, the Waegner. This hotel dates from 1950 and is on the same street and just four blocks away, closer to the center. The 35 rooms here are all carpeted and have TVs, minibars, sofas, large closets, and baths with fairly old fixtures, including showers. There's a pleasant sitting room with comfortable furnishings plus a large, undistinguished restaurant. If you choose to eat here, the seafood selections, such as *gambas* (prawns) a la Riviera, are generally best.

GRAN HOTEL OSORNO

Calle O'Higgins 615, phone (64) 23-2171.
Category: B
Rates: $15/$24 S/D incl. tax and breakfast. All major credit cards.
Directions: Facing the main square.

Half a century old and once the city's finest hotel, the Gran has been recently renovated and now fills a badly needed gap in the city's meager mid-range lodging resources. The exterior of this five-story structure is hardly impressive, but upon entering you'll see that this old building facing the Plaza de Armas was once indeed grand. The 50-foot-long lobby soars a full two stories upward and is larger and potentially grander than any room in the slightly newer, more upmarket Waeger nearby. Most unusual is the art deco ceiling which consists of hundreds of round pieces of glass that spray filtered sunlight throughout the lobby. This is the best place to watch all the action. There are numerous sitting areas with comfortable chairs, sofas, rugs, and coffee tables with brass lamps. For those without wheels, you can always find a taxi waiting just outside.

Rooms here are smaller than standard and quite presentable, with wide single beds, papered walls, industrial carpeting, floor-to-ceiling draperies, TVs, telephones, and decent attached combination bathrooms with tile floors and ordinary fixtures. There's also a restaurant that features a set menu each day for just $3. The food isn't bad considering how cheap it is to eat here.

First Alternative: **RESIDENCIAL RIGA**
Calle Antahuer 1058, phone (64) 23-2945

An excellent alternative to the Orsono is the Riga, which is a homier B&B away from the center and about a third less expensive than the Gran. It's also very popular, so during the summer season you'll have to call ahead.

Second Alternative: **VILLA EDUVIGES**
Calle Eduviges 856, phone (64) 23-5023

For a place fairly close to the center, try this friendly B&B, which is between Bilbao and Mañuel Rodriguez, eight short blocks southeast of the Plaza de Armas and five blocks south of the bus terminal. It's of similar quality, style and price, with rooms for about $12 and, like the Riga, it has a good supply of hot water and serves breakfast.

Lake Puyehue

GRAN HOTEL TERMAS DE PUYEHUE
Ruta 215, Km 76, Entre Lagos
Osorno phone (64) 235-157
Osorno telex 232157/273146
Santiago phone (2) 231-1004
Santiago telex 240572
Category: Deluxe
Hot-springs resort, 100 rooms, heated indoor pool, thermal baths, tennis, mini-golf, game room, riding stables, boats for fishing and water skiing (or just relaxing), and a childrens' play area.
Rates: $38-$42/$52-$57 S/D incl. breakfast & tax (less from 5/1 to 12/14). Major credit cards are accepted.
Directions: Just outside Entre Lagos on the International Highway (Route 215) from Osorno to Arentina, 76 km (50 miles) east of Osorno and 4 km before Aguas Calientes. It's just off the road and within view of Lake Puyehue. Frequent public buses that run from Osorno to Entre Lagos, Puyehue and Aguas Calientes will drop guests at the hotel; the trip takes 2 hours.

Constructed between 1939 and 1947, this well-known complex has been a favorite with Chilean families for years. It has a prime location on some extensive, wooded and verdant grounds within view of Lake Puyehue and several miles from Puyehue National Park. The thermal baths are the main attraction here, so be prepared for bathing with large crowds! There are several baths, including an enclosed one with 100°F water and an outside one, Los Baños de Barros, with 106°F water. Some of the older crowd come looking for relief from their rheumatism, arthritis, or skin diseases, and to pass away time playing dominos, cachos, or naipes in the bar. Others visit to enjoy both the baths and some of the many sporting activities offered here, which include riding and fishing. There's even an enclosed tennis court now. Excursions to the nearby volcano, Casablanca, can also be arranged; it's fairly easy to climb during the summer and serves as the skiing center for this area during the winter season.

The lodge itself is an attractive stone and wood structure, both inside and out. The restaurant is trimmed with local handicrafts and wrought iron lighting fixtures and has an international menu with an emphasis on seafood and beef. They have a captive audience so it's not surprising that meal prices, even for breakfast, are quite high by Chilean standards. Even with the hotel's first-rate facilities and beautiful scenery, room prices likewise seem excessively high, especially during the peak season. Units with lake views are dearer still. All have carpets, heating and medium-size bathrooms with combination baths.

First Alternative: **NILQUE MOTEL**
Located on the shore of Lake Puyehue, Osorno phone (64) 234-960

This similarly-priced lakefront resort with its own private beach is much smaller (only 40 cabins) and is probably the country's top family resort. Activities include horseback riding, fishing, and boating, plus there's a childrens' play area.

Second Alternative: **PUB DEL CAMPO**
Entre Lagos

Both the Termas de Puyehue and Nilque are lovely, but they're also a bit over-priced. If you're here during peak season, consider heading into town and checking out this small but popular Swiss-run hotel. The rooms are fine and cost only a fraction of those at the Termas de Puyehue. Meals are excellent.

Puerto Octay, Frutillar & Puerto Varas

HOTEL CENTINELA
Peninsula Centinela, Pt Octay
Phone (649) 22
Santiago phone (2) 223-2497/251-2135
Category: B
15 rooms & 18 cabins, rustic lodge, overlooking lake, restaurant and bar.
Rates: $24/$15 per room incl. breakfast & tax, $47/$40 per cabin (about 20% less 3/1-10/31). Visa & Diners credit cards are accepted.
Directions: On Centinela Peninsula, 3 miles south of Puerto Octay. If you arrive in Puerto Octay by bus, you may have to walk, as the village has only one unmarked taxi. The friendly owner of the general store next to the bus station will help you look for it. Regardless, the 1-hour walk is delightful and easy to follow.

Built around the turn of the century as a summer house for political and artistic Chilean celebrities and in operation as a hotel since 1942, this marvelous rustic place is situated on 22 acres of heavily wooded land on the tip of beautiful Centinela Peninsula, overlooking Lake Llanquihue. Part of the fun of staying at this tranquil place is just walking around the unkempt grounds and swimming in the lake. You may even encounter a few wandering cows munching on the wild flowers. Another attraction is Puerto Octay, a truly delightful village reminiscant of a European town with its quaint homes and extravagant, turn-of-the-century architecture. It's full of people of Germanic descent and has attractive vegetable gardens everywhere you look.

During the long summer months guests at this friendly establishment can sit in the windowed dining room or out on the front tile terrace until 9:30 p.m. and watch the sun set on three (yes, three!) volcanoes. The cast iron stove in the large dining area makes it a good place to sit when the weather is chilly. The meals, which are quite good and cost about $6 with wine, are served family style, usually with two choices for the main dish, such as roasted chicken or roasted beef.

The main sitting room in this wood-framed, shingle-roof lodge is two stories high, with a pointed exposed-beam ceiling dominated by a brass chandelier and a huge painting on the second floor level. Guests can look down from the second floor as a wooden balcony runs along the front and back sides on this level. The room is rustic and sparsely furnished with rugless wide-board flooring, wooden walls, and several ordinary but functional sofas and armchairs. A single stove supposedly heats this spacious area during the fall to spring months, but don't expect it to be toasty. Next to it is a smaller sitting room without heating that's cozier and more homey. It has matching sofas, chairs and coffee tables made of wicker, as well as five or so other comfortable chairs. For entertainment guests can head for the small card room, which has plain wooden tables and views of the lake.

The standard rooms in the main house are a bit small, with low ceilings, but they have so few furnishings that they are not cramped. Two single beds with foam mattresses that sag just a bit, a small wooden table, a built-in closet, a wash basin, and an overhead light bulb are all you will find. Rooms 5, 7, 9, 10 and 11 have both lake and volcano views; others have views of one or neither. Not surprisingly the bathroom facilities are quite old, but they are in good working order and the hot water supply is reliable, plus the towels are thick. The more expensive units have private baths; others have shared ones. In back you'll find 18 new A-frame cabins; all have great views of the lake and over half of them also have kitchenettes.

***Alternative:* HOTEL HAASE**
Calle Pedro Montt 344, Puerto Octay, phone (649) 213
Rates: $8/$12 S/D incl. tax. No credit cards are accepted.
Directions: 1½ blocks south of the town plaza.

Travelers who would rather be in the heart of this picturesque village may prefer the friendly Hotel Hasase, which in its own way is as unique as the Centinela. It's a spacious place with high ceilings and several dining rooms, and is run by a wonderful elderly woman of German descent who is usually delighted to show guests around.

HOTEL FRUTILLAR
Ave. Philippi 1000, Frutillar, phone (65) 42-222/277, telex 370168, Santiago phone (2) 394-422
Category: A
Rates: $33/$42 S/D incl. breakfast & tax; 33% less 3/15-12/14. Major credit cards.
Directions: In the center of Frutillar on the main drag.

Frutillar is also very picturesque, but it's a good deal more touristy and expensive than Puerto Octay and things don't seem as authentic. The best time to visit is during the last week of January when Frutillar holds its famous music festival, an annual tradition since 1968. However, getting a room anywhere in town is extremely difficult then. There are only a handful of full-scale hotels in town; the other options are all B&Bs. One is the modern two-story Hotel Frutillar which is in an unbeatable location, literally on the lake's edge in the heart of town. Rooms here are carpeted, heated, have knotty-pine walls on one side, vanity tables, comfortable beds, and modern combination baths. Half of the 32 units have views of the lake, so try to reserve one of them, as the sight is truly exceptional.

Unfortunately, the ambience here is fairly dreadful, the saving grace being the hotel's exceptionally friendly management. The public areas are functional and the quality of everything, from the walls to the furnishings, is entirely ordinary. They have parquet floors and a few throw rugs here and there. Knotty-pine walls are offered in some of the rooms. The main sitting room is furnished with flimsy cushions, a modern brick fireplace, several rugs, plain white curtains, solid wood chairs, and several plants – hardly anything special. The restaurant has a similarly cold feel to it, but the lake views from here, as throughout the hotel, are great. For better food and ambience head for the **Club Alemán**, just 200 yards northward on the same street.

Alternative: HOTEL SALZBURG

This newer country-style hotel in Frutillar has a more interesting atmosphere and is a better alternative if you can afford to pay a little more. It has modern rooms, a sauna, and a good restaurant. The management will gladly arrange tours and fishing trips for its guests as well as rent mountain bikes.

HOSPEDAJE WINKLER

Ave. Philippi 1155, Frutillar
Phone (65) 42-388
Category: B
10-room B&B, plus cabins.
Rates: $10 per person incl. breakfast & tax, 33% less 3/15-12/14. No credit cards accepted.
Directions: Near the center of town, south of Hotel Frutillar and facing the lake.

Formerly called the Mahler, this friendly place on the main drag near the heart of town is definitely one of the best B&Bs here. As you're walking along Philippi, look for an attractive two-story house painted green and white, built of stone on the first floor and wood on the second. Directly facing the lake, it's very well maintained with a small tidy lawn in front.

On arrival you'll probably be led to the small home-like living room, which is the only place to spend your spare time here. The rooms, which are not cramped, have average-quality beds, fairly large mirrors, and adequate closet space, but no rugs or reading chairs. The nicest ones here have tiny private baths and hot showers. There are also cabins in back and YMCA members are offered discounts.

Alternative: HOSPEDAJE LAGO AZUL

Avenida Philippi 1175, Frutillar, phone (65) 42-338

If the Winkler is full try this similar identically-priced B&B just two doors down and closer to the center. It's a two-story, blue-striped house and not marked. The owners are very friendly and cater primarily to families. The guest rooms are fairly large and have beds that are marginally comfortable. The bathrooms here are small and have hot-water showers, but not tubs; only a few of the 12 rooms have private baths. A good breakfast is included in the room price.

HOTEL LICARAYEN
Ave. San José 114, Pt Varas
Phone (65) 23-2305/23-2955
Category: A
18 rooms, open year round, central location, lakefront hotel, restaurant and bar.
Rates: $33-$44 per room including tax and breakfast (33% less from mid-March to mid-December). All major credit cards.
Directions: 3 blocks from the heart of Puerto Varas, facing the lake.

With some 30,000 inhabitants, Puerto Varas is the largest town on Lake Llanquihue; it's also one of the least interesting. There are, however, some good beaches just a short walk from the heart of town. The beaches are one reason why the Licarayén, which faces the water, is so popular and such a good choice in this city.While this three-story chalet looks like a modern and somewhat unusual private residence with many angles, it's been a hotel since it was constructed in 1970. A newer section was added in the mid-1980's. The exterior is quite attractive, with plants and several trees around it.

Those guests not on the beach can usually be found lounging on the long wooden sundeck which extends around most of the front section of the building. In the evening a popular place to spend time is the main sitting room, which is clean and pleasant, but not particularly striking. This room has a couple of reasonably comfortable sofas and chairs, a few flowers here and there, two large arched windows facing the lake, plus a small adjoining bar where drinks are served.

The Licarayén has first-rate rooms, the best being the six in the new section. Most of them have views of the sea and three have jacuzzis. These newer units are slightly smaller than standard and have new carpets, twin beds with thick bedspreads, matching draperies, good lighting for reading in bed, breakfast tables, TVs, heating, ample closet space, and modern tile bathrooms with lots of counter space and combination baths. The other rooms, a few of which have balconies, are a bit smaller and 25% cheaper. They have older furnishings, including carpets, TVs, heaters, telephones, and bathrooms with showers, but no tubs.

Alternative:
HOTEL BELLAVISTA
Avenida Vicente Peréz Rosales 60
Phone (65) 23-2011/2.
Rates: $30/$37 S/D incl. tax during the high season (1/1-3/15); $24/$29 S/D any other time. All credit cards.
Directions: On the beach road leading east towards Ensenada, 5 blocks east of the Licarayén.

As the Licarayén is heavily booked during the summer season you'll probably have to look elsewhere if you haven't reserved in advance. The pickings in Puerto Varas are slim, but if you must stay here your best bet is the new Bellavista, a five-story, 27-room establishment which is nearby and has a very friendly uniformed staff. It lacks any semblance of character, but has two very good features – proximity to a good beach (just 50 yards away) and rooms (all facing the lake) providing fantastic views of Osorno Volcano. The rooms have TVs and modern combination baths. There's no restaurant, but guests can get breakfast and snacks anytime during the day at the cafeteria here.

Ralún, Ensenada, Petrohué & Peulla

HOTEL RALUN
Ralún
Phone (65) 25-2100
Telex 240048/240049
Santiago phone (2) 698-1881
Category: Deluxe
Secluded fishing resort, lakeside stone lodge, 8 rooms and 12 cabins, open year round, fishing, private beach, tennis, sailboats, horseback riding, water skiing, kayaks, lake excursions, sauna.
Rates: $65/$70 S/D incl. tax, $54/$60 S/D low season (4/4-12/15); 35-50% more for cabins for 4-6 persons. All major credit cards are accepted.
Directions: On the southern end of Ralún, which is a village 61 miles/96 km east of Puerto Montt via Puerto Varas and Ensenada (20 miles/31 km south of Ensenada). Hotel transport is available daily to/from Puerto Montt; the trip takes 2 hours.

The main attraction of this lovely remote resort, which overlooks Reloncair Estuary, is fishing. Indeed, this is probably the premier river-fishing resort in South America. Anglers primarily from North America come here every year, mostly from November through March, to test their skill and luck in the nearby streams and lakes. The main catch is brown or rainbow trout (usually in the one- to five-pound range) and salmon. Even if the ol' man is the only angler, other members of the family will hardly die of boredom. The deep green estuary in front of the hotel affords guests the opportunity of learning or testing their skills at sailing, sailboarding, water skiing, or flat-water kayaking and canoeing. Interested guests can get all the necessary equipment at the dock below the hotel. Those less vigorous may prefer soaking up some rays at the hotel's private beach, taking a cruise around the lake, hitting some tennis balls, relaxing in a sauna, or playing billiards and ping-pong.

The main lodge, which burned down in 1992, is being rebuilt. It was attractive and perfectly located with a large lawn sloping gently down to the lake. The best views of the lake and the beautiful surrounding mountains are from the outdoor terrace just outside the restaurant. A small, rocky stream meander through the hotel's public areas, filling the lounge, bar and restaurant with the sound of trickling water. The lakeside wall of the lobby is mostly glass and the A-frame ceilings reach three stories high.

The main dining room is famous for its seafood; dishes, which are listed on the menu in English and Spanish, include poached trout in butter and wine sauce, fish *papillote* (cooked in paper to preserve the flavors) with tomatoes, olives and wine, and sauted sole with mushrooms, parsley and cream. There are also various meat dishes, such as country-style rabbit casserole, and soups, including gaspacho, plus a dessert tray. In addition, the atmosphere is lively and the lake views are unbeatable. Most important, however, the service is truly superb.

The individual cabins did not burn down because they are 50 meters or more from the main lodge. Two of their nicest features are stone fireplaces and individual porches with deck chairs. Just don't expect to have a good view of the lake, because the nearby trees tend to block that angle. The cabins vary in size, sleeping from four to six people. All are spacious, with double beds and sofa beds, comfortable chairs, TVs/VCRs, minibars, wide-board flooring, white throw rugs, lots of closet space, telephones, piped-in music, and private bathrooms with floors and walls of pink tile, combination baths, and bidets. While the Ralún attracts mainly families, there are also some rooms in the main lodge for couples, which are at least a third less expensive.

HOTEL ENSENADA
Ensenada
Phone (65) 23-2888
Puerto Varas telex 370018
Pueto Montt phone (65) 25-2363/3325
Category: A & B
20 rooms, 2 stories, rustic shingle house, open only 12/1-Easter. There is also a cheaper hostel on grounds. Fishing, heated pool, sauna, tennis.
Rates: $52-$63 per room ($42 with shared bath) including tax, breakfast, and dinner; $18 at the hostel including tax only. No credit cards are accepted.
Directions: On the main drag in Ensenada, facing Lake Llanquihue, 41 miles/65 km northeast of Puerto Montt.

This charming establishment, the older section of which dates from the turn of the century, caters primarily to anglers, guiding them on trips to nearby rivers and lakes. But it offers an entirely different ambience from that of the Ralún – a homey, tranquil one with antiques and regional cuisine. It is probably more suited for those without young children. The main building, a two-story structure which was once a house, is right out of a picture book, with its white picket fence, huge lawn with flowers and 40-foot cedar trees, shingle roof, and long front porch slightly overgrown with crawling vines and lined with brightly colored, wooden chairs. From the porch guests can see the near-perfect Volcano Osorno in the distance, but the lake, which is only 200 yards away, is largely blocked from sight by trees.

The public areas on the ground level, which include a lounge, a reception, and a restaurant, are all wonderfully decorated. The best place to meet people is the main lounge, which is sort of a turn-of-the-century museum and has ornate Victorian furnishings, old photographs and posters on all the walls, plus natural wooden floors, walls and beam ceilings. The sofas and matching chairs are simply fantastic, with high elaborately carved wooden backs and covered in old-design flowery material. In the center is a magnificent cast iron stove with various pots on top, and to one side is an antique upright piano.

Most fascinating, perhaps, are the knick-knacks found throughout the public rooms. They number a hundred or so and are all about as ancient as you'll find in this area. Among these relics are an old coffee grinding machine, record players, a commode, ski poles, car wheels and fenders, hand grinders, wall telephones, sewing machines, a water pump, a cash register, and a rifle. Be sure to ask the owner to show you how the two laundry machines flanking the entrance work – hand-operated and fire-heated, they are true marvels of engineering.

On the same floor you'll find the restaurant, which serves delicious meals and features cuisine of the southern region. The rooms and baths upstairs are a bit rustic and on the small side, with fairly low ceilings. They are comfortable, spotlessly clean and provide all the basic necessities. The oldest units have shared baths and are the least expensive; rooms with private baths are 25% more, while the newer, more deluxe *especiales* are dearer still. All prices include a free cocktail every evening from the bar. Those traveling on a tight budget can stay at the newly-opened *hostal* on the grounds. Rooms with baths here are decent and cost less than half the price of those in the main hotel. Guests can also economize by cooking in the *hostal's* facilities.

Alternative: **HOSTERIA RUEDAS VIEJAS**
Ensenada, phone (65) 23-312/23-775
Rates: $15 per room incl. tax; all major credit cards are accepted.
Directions: 300 yards west of Hotel Ensenada on the same highway.

If the Ensenada is full or closed, try the nearby Ruedas Viejas, which is similar in quality to the *hostal* at the Ensenada. Like the Ensenada, it's about 200 yards from the lake, but it's open year round and has a restaurant and a bar with a TV. Rooms are medium size and have small wood-burning stoves, twin beds, chairs, and private baths with hot-water showers.

HOSTERIA PETROHUE
Puerto Montt phone (65) 25-4646
Puerto Montt telex 370002
Category: B
Modernized old lakeside lodge, open year round, restaurant, laundry service.
Rates: $17/$25/$28 S/D/T incl. tax (less from 4/15 to 11/15). Travelers' checks & US dollars accepted, but no credit cards.
Directions: In Petrohué on the western shore of Lake Todos Los Santos, next to the ferry landing.

Virtually at the foot of Osorno Volcano, this country-style lodge of local wood construction was built for Queen Elizabeth's visit in the 1960's and is now a popular overnight stop for those coming or going to Bariloche,

Argentina. The floors, ceilings and most of the walls are made of wide, natural wood boards. Most guests gather in the restaurant or the adjoining lounge. The latter has an unusual all-wood clock with wooden pieces inside ticking away and a large metal fireplace which is used nightly (except during the peak of the summer season). During the winter months guests, sitting on comfortable sofas, chairs and padded rockers, can huddle up in front of the fire. A string of connecting windows permits views of the lake, but trees obstruct much of the panorama. Other furnishings are likewise entirely in keeping with the environment, including an old wooden chest, wooden tables with solid-wood chairs, and throw rugs.

The adjoining restaurant is similar to the lounge with rugless, hardwood floors, all-wood chairs and tables, and exposed-beam ceilings. It's a large area with many tables so as to accommodate the heavy tourist traffic during the summer months. Indeed, the entire hotel has lost some of its charm by becoming a bit commercialized. In the process of catering more often to tour groups, it has been modernized, made somewhat more comfortable, and expanded from its original eight rooms. At lunch there may be Chilean folksinging for entertainment.

The older rooms here are fairly small and have knotty-pine floors and walls, reasonably comfortable beds with thick blankets, throw rugs, side tables with candles, built-in cabinets, and small private baths with hot-water showers. The newer units are larger and have more comfortable furnishings and updated baths.

RESIDENCIAL PALOMITA
Peulla
No phone
Category: C
4-room rustic hostel, restaurant, friendly staff.
Rates: $10 per person incl. tax, breakfast & dinner. No credit cards.
Directions: Across the bridge from Hotel Peulla in Peulla, which is on the opposite (eastern) shore of Lake Todos Los Santos from Petrohué.

A small *residencial*, the Palomita is inexpensive and much better value than the relatively pricey Hotel Peulla, which offers the only other accommodations in town. The four guest rooms, located in the remodeled attic of this rustic old home, are small but adequate. The beds are comfortable and rooms are generally clean but old; several have a spectacular view of the lake and the snow-capped volcanoes outside of Peulla. There are also separate hot-water showers with towels provided. In addition, you're sure to find the staff exceedingly warm and friendly and the family-style meals they prepare are quite tasty – they'll even make last-minute changes for vegetarians.

Most important perhaps, the Palomita offers the opportunity of passing time with a friendly Latin family instead of with other tourists. If it's full, ask them to point you to similarly-priced private residences that accept travelers. And even if Hotel Peulla, which is just 50 metres away, is too expensive for your budget, you can always walk over there and enjoy its garden, cocktail lounge and restaurant.

Alternative: HOTEL PEULLA

Peulla, phone (65) 25-3253, Puerto Montt phone (65) 25-4646, Puerto Montt telex 370002

Hotel Peulla, situated half a mile from the ferry landing in Peulla, is a large, well-maintained establishment which caters to tour groups and has a beautiful setting overlooking the lake and mountains. It has 53 rooms, a good restaurant and bar, and an attractive garden. It is owned and run by a Chilean, Alberto Schirmer, and his Californian wife. They also own Hostería Petrohué and the ferry connecting Peulla and Petrohué.

The units here are more spacious than those of Hostería Petrohué, but they are also over double the price (which includes breakfast and dinner). Prices are slightly lower if you reserve yourself (rather than through an agency) or visit between 4/15-11/15, but this place can be quite cold then. If the Peulla is too expensive for your budget and a *residencial* like the Palomita doesn't sound like your cup of tea, consider staying the night in Petrohué instead of in Peulla.

Puerto Montt

HOTEL VICENTE PEREZ ROSALES

Ave. Antonio Varas 447
Phone (65) 25-2571/2
Telex 270056
Category: A
82 rooms, central, good harbor view, restaurant, car rental desk, travel agency, shops, barber shop, beauty parlor.
Rates: $66/$74 S/D incl. tax, about 20% less 3/15-12/31. Diners and AmEx only.
Directions: 1 block from the Plaza de Armas, facing the water, Reloncavi Gulf.

The city's top address has been for many years and remains this modern six-story hotel in the heart of town overlooking the harbor. The exterior faintly resembles that of a chalet, but as you enter, you'll quickly realize that this is no homey Swiss inn. The lobby is huge and modern, with 15-foot ceilings, floor-to-ceiling windows, intriguing floor lamps made of tree branches with plants growing out of the brass-pot bases, potted plants here and there, and soft music playing in the background. The furnishings, while not terribly interesting, are comfortable, with various sofas and chairs, plain carpets, and frequent art exhibits on the walls. The centerpiece is a dark stone fireplace fashioned from the bow of an old sailing vessel. It includes a mermaid and a small sail.

Adjoining the lobby is a large hotel-like restaurant, which has the same high ceilings, another large stone fireplace, and linoleum flooring. Except for the grand piano in the corner, the furnishings are hardly distinguished. The best feature is that the port-side wall is almost all glass and lined with plants, thus affording suberb views of the harbor and adding a touch of warmth. The evenings often bring with them a local pianist to play while you dine. The bilingual menu is impressive, with a three-page wine list. The meals, however, are unexceptional. The best dishes are, of course, seafood. The *congrio Margarita* (eel with cream sauce), *corvina* (sea bass) prepared four different ways, breaded abalones, Chilean fish chowder, and king-size crabs are all worth a try. There's also a wide assortment of desserts including baked Alaska. For a change, you might try the **Restaurant Centro Español** nearby at O'Higgins 233, one block from the Plaza de Armas; paella is one of the specialties.

The rooms here are comfortable and spacious, but they're also a bit utilitarian. The standard ones have TVs, industrial carpeting, minibars, unadorned walls, comfortable chairs, and tile baths. They also have either city views or, more picturesque, harbor views; a few even have balconies. The units on the second floor are more modern and slightly better, so request one of those or one with a balcony. Finally, for tour, travel, and car rental information, you need only inquire at the travel agency here or at the large Andina del Sud agency next door.

HOTEL COLINA
Avenida Talca 81
Phone (65) 25-3502
Category: A
50 rooms, waterfront, modern, central location, restaurant and bar.
Rates: $42 per room incl. tax ($25 per room 3/15-11/30). All major credit cards are accepted.
Directions: Overlooking the port, 3 blocks west of the Plaza de Armas.

A good and less expensive alternative to the Rosales is the Colina, which offers similar scenery and is just two blocks away, overlooking the harbor. A modern five-story building, it's in good condition, with a presentable exterior combining natural wood and rough cement painted white. Upon entering you'll find a spacious and respectable lobby with carpeted floors, modern sofas and chairs, glass-top coffee tables, and wood and white plaster walls. An unusual wood carving decorates one of them. Guests gather either here or in the bar downstairs, which has a fairly inviting atmosphere.

Next to the bar is the main restaurant. It is nothing special – plain carpeted floors, ordinary furnishings, and no views. It does have, however, a passable menu with a wide variety of dishes, including *salpicon mariscal* and *caldillo marinera*, which are local seafood dishes, plus a variety of desserts, the most popular being peach melba.

The rooms on the top four floors are quite acceptable, but a bit cramped. They have industrial carpets, TVs, natural wood walls, built-in closets, comfortable twin beds with a single light between them, and tile baths with ordinary fixtures, linoleum floors, showers and bidets.

Alternative: **HOTEL VIENTO SUR**
Calle Ejército 200, phone (65) 25-8701, fax (65) 25-8700
Rates: About $45 per room incl. tax. All major credit cards are accepted.
Directions: On Calle Ejército, which is five blocks east of the Plaza de Armas.

If the other two are full, try the new Viento Sur. It's not on the water, but offers value, plus guests have access to a gym and sauna. There's a good restaurant as well.

HOSTAL PANORAMA
Calle San Felipe 192
Phone (65) 25-4094
Category: B-C
20 rooms, great harbor views, restaurant, terrace.
Rates: $18/$23 S/D incl. breakfast & tax (25% less 2/15-12/14). No credit cards.
Directions: 3 blocks northeast of the Plaza de Armas and up a long flight of stairs starting at the junction of San Felipe and Benavente.

Pickings are slim among category B hotels. One that has a very friendly staff and has been popular for years with overland travelers is the Panorama, which is on a bluff with great views of the harbor and only a 10-minute walk from the Plaza de Armas. The views are particularly good from the breakfast room and the front terrace, which has a few chairs for sunning. The only place to sit down and unwind other than the patio is the restaurant. This is a fairly large area with thin carpeting, a large-screen TV, and numerous plain tables with flowers during the summer. The meals are wholesome; for $3 you can fill yourself to the brim!

Some people complain that the rooms are a bit damp; they are also smaller than standard. The pluses outweigh the minuses, however, as they are all quite bright with large windows, offer marvelous views of the port, are fully carpeted, and have telephones, simple but comfortable beds, and private baths with hot-water showers.

Alternative: **RESIDENCIA PARTICULAR DE ALDA GONZALEZ**
Calle Guillermo Gallardo 552, phone (65) 25-3334
Rates: $15/$10 per room with bath incl. tax & breakfast. No credit cards.
Directions: 5 blocks north of the intersection of Gallardo and Avenida Antonio Varas, which is a major downtown intersection.

Many of the cheaper category C establishments are a good walk from the heart of town. One that is only five blocks from the center is the Alda González. Alda is very pleasant and friendly, and her husband is a real character who loves to chat and is as entertaining as they come. If having a central location or the chance to interact with the locals are top priorities in addition to low price, this old three-story *residencial* can be recommended. Moreover, unlike most B&Bs, they allow use of the kitchen for preparing lunch or dinner (breakfast is provided). You also have access to the sitting room for talking and watching TV.

The guest rooms are clean but hardly anything to write home about; knowing something about them, however, can improve your chances of getting a good one. Some of the beds, for example, are very soft, so you may want to check them first. Also, if you take a room with shared bath, request one located away from the communal bathroom; the walls are paper thin and you'll have to put up with every noise from therein. And be prepared for some temperamental showers – the water vacillates between scalding hot and icy cold. Finally, bring your own towel, soap and toilet paper because, as in many cheap guesthouses in Chile, these items are not provided.

Chiloé Island

Ancud

HOSTERIA ANCUD
Calle San Antonio 30, phone (656) 2340/2350, telex 275002. Santiago phone (2) 696-6826, Santiago fax (2) 696-5599
Modern rustic, facing ocean, 24 rooms, restaurant, bar, laundry.
Rates: $40/$60 S/D incl. breakfast & tax, $29/$36 S/D in low season (4/1-11/30). All major credit cards.
Directions: On the northern edge of town overlooking the bay, a 10-minute walk to the center.

Ancud's leading hotel for many years, this modern and attractive A-frame *hostería*, while hardly deluxe, has no serious competitors in this picturesque seaside town on Chiloé Island. The setting, on a hill beside Fort San Antonio and a hundred meters across a large lawn to the water, couldn't be better. Constructed of wood and large gray stones with a glass wall facing the sea, the Ancud has a bold design on the outside and an inviting atmosphere inside.

Upon entering you'll notice one of the two principal fireplaces on the main floor. It's almost always lighted (except during the hot summer months) and seemingly beckons travelers to come inside and warm up. The atmosphere throughout the hotel is fairly rustic as the walls are made of exposed logs and stone while the ceilings and floors are entirely of wood. Further inside you'll come to an area that soars some 30 feet high with a glass wall on the sea side. The window offers magnificient views of the water and the few plants scattered here and there add warmth to the room. Adjoining it is a smaller sitting area which is spacious and has wooden floors, comfortable sofas, modern armchairs constructed of wood and leather, fine Chilean rugs, and a huge round metal fireplace. A fire is usually roaring here, too. This is a popular place to sit and watch TV. When guests get thirsty or want a snack, they need only walk over to the cafeteria next door which, again, proves a good place to admire the scenery outside. The main restaurant is downstairs. It has glass on three sides and overlooks the bay. Chances are you'll find the tablecloths in festive colors, brightening up the place quite a bit. The menu offers many selections, including salmon, *congrio* (eel) and *corvina* (sea bass), prepared in a variety of ways, filet mignon, chicken *al whisky*, and oysters. It also serves excellent desserts such as banana split and pancakes with rum.

The nicest feature of the rooms is that they all have views of the water. They are attractive and standard size with wide-board flooring, twin beds with wool covers and reading lights, walls made of exposed logs, spacious closets, but no phones or reading chairs. Each unit has a small private bathroom with black tile floors, ordinary fixtures, showers and thick towels.

HOSTERIA WECHSLER

Calle Lord Cochrane 480, phone (657) 2318.
Category: B. 26 rooms, bay view, open year round, restaurant.
Rates: \$15/\$25 S/D incl. tax, \$10/\$17 S/D 4/15-12/14. No credit cards.
Directions: In the center, 2 blocks north-west of the bus station on the bay-front road headed towards Hostería Ancud.

From the outside this three-story structure is ordinary looking and not particularly inviting. Inside, however, it's clean and comfortable and the water is only 100 yards away, so many of the guest rooms have good views of the bay. Rooms are standard size and quite decent; the floors, walls and ceilings are all of wood construction. Each unit has a large wooden closet, two comfortable single beds, throw rugs, plain wooden chairs, and TVs available on request. Half of the rooms also have private baths with tile walls and combination hot-water baths. The main public room is a large wooden-floor combination restaurant/lounge with brightly-colored tablecloths; guests can get breakfast here as well as drinks throughout the day from the tiny bar. At one end of the room is a sofa and matching chairs surrounding the TV. All in all, despite some new competition, the Wechsler remains a good choice in its category.

Castro

HOTEL UNICORNIO AZUL

Ave. Pedro Montt 228
Phone (657) 2359
Category: A
18 rooms, charming gothic residence, restaurant.
Rates: $56/$64 S/D incl. tax & breakfast; $36/$44 from 3/16 to 12/15. All major credit cards.
Directions: Not far from the center and near the water.

A lovely old hotel dating from 1910, the year of Haley's Comet, the Unicornio Azul was reconstructed in 1986 when Haley's Comet last passed the earth. These events were perhaps not by chance as the hotel has a definite mythical ambience, with a mystical unicorn dominating the decor. And with its distinctive pink walls, blue roof and numerous gables, this gothic-looking establishment also has a striking exterior.

Eight of the 18 rooms have small balconies and views of the Bay of Castro. All units are large, with comfortable beds and spacious private baths. Each gable has a small niche for sitting – perfect for enjoying a good book and a quiet moment. When guests tire of reading they can rent movies to watch in the sitting room. Or they can stroll through the enchanting garden in back. All in all, this fantasy-filled residence, which has a professional and amiable staff, is a delightful retreat and is highly recommended despite the somewhat high prices.

HOSTERIA DE CASTRO

Calle Chacabuco 202
Phone (657) 2301/2
Telex 275507
Category: A
Modern, rustic, facing ocean, 29 rooms, restaurant and bar.
Rates: $44/$53/$64 S/D/T incl. tax & breakfast; $22/$26/$27 S/D/T in low season (3/16-12/14). All major credit cards.
Directions: 2 blocks southeast of the Plaza de Armas at the corner of Thompson and Chacabuco, overlooking the bay.

Equally high on ambience but of a different sort, this more modern, four-story A-frame *hostería* is quite striking. It has a tall, sloping, shingle roof and a rustic interior similar in inspiration to that of the Hostería Ancud. An interesting architectural feature is the central area of the roof; it's all glass, spreading light and heat to the hallways below.

If you pass the reception you'll come to the spacious main lounge, which has several sitting areas with comfortable sofas and chairs, plus a TV and a few large plants to fill up space. The wide-board floors with wooden pegs add a nice touch, but what makes this room special is the all-glass wall on the bay side, which affords superb views of the port. Guests searching for a cozier environment can try the adjoining bar. The room is rugless and may feel slightly cold but, when there's a roaring fire in the fireplace, it's a good spot to spend time. The snack bar has an identical wrought iron fireplace and is also a popular room.

On the level below is the main restaurant. The floors are bare and the furnishings are plain, but the two copper chandeliers and the two-story glass wall facing the port more than make up for what this room lacks in ambience. The menu is unimaginative, which suggests that the meals may be the same. As in most restaurants in southern Chile, fish is the specialty; the selections include salmon, red snapper (*perjerrey*), eel (*congrio*), oysters, and sea bass.

Half of the rooms here face the water and, although they are smaller than standard, they are heated and offer comfortable beds, wallpaper, telephones, stylish brass lamps, linoleum floors, and simple bathrooms with somewhat dated fixtures and showers. Ask for a unit with carpeting, a TV and a combination bath; they are only slightly more expensive and worth the few extra dollars.

***First Alternative:* HOTEL GRAN ALERCE**
Calle O'Higgins 202 y Gabriella Mistral
Rates: $44/$52 S/D incl. tax & breakfast, lower in off-season. Major credit cards.
Directions: 4 blocks north of the Plaza de Armas and 2 blocks from the municipal bus station.

This similarly-priced three-story establishment that opened in 1989 is no match in terms of ambience. It does, however, offer better, more modern rooms, with TVs, heating and hot-water showers.

***Second Alternative:* HOSPEDAJE DE JESSIE TORO**
Calle Las Delicias 287.
Rates: $8/$13 S/D incl. tax & breakfast. No credit cards are accepted.
Directions: On Calle Delicias, not far from the center.

For a less expensive B&B, try Jessie Toro's place. He has a very friendly family and clean spacious rooms with hot showers.

Easter Island

HOTEL HANGA ROA
Avenida Pont, Hanga Roa, phone 395334/396834, fax 395334, telex 240118
Ocean-edge, 60 rooms, modern, restaurant, pool, souvenir shop, laundry, lectures with slides, car rental desk.
Rates: $140/$197 S/D incl. tax & breakfast; $90/$116 S/D May-August. No credit cards.
Directions: On the southwestern side of town, 100 meters from the ocean and within walking distance of the center.

The Hanga Roa has been the town's leading hotel for years, as well as being the most expensive. A one-story structure perched on the ocean's edge outside of town, it borrows heavily from the island's Polynesian influence, with reed ornaments, wood planking, walls of carved volcanic stone, and local paintings. The restaurant offers decent food and superb views of the sea, and there are several shops with a good selection of the local handicrafts.

Guests spend a lot of time at the circular pool, which overlooks the ocean. It's surrounded by a sundeck furnished with chairs and umbrellas. The standard size rooms are rather modest for the sky-high prices, but on Easter Island all accommodations are over-priced. They have wooden walls, floor-to-ceiling windows, terraces facing the pool, telephones, and hot-water private baths, but no TVs.

First Alternative: **HOTEL IORAMA**
Avenida Ana Magara, Hanga Roa
Rates: $83/$131 S/D; $55/$75 S/D May-Aug. (incl. breakfast & tax). No credit cards.
Directions: On the outskirts of town not far from the airport.

This friendly 14-room hotel is nicer and a better buy than the Hanga Roa as it has very nice rooms for a third of the cost. There's also a good restaurant, a pool and fine ocean views to boot.

Second Alternative: **INN AT TAHAI**
Calle Simón Paoa, Hanga Roa
Rates: $40/$75 S/D incl. tax & full board (lower in off-season). No credit cards.
Directions: On the northern outskirts of town, before the museum and within walking distance of the center.

María Hey's guest house, also known as Pensión Tahai, offers travelers a better deal – a clean bungalow, cold-water showers, and decent meals for a fraction of the cost of the other inns. She also has a pretty garden and lounge, both of which are enjoyable places to relax. If her place is full, try **RESIDENCIA HANGA ROA REKA**, which is a similarly-priced guest house and permits camping for only $10 a person.

Colombia

One of the countries most overlooked by travelers to South America is Colombia, in large part because of the perception that wars among drug cartels and periodic guerrilla attacks make traveling here dangerous. In reality, travelers were never the object of these attacks; moreover, the problems themselves have greatly diminished in recent years. Petty thieves, not bombs, are the main worry for foreign travelers today, but no more so than in Brazil or other South American countries. As a result of the improved crime rates, tourism here is on the rebound.

For travelers who appreciate hotels with character, Colombia is the place to be, as it has more interesting places to stay than any country in South America. In Bogotá, the third highest capital city on the continent, the choices include a 1940's mansion and several old colonial residences, all of which have been converted into hotels. In addition, it has a swanky apartment-style hotel with the best restaurant and service in Colombia.

Traveling northeast from Bogotá through some strikingly beautiful hills that are often enshrouded in clouds, you'll come to several small towns – Villa de Leiva (the entire town has been declared a national monument), Paipa (a hot springs resort), Duitama and Sogamoso – which have an unusually large number of centuries-old *haciendas* that have been converted into charming places to stay. Alternatively, you can head southwest towards the sunnier and warmer resort town of Giradot which is set along a river and has several laid-back hotels geared mainly to weekend visitors from Bogotá. Further west of Bogotá are the modern cities of Medellín, in a beautiful undulating setting and with the continent's only monorail, and Cali, which has a river flowing through the center. The best time to visit Cali is the last week of December, when it comes alive for its annual fair. The fair features bullfights every day and masquerade balls at night. The port city of Buenaventura is nearby, but it has little to offer travelers except a marvelous Beaux-Arts hotel dating from the early part of the century that has been restored to its former grandeur.

A few hours south of Cali is Popayán, which is full of old colonial buildings and is one of the country's most picturesque towns. In the same direction is San Agustín, a world-famous archaeological site dating back to 3300 B.C., with hundreds of large rough-hewn stone figures of men, animals and gods of mysterious origin. Both places have lots of old residences that have been converted into hostels; Popayán also has a former monastery that is now a hotel. Further south still is Laguna la Cocha, a beautiful lake and a great place for a quiet retreat. The best place to stay there is a rustic, old lakefront lodge which is Swiss-run and will make you think you're in the old world.

Colombia's most famous resort city is Cartagena which, even during the worst days of the drug wars, continued to attract hordes of foreign tourists. The principal attractions are the beach and the old walled city, still largely intact. Buildings date back centuries and include several that have been converted into truly splendid bars and restaurants. For those who like to poke around on foot seeing how people spend their time, this walled city is fantastic. You can take a horse-drawn carriage out to Bocagrande, the city's main beach, where most hotels are located. Keep an eye out for one Mediterranean-style resort that is reminiscent of south Florida's grand hotels built in the 1920's. This beach section is what attracts most Colombians and it's also where most of the action is these days. As a diversion, you can take a boat ride out to the Rosario Islands, where there are several rustic hotels, deserted beaches, and numerous coral reefs for snorkeling.

Further west along the northern coast of Colombia are Barranquilla (the country's major port) and Santa Marta-El Rodadero (another popular beach resort). And far out into the Caribbean, some 180 km/590 miles east of Nicaragua, is the island of San Andrés, which is where Columbus landed on one of his voyages to the New World. Today, this customs-free port is a popular destination for Colombians because they can alternate between vacationing on the beach and shopping like mad. For foreigners the major attractions in addition to the beach are snorkeling and skin diving in the coral reefs offshore. In short, Colombia offers a number of interesting places to visit, and the wide variety of delightful places to stay enhances considerably the appeal of traveling here.

Bogotá

HOTEL CHARLESTON
Carrera 13 No. 85-46
Phone (1) 257-1100/218-0590
Fax (1) 218-0605
Telex 44355
Category: Deluxe
Exclusive, choice area of town, 32 suites, superb restaurant, car rental, piano bar, English spoken.
Rates: $150/$160 S/D incl. tax. All major credit cards.
Directions: On a quiet residential street in the exclusive, northern "El Lago" district, which is the city's trendiest restaurant-nightclub area and safer than most.

If good service counts, stay at the Charleston; it offers the best service of any hotel in Colombia, if not all of South America. The same can be said of the restaurant here. It's the only hotel in this book besides the Casa Medina which rates being called deluxe and doesn't have a pool or lake – which says a lot about the quality of everything else. The one thing it lacks, besides a host of amenities, is an interesting facade. The building is a modern brick construction, five stories high, and very sophisticated, but not striking. Indeed, it looks more like a townhouse than a hotel. Understated luxury, you'll find, is the theme throughout.

You'll immediately sense that this place is a step above the rest from the cozy lobby. It has checkered marble floors, wood-panelled walls, elegant brass-based lamps, Queen Anne chairs, fresh flowers, and a highly professional English-speaking staff at the reception desk. If you head into the sitting room and take a seat at one of the white marble-top tables, you'll promptly be offered a drink from the bar. The sitting room is carpeted, with wood-panelled walls and is filled throughout with the sounds of classical music.

Even if you've only come for a meal, you'll find the experience memorable. **La Biblioteca**, as the adjoining restaurant is called, has one wall with stained-glass windows, another with several old prints and gilt-framed mirrors, and another lined with books, including a few in English. It gives the room a club-like ambience. The food, however, is French and hardly typical club fare. For starters you might try a cold *salmón de lago marinado en mostaza Dijón* (lake salmon marinated in Dijon mustard sauce) or their superb hot broccoli mousse with Bearnaise sauce. As a main course why not opt for the *langostinos a la plancha con salsa buerre blanc* (grilled crayfish with white butter sauce) or the *estofado de pollo y langostinos con champinones y arroz pilaf* (a chicken and crayfish dish with mushrooms and rice pilaf)? And their *crèpes soufflés de limon y semillas de hinojo* (fennel seed and lemon soufflés) are outstanding. As the dining area has space for only about 40 people, reservations are essential.

The guest rooms, which are single-room "suites," are all ultra-posh, with plush carpets, air conditioning, cable TV, glass-top breakfast tables, double queen-size beds, thick bedspreads, papered walls, walk-in closets, and modern double-room bathrooms with long, marble-top counters, carpeted floors, and tile showers. Guests receive a copy of the local newspaper each day at their door; their shoes will be there as well if they were left the night before to be shined. With service like this, the Charleston is virtually in a class of its own.

HOTEL CASA MEDINA

Carretera 7 No. 69A-22
Phone (1) 212-6657
Fax (1) 212-6668
Telex 42639
Category: Deluxe
Stately historic landmark, midtown, 24 rooms plus 28 newer units in annex, restaurant and bar.
Rates: $150 per room incl. 15% tax. Major credit cards.

Directions: In midtown on a major north-south artery, between the downtown commercial area and the trendy northern district.

If looks count, stay at the Casa Medina, an historic 1940's landmark that has been converted from an apartment building into a luxurious hotel. Declared a national monument in 1985, this four-story hotel in midtown has a stately stone and brick exterior and faces a busy thoroughfare. As the doorman ushers you inside you may sense that you're entering a prestigious men's club, not a hotel. There are no moose heads, but just about everything else you'd expect of a club lobby is here – a well-used stone fireplace, a small ticking clock over the mantel, parquet floors, oriental rugs, several old oil portraits, large windows, fresh flowers, comfortable seating arrangements, and an impressive winding stairway towards the rear.

To one side is the main sitting room which has a similar well-used fireplace, Victorian furnishings, including a relaxing sofa and several matching chairs, a huge gilt-framed mirror, fresh flowers, brass table lamps, and the latest editions of *Time* and *Newsweek*. The accommodations are all upstairs and in the new annex. They vary in size, design and decor, but all have carpets, comfortable beds, air conditioning, cable TVs, minibars, ample closet space, and tile baths. A few offer fireplaces as well.

One of the Medina's major attractions besides its traditional, formal appearance and top-notch service is its restaurant. Majestic in size (14-foot ceilings) and English in appearance, it is dominated by an elegant old chandelier. It features excellent cuisine, gold-trim plates and real silverware, along with truly superb service. The decor is fitting – parquet floors, exposed-beam ceilings, huge floral arrangements, Louis XIV side tables, wainscoting, massive windows with formal curtains, and tables with leather armchairs. On the bilingual menu you'll find numerous French selections including, as an *entrada*, warm eggs piperade style and cold asparagus with mousseline sauce. As a main course, try breast of chicken in fig sauce or beef en croute with port wine. Profiterole with hot chocolate sauce and the restaurant's superb coffee make a fitting end to a great meal.

First Alternative: **HOTEL LOS URAPANES**

Carrera 13 No. 83-19, phone (1) 218-5065/218-1188, telex 42378, fax (1) 218-9242
Rates: $100 per room incl. 5% tax ($131 for suites). All major credit cards.
Directions: 2 blocks south of the Charleston on the same street.

This modern five-story hotel is an excellent and less expensive alternative to the Charleston, and it's in the same trendy neighborhood, too. The hotel's size (51 units) and ambience are similar to the Charleston's, and there's an emphasis on good service. The small six-table restaurant, however, is not in the same league, although the food is quite good. The regular *sencilla* rooms have thick carpets, plush bed covers, cable TVs, desks, ample carpet space, and modern tile bathrooms with showers and lots of counter space.

Second Alternative: **HOTEL LA FONTANA**
Calle 127 No. 21-10, phone (1) 274-0200/274-7868, fax (1) 216-0449, telex 45382
Rates: $161/$207 S/D incl. 15% tax. All major credit cards are accepted.
Directions: In the exclusive upper northern section of Bogotá, beyond the restaurant district.

Facing the city's largest shopping center and surrounded by gardens, the popular Fontana is the furthest north of the major hotels and a good choice for those who want to be in a relatively safe area away from the center of town. With 152 rooms, it's more manageable than the 729-room Tequendama Inter-Continental (the city's top large hotel). It's also more attractive, with towers grouped around a central patio, resembling a medieval village. The Fontana reputedly has the best seafood restaurant in town. The rooms are attractively decorated and have cable TVs, combination baths with hair dryers, and space heaters upon request.

HOTEL BELVEDERE
Transversal 18 No. 100-16, phone (1) 257-7700, fax (1) 257-0331, telex 44523
Category: A. Modern, good area, 36 rooms.
Rates: $77/$93 S/D incl. tax. All major credit cards accepted.
Directions: In the exclusive northern section of the city, 15 blocks north of the city's best restaurant/nightclub area.

Recently redecorated and well maintained, the ultra-modern Belvedere offers the best value of any of the city's top hotels in the fashionable northern side of the city. With only 36 rooms, it can also offer more attentive service than its numerous competitors. In addition, it's conveniently located near the swanky Unicentro shopping mall and not far from the city's top nightlife area. You'll need taxis to go anywhere, but they are easy to find as the hotel faces a major street.

The entrance of this sedate six-story structure opens onto a tastefully decorated small lobby with cocoa-color walls and numerous plants and fresh flowers. The furnishings are all contemporary and stylish, including those in the adjoining restaurant, which overlooks the street. Seafood dishes are the specialty here, and the restaurant boasts an extensive wine cellar. Other amenities include a bar in the reception area, which has live music on weekends, carpeted meeting rooms, and private parking.

The guest rooms are stylishly decorated with dark beige or blue carpets and matching draperies, bedspreads and upholstery. The standard units are air conditioned and have cable TVs, minibars, telephones, ample closet space, and modern tile bathrooms with showers and marble counters. The more expensive suites have the same features, plus minibars and kitchenettes.

HOTEL CENTRO INTERNACIONAL
Carrera 13A No. 38-97
Phone (1) 288-5566/232-6834
Fax (1) 288-0850
Category: A
Modern highrise, near US embassy, 64 rooms, travel agency, gift shop, English spoken.
Rates: $38/$52 S/D incl. 10% tax; $50/$63 S/D suites. All major credit cards accepted.
Directions: In midtown, 2 blocks from the US Embassy, 20 blocks north of the old commercial center, and 45 blocks south of the trendy northern restaurant/night-life area, with easy access to taxis.

In Bogotá, a city long noted for street crime, a hotel's location can be the deciding factor for many travelers. Most lower-to-mid-range hotels are in the crime-ridden downtown area. One exception is the Centro Internacional in midtown and only two blocks from the U.S. Embassy. It has lots of shops nearby and is very accessible to taxis. An equally attractive feature is that the rooms are a real bargain, and the staff is quite helpful to boot. It's hardly surprising, therefore, that the hotel is often fully booked. Be sure to make advance reservations.

Especially popular with both foreign and local business people, this modern six-story establishment won't win any awards for its public areas, but they are quite neat and presentable. Adjoining the small functional lobby, for example, is a modern area with leather sofas, attractive blue-gray industrial carpeting, several flower arrangements, brass lighting fixtures, and a TV. Overlooking this area is the dining room, which has a bright atmosphere and features a stone wall lined with plants. The menu is fairly simple, with about 15 main courses to choose from, including *cazuela de mariscos* (seafood stew), pork chops with apple sauce, several spaghetti dishes, as well as sandwiches. The food is mediocre, but several restaurants within easy walking distance provide an alternative to eating here. But beware; Petty thieves definitely exist in this area, especially at night.

The standard accommodations are smaller than average. They offer industrial carpets, comfortable beds, TVs, telephones, small desks, unadorned white walls, ample closet space, dressing mirrors, and tile bathrooms with ordinary fixtures, including showers. Take a tip from U.S. Embassy personnel who frequent this place – the hotel's two-room apartments cost only about $8 more and are well worth the difference.

First Alternative: **RESIDENCIAS TEQUENDAMA**
Carrera 10 No. 27-51 Interior 150, phone (1) 286-1111 x 3315, telex 42627, fax (1) 282-2860
Rates: $59 per suite incl. tax. All major credit cards are accepted.
Directions: In lower mid-town, just north of the Tequendama Inter-Continental on the same block.

If you'll be staying two weeks or more, by all means stay here. The area is not the safest, but this all-suite aparthotel connected to the Tequendama Inter-Continental (with which it shares a telephone and fax) is unquestionably the best buy in Bogotá. The rooms are available only for stays of two weeks or more. However, when business is slow, exceptions are occasionally made, so it may be worth inquiring. The magnificent suites are very comfortable and have two spacious, attractive rooms, cable TVs, and well-stocked kitchenettes. Guests have full access to all the many facilities of the Inter-Continental. These include a pool and health club.

Second Alternative: **HOTEL NEUCHATEL**
Calle 90 No. 7A-66, phone (1) 218-3848, fax (1) 218-1568, telex 45403
Rates: $58/$65 S/D incl. 5% tax. All major credit cards are accepted.
Directions: On a quiet street in the exclusive northern area of Bogotá, 10 blocks east of the lively restaurant and nightclub area and 2 blocks west of Carrera 7, a major north-south artery.

If a well-managed upmarket B&B sounds appealing, try the homey 20-room Neuchatel. Owned and run by a very friendly man, it's an attractive two-story house with a nice lawn and trees in front, and the location is the choicest residential area of the city. Indeed, some of the city's best restaurants and nightclubs are not far away. The hostel features a home-like bar with captain's chairs, a cozy private dining room with good food, and a living room with a fireplace, comfortable leather sofas and stacks of magazines. The rooms are modest in size, individually decorated and reasonably attractive, but nothing special. They have twin single beds, carpeting, TVs, breakfast tables with captain's chairs, and tiny bathrooms with showers. There are also some larger, slightly more expensive units with queen-size beds and skylights. Note: To get a taxi, you'll have to call or walk two blocks to hail one.

HOTEL SAN DIEGO
Carrera 13 No. 24-82, phone (1) 284-2100
Category: B. Modern highrise, downtown, 34 rooms, restaurant, bar, laundry service.
Rates: $25/$32 S/D incl. tax. All major credit cards, but not AmEx checks.
Directions: On the edge of the old business area and across from the landmark Tequendama Inter-Continental, bordering an unsafe area.

Price-wise, one of the best deals in Bogotá is the San Diego, directly across the street from the huge Tequendama. That street is the dividing line between the unsafe downtown area and the somewhat safer midtown area, hence this establishment's location is better than most in its class.

In addition to the hotel's favorable prices and acceptable location, Colombian business people, to whom it caters, seem to like the fact that this modern highrise is also quite presentable in appearance, both inside and out. The two-story lobby, for example, is clean and spacious, with attractive ceiling lights, stone floors, and a sitting area that has reasonably comfortable sofas and chairs. Adjoining the lobby is a small bar/restaurant serving decent food.

The guest rooms are surprisingly spacious, with two queen-size beds, linoleum floors, TVs, desks, several chairs, and good views of the city. The tile bathrooms are also quite spacious, with modern fixtures, including showers and long mirrors. In short, for the price, it's hard to find fault with the San Diego.

HOSTERIA DE LA CANDELARIA
Calle 9 No. 3-11
Phone (1) 342-1727, 242-1727/283-5258
Category: B
Old house, historic section of town, 11 rooms, restaurant, laundry service.
Rates: $23/$29 S/D incl. tax. All major credit cards.
Directions: Downtown in the old La Candelaria district, 5 blocks east of Plaza Bolívar.

If you're searching for colonial atmosphere, look no further than La Candelaria, which was formerly a colonial residence and is one of the city's few hotels of that era. This small 11-room hostel is a real gem and is only four blocks from Universidad Libre at Calle 8 and Carrera 6, one of the city's liveliest and most interesting areas, with throngs of students crowding the numerous coffee and sandwich shops after classes. To absorb a bit of Latin atmosphere, both present and past, stay here in the center of the city's old historic district at this relatively unknown *hostería*. Just beware: while the hotel is on a quiet side street, the area is dark at night and noted for thieves.

The Candelaria is a rare find in a South American capital city. Virtually all hotels of this type have gone either into disrepair or out of business. Not fancy, but very well maintained, the Candelaria offers simple unheated rooms with exposed-beam ceilings, wooden floors, thick rugs, old photographs on the walls, and genuine antique furnishings. The carved wooden beds have headboards, footboards, and layers of blankets. There are vanity tables in some rooms, with large round mirrors and small sleigh-like stools. There's also a reliable supply of hot water in the private tile baths, which have showers and other fixtures in good working order.

In the lobby you'll find all kinds of notices on the wall, some of upcoming events. If you have any questions the exceptionally friendly staff at the reception desk will be more than delighted to answer them. The large central patio further inside has been covered with glass and converted into a greenhouse-like restaurant with festive tablecloths, tile floors and a collection of interesting abstract paintings by local artists for sale. This is a wonderful place to take breakfast or lunch and, on Thursdays and Fridays, there's musical entertainment. For dinner you'll have to eat elsewhere unless you've booked in advance. If you wander around you'll find no fewer than four adjoining drawing rooms, all carpeted, pleasantly quiet, and featuring antique furnishings – perfect for reading or talking with friends. If you like the fresh air, you may prefer relaxing in an armchair outside your room, overlooking a small grass-covered courtyard. The area is surrounded by potted plants, flowers and vines growing on the walls. This *hostería* is unusual in offering so many public areas, which makes for meeting other interesting travelers who have stumbled upon this unheralded gem.

HOTEL LAS TERRAZAS
Category: B
Calle 54A No. 3-12
Phone (1) 255-5777
Telex 43137
Modern, residential area, 32 rooms.
Rates: $28/$37 S/D incl. tax. All major credit cards are accepted.
Directions: In a mid-town residential area, 30 blocks north of the commercial center & 3 blocks east of Cra. 7.

Finding an inexpensive hotel that's neither in the risky downtown area nor far from the center is no easy feat. One that fills the bill is the Terrazas, a modern architecturally-striking establishment in midtown. It is conveniently located several blocks off a major north-south artery in a quiet residential neighborhood at the foot of the mountain overlooking the city.

The exterior of the building is all red brick, while inside knotty-pine trimming predominates. The guest rooms are small and a bit plain, but quite neat. They feature knotty-pine ceilings, closets and doors, and have linoleum floors, somewhat worn industrial carpeting, plain beds, color TVs, telephones, straight-back chairs, and tiny tile bathrooms with thick white towels and modern fixtures, including showers. Laundry service is also available.

The public areas, which are also well maintained, consist of a cozy lobby with knotty-pine ceilings, several sofas, brass lamps and a small bar with a TV. There's a reasonably attractive dining room with checkered tablecloths and a red tile floor. It's well used by guests, most of whom are foreign travelers. The food is adequate and prices are moderate; about $1.25 for a continental breakfast, $4 for most main courses, and $5 for a half-bottle of wine. The selections include Spanish omelettes, *cazuela de mariscos* (seafood stew), filet mignon, fried chicken, and wines from Chile, Argentina, France and Spain. All in all, the Terrazas is a good, safe choice for low-budget travelers.

First Alternative: **HOTEL LE MIRAGE**

Carrera 15 No. 102-12, phone (1) 256-1955/610-3036
Rates: $27/$30 S/D incl. tax. All major credit cards are accepted.
Directions: Going north on the busy north-south Avenida 15 (not Carrera 15), take a right at Calle 102 and go one block; it's on the corner of Carrera 15.

This cozy six-room B&B is in a strikingly modern two-story house set in a quiet, guarded residential area. It may be the best option for those wanting to be on the safer northern end of town and/or near the city's best restaurant and nightclub area. Rooms are carpeted, they have TVs, and the English-speaking staff provides excellent service. The public areas include a small carpeted lobby with numerous modern paintings on the walls, plus a cozy dining area with three tables and wicker chairs.

Second Alternative: **HOSTAL ARIAS**

Carrera 33 No. 95-74, phone 218-4167/236-0086
Rates: $22/$25 S/D incl. tax & full board (required). Credit cards are not accepted.
Directions: Not far from the well-known Clínica Barraquer and Hotel Bogotá Plaza, it's in the northern district, 3 blocks from Cinemateca La Castellana and about 5 blocks east of the wide, north-south Autopista Norte. If you're coming by bus, head north on Carrera 14, which eventually becomes Autopista Norte, and get off about 100 meters after passing over the 1st bridge. Walk eastward for about 5 blocks and ask a passer-by; everyone knows this place.

Most of the cheaper category C hotels are in the unsafe, downtown area. One exception is the homey Arias, formerly the Moreno, not far from the Mirage. It's a small family-run B&B on a residential street lined with two-story row houses. Gloria Gaona, the friendly manager, will make you feel right at home and offer you a drink or a meal anytime. There are seven cramped rooms that offer comfortable beds and private baths with hot-water showers. There's also a comfortable sitting room and dining area.

Eastern-Central Region

Paipa-Lake Sochagota

HOTEL PAIPA
Lake Sochagota, Paipa
Phone (87) 850-944
Bogotá phone (1) 232-6146
Telex 46241
Category: Deluxe
Modern, lakeside, 102 rooms, pool, tennis, water skiing, disco, billiards, ping-pong.
Rates: $90/$121 incl. 15% tax. All major credit cards are accepted.
Directions: Outside Paipa, a 3.5-hour drive northeast of Bogotá (173 km) and an hour beyond Tunja. At Paipa, turn right (south) and go about 4 km around Lake Sochagota; it's on the southwestern side.

The top hotel in the Paipa area is this very modern four-story resort, which has an unusually stark, monolithic appearance. It is the only deluxe hotel in the eastern-central region of Colombia. The facilities here include several flood-lit tennis courts, a rather oddly-shaped pool, a playground, billiard tables, ping-pong, several bars and a disco – quite impressive! Guests can also ride horses or try their hand at water skiing – Sochagota Lake is only 100 meters away. The accommodations inside this squarish red brick structure are thoroughly modern and plush, with TVs, minibars and combination tile baths; they are also frequently full on weekends.

The public facilities feature plush leather sofas, expensive modern paintings, and marble floors. You'll find a cafeteria, the **Bachué**, on the main floor, but for a truly exquisite meal, go for the **Zipa** restaurant downstairs. The menu includes such exotic selections as shrimp bisque with cognac, roast duckling in pitahaya (a locally-grown fruit) sauce, smoked trout, and seafood casserole Bali style. Meals here are relatively expensive and, for those who can afford an occasional splurge, they can be a real treat.

HOTEL SOCHAGOTA
Lake Sochagota, Paipa
Phone (87) 850-011/2/3
Bogotá phone (1) 248-1956
Telex 46265
Category: A
Modern, lakefront, 63 rooms & cabins, tennis, pool, hot baths, water skiing, billiards, children's playground.
Rates: $49/$67 S/D incl. tax; $80 for cabins. All major credit cards are accepted.
Directions: On the same road as Hotel Paipa, 2 km before it.

One of the most popular hotels in eastern-central Colombia is the Sochagota, which is part of the nationwide Herman Morales chain and overlooks Sochagota Lake just south of Paipa. One of the main attractions of the Paipa area is the hot springs, but this nearby resort offers a lot more: a heated pool, tennis courts, billiards, basketball, a children's playground, water skiing, and a launch for excursions on the lake.

The public areas include a large high-ceiling lobby with a glass wall facing the lake, comfortable sofas and chairs, shag rugs, and numerous ferns and other plants. This and the pool are the best places for relaxing. You can also get good views of the lake from the restaurant, but it's a modern low-ceiling room and not nearly so inviting.

The most appealing feature of the guest rooms is that they all offer superb lake views. They have twin beds, good quality carpets, color TVs, telephones, closets, modern reading chairs, and tile bathrooms with showers. In short, while the Sochagota lacks the inherent interest of some of the region's old *haciendas*, it does offer a lot more in terms of location and amenities.

Alternative: **HOTEL CASA BLANCA**

For accommodations at about half the price, try the friendly Casa Blanca, which is on the southern outskirts of Paipa and near the lake, before Hotel Sochagota and on your left. Modern and attractive, it's a three-story A-frame structure with a red tile roof and freshly painted white walls. There are about 10 rooms, a restaurant, and private parking.

Villa De Leyva

HOSTERIA DEL MOLINO LA MESOPOTAMIA
Calle del Silencio
Phone (87) 320-235
Bogotá phone (1) 213-3491
Category: A
400-year-old mill, 34 rooms, small pool, restaurant and bar.
Rates: $21-38/$36-62 S/D incl. tax, (10% discount for booking 10 days in advance). Closed the first week of January. All major credit cards are accepted.
Directions: On the eastern edge of town, a 10-minute walk to the center.

If the idea of staying in an old mill constructed in 1568 sounds interesting, you'll undoubtedly enjoy a weekend here. The unique Molino la Mesopotamia is one of the most famous hotels in Colombia. Indeed, there's no hotel in all of South America quite like it. Some 50 meters above the main building is a small spring-fed pond constructed to run the mill's stone wheel that once ground corn. The water in the pool is crystal clear and warmed by the sun, so guests can use it for swimming, except during the coldest months when you may find it rather chilly!

The original mill is now the restaurant. It is located downstream of the pond and sits directly over the water. Eating here with the sound of rushing water below is simply unforgettable. A typical home-cooked meal costs about $6 and is very satisfying. Wide-board flooring, an exposed-beam ceiling, a painting on the wall of the last supper, and old wooden chairs and tables complete the picture. Afterwards, you can have a nightcap at the bar. It's rustic and cozy, with an old bread oven at one end, wooden benches and tables, a crocodile skin covering one of the walls, and two small stained-glass windows that allow only a small amount of light into this den-like room.

The hotel consists of several additional buildings connected by a stone walkway. The beautiful gardens with trees and bushes all around tend to block views of the surrounding area. Rooms in the main building are filled with the sound of trickling water and are appropriately furnished with antiques. The main sitting room, for example, has several old tapestries, the original tile flooring, old sofas covered with velvety material, high-back armchairs, carved furnishings, several antique tables, and an old printing press.

The more expensive guest rooms have equally ornate furnishings: canopied beds, creaky old floors, antique bureaus, comfortable chairs, and private baths with old fixtures, including showers. The less expensive accommodations are smaller and have simpler furnishings. But you'll do better splurging on one of the higher-priced units, such as room 10 or 11. Staying in one of them will make a weekend here far more memorable. If you reserve at least 10 days in advance the room cost will be reduced by 10%.

Alternative: **HOSPEDERIA EL DURUELO**
Villa de Leyva, Bogotá phone (1) 245-1470
Rates: $38/$56 S/D incl. 5% tax. All major credit cards are accepted.
Directions: On the eastern edge of town, 6 blocks uphill from the town plaza by way of Calle 13.

In the foothills on the edge of town, the popular Duruelo, which dates from the early 1980's but has a colonial-era appearance, is the town's newest and largest hotel. It has the most amenities, including a clay tennis court in good condition, horseback riding, a gift shop, billiards, a card room, and a restaurant. It's a large 65-room complex with a number of two-story tile roof buildings connected by covered walkways. In back there are spacious lawns with lots of flowers and bushes. The public areas have old-style furnishings, high ceilings with exposed wooden beams, wrought iron lighting fixtures, tile floors, and throw rugs. The colonial theme continues in the guest rooms, which have comfortable beds and reading chairs, fine carpets, and modern tile bathrooms with showers.

HOSPEDERIA EL MESON DE LOS VIRREYES
Carrera 9 No. 14-55
Phone (87) 320-252
Bogotá phone (1) 223-9302
Category: B
Restored colonial house, central, 16 rooms.
Rates: $23/$56 S/D incl. 5% tax. All major credit cards.
Directions: 2 blocks north of the town plaza.

An excellent, less expensive alternative to the Mesopotamia is the Mesón de los Virreyes, which is a lovely remodeled house closer to the center. The shady courtyard in back is filled with potted flowers and, in the center, there's the original stone fountain which no longer functions. Surrounding this area is a porch with wooden benches and cheap paintings on the walls. Guests can hang out here or in the restaurant. The food, which comes in ample-size portions, is served in a cheerful room with lots of sunlight, checkered curtains and high ceilings. The decor is fitting – wrought iron lighting fixtures, wooden high-back chairs with leather seats, and 12 or so tables.

No two guest rooms are configured alike, but they are generally on the small side. Each has carpets, wood-beam ceilings, plain white walls, antique furnishings, colonial-style beds with blankets on top, and tiny private baths with showers.

Alternative: **MESON DE LA PLAZA MAYOR**
Carrera 9 No. 13-51, Bogotá phone (1) 218-7441
Rates: $31/$46 S/D incl. 5% tax. Diners and Visa accepted.
Directions: In the center facing the main square.

This 17-room hotel in the heart of town is slightly nicer and, if you don't mind paying a little more, is a good choice. The Los Virreyes, however, does offer better value for money. The Plaza Major, which is named after the town's main square which it faces, is a beautifully restored colonial house with two flowery courtyards. The cozy and inviting restaurant has wall-to-wall carpeting, and the sitting room has antique furnishings, throw rugs, exposed-beam ceilings, and a TV. The guest rooms, which are quite nice and not cramped, feature high ceilings, antique beds with brightly colored blankets, the original wide-board floors, old bureaus, and private baths with showers. A major plus of the Plaza Mayor is the owner, Mauricio Ordóñez, who likes to chat with the guests and speaks English as well.

HOSPEDERIA EL MARQUES DE SAN JORGE
Calle 14 No. 9-16
No phone
Category: A
Restored colonial house, about 10 rooms, restaurant, and courtyard.
Rates: $11 per person incl. tax. No credit cards.
Directions: 1 block north of Plaza Mayor, around the corner from Los Virreyes.

The San Jorge is a great place to stay at a low price. It is conveniently located and has a good atmosphere. Like many hotels in town, it is an attractive single-story colonial house that has been converted into an inn. There is a traditional courtyard, potted flowers seemingly everywhere, and an old stone fountain in the center which, unfortunately, no longer works. This area is enclosed by a covered walkway with old-style benches and chairs. Most guests gather there or in the attractive restaurant, which has about six tables with brightly colored tablecloths. The rooms, most of which open onto the porch, are small, basic and somewhat dark, with twin beds, unadorned walls, and shared tile baths. The baths have clean modern facilities, including showers.

Sogamoso-Duitama

HOSTERIA SUESCUN
Km 4 Vía Sogamoso-Duitama, Sogamoso
Phone (87) 706-828
Bogotá phone (1) 271-1251
Category: A
Old *hacienda*, 16 rooms, extensive grounds, restaurant.
Rates: \$38/\$49 S/D incl. 5% tax. Diners card.
Directions: Near Sogamoso, a 4-hour drive (210 km) northeast of Bogotá via Tunja, Paipa and Duitama, then south at Duitama for 25 km towards Sogamoso. The hotel is well marked, 4 km before (north of) Sogamoso on your right and 250 meters off the paved highway.

If you're in Bogotá and are looking for a relaxing weekend retreat, consider Hostería Suescún. Although it is a four-hour drive from Bogotá, it may be just what you're looking for. Simón Bolívar stayed here in 1819, and so have many other famous Colombians, especially writers. Still patronized by Bogotá's social elite, this four-century-old *hacienda*, which was originally a monastery, was converted into a delightful hotel about 45 years ago. As you turn off the highway onto the dirt road leading to the *hostería,* you'll probably see black cattle and several dozen racing horses grazing here. There's also a professional jumping arena. Don't mess with the bulls. Some of them are being trained for the bull ring and can be quite "bravo."

A bit further on you'll come to the *hacienda* itself, surrounded by shade trees and covered with Spanish moss. Walking around the grounds is a treat. Everywhere you go you'll hear the soothing sound of trickling water, which runs along an intricate network of rock-built troughs throughout the grounds. If you're the more sedate type, you can simply sit out on the front veranda, which is lined with numerous comfortable chairs and several leather sofas. From here you can admire the old three-story bell tower, which is floor-lit at night.

Inside there are no fewer than four living rooms to relax in, one a card room and another set up to watch TV. The ambience is homey and old style – 13-foot ceilings, fascinating old Colombian lithographs lining the walls, comfortable sofas and chairs, white shag carpets, soft music playing in the background, a large fireplace, colorful flowered curtains, and flower arrangements here and there. The dining area is similarly divided into several rooms. All have old wooden armchairs with leather seats, tile floors, and flower arrangements on all the tables. A three-course meal costs only about $6 and, even though the choices are very limited, with selections such as baked chicken and breaded pork chops, the meals are quite good.

The guest rooms are all configured slightly differently, but most have 10-foot ceilings and white walls, queen-size beds with checkered blankets, thin carpets, telephones, closets, windows with interior shutters, and bathrooms with old fixtures in good working order. Make time to come here; you'll find the experience truly unforgettable.

HOSTERIA HACIENDA EL CARMEN

Calle 8 No. 35-14, Duitama
Phone (87) 602-307
Categoy: A
Old *hacienda*, in town, 18 rooms, restaurant, sauna, gym.
Rates: $25/$34 S/D incl. 5% tax. All major credit cards.
Directions: In Duitama, a 10-minute drive north-east of Paipa. The main road skirts the southern edge of Duitama; a wide avenue leads from it to the center. The turn-off for the hotel is 100-200 meters up this avenue, on the left.

Another wonderful place nearby, in Duitama itself, is El Carmen. This 200-year-old *hacienda* was converted into a hotel in 1987. After all these years it's still in the Salamanca family. The friendly manager, Luis Alejandro Alarcón, will be proud to show you the hotel's numerous facilities, which include a fully-equipped gym, a sauna, an attractive restaurant, two patios, and a small garden outside. The *hostería's* two patios, which are glassed in like greenhouses, are sunny and particularly nice as they are a bit warmer than the outside temperature – a great plus for this slightly chilly region. They have comfortable arrangements, fireplaces, tile floors, walls adorned with various knick-knacks, ferns and other plants, and soft music playing in the background. At noon these two patios can be toasty warm, even though the temperature elsewhere may be nippy. The patios are where most guests gather, day and night. The dining room, which overlooks one of the patios, serves very good Colombian and international fare.

The 18 guest rooms are quite attractive and not at all cramped. They have fine industrial carpets, comfortable beds, color TVs, telephones, French doors which open onto the patios, spacious closets, and all-new bathrooms with modern fixtures. In short, if you're looking for a very moderately priced place with excellent facilities and colonial charm, the Carmen is hard to beat in the Duitama-Paipa area.

HOSTERIA SAN LUIS DE UCUENGA
Km 7 Vía Duitama-Belencito, Duitama
Phone (87) 603-260
Bogotá phone (1) 218-0321/76
Category: A
Old *hacienda*, rural area, gardens, 22 rooms, restaurant, volleyball.
Rates: $31/$38 S/D incl. tax; $55 for suites. All major credit cards are accepted.
Directions: 7 km northeast of Duitama on the highway to Belencito, just off the road.

A delightful place to stay just outside Duitama is the picturesque well-known San Luis de Ucuenga, a 200-year-old *hacienda* that was converted into a hotel during the 1960's. This peaceful establishment has an authentic feel about it, not having changed much over the years. It features antique furnishings in all the rooms, somewhat chilly guest rooms with fireplaces, wooden porches and hanging potted plants, tall trees in the yard where birds chirp away, and a fruit orchard in back with flowers everywhere.

There's a fairly elegant dining room with a fireplace and a TV room. The best place to relax is unquestionably outside in the back yard where soft, recorded classical music can usually be heard. This area is especially nice during the peak December-February period when the weather in this region of Colombia is at its finest. At other times of the year the skies are mostly cloudy and the air is a bit crisp, but it's still pleasant. Tables and chairs are set out on the lawn for the guests to use as they like; there's also a grass volleyball court, plus swings and a see-saw for the kids.

There are two classes of accommodations. The standard units, which are of modest size, tend to be a bit chilly at times. They have carpets, antique furnishings, comfortable old beds with heavy blankets, telephones, sofas, unadorned white walls, and tile bathrooms with showers. The more expensive "salons" have all the above plus fireplaces, breakfast tables and finer antique beds.

First Alternative: **HACIENDA PUNTA LARGA**
Km 7 Vía Duitama-Belencito, phone (87) 602-139/605-841, Bogotá (1) 256-1643/218-0321
Rates: $25/$31 S/D incl. tax ($30/$46 S/D suites). All major credit cards.
Directions: Across the street from the Ucuenga.

A stone's throw from the Ucuenga is the 30-room Punta Larga, which is a restored *hacienda* with slightly cheaper accommodations and a beautiful courtyard full of flowers. Built on a ledge with great views of the nearby valley, it's an old place. Some sections date back 200 years. Most of the complex, however, dates from the 1970's, when it was converted into a hotel. The decor of the guest rooms is singularly uninspired, and even the suites lack fireplaces. If you take a unit in the original section, which unlike the newer section has no good views, it will at least make you feel as though you're stepping back in time. The restaurant has a new feeling about it despite attempts, such as the exposed-beam ceilings, to make it look old, and the food is rather ordinary. The Punta Larga also offers guests a game room with billiards and ping-pong.

Second Alternative: **HOTEL MARANTA**
Carrera 16 No. 17-36, Duitama, phone (87) 602027/603995
Rates: $19/$24 S/D incl. 5% tax.

For a less expensive category B alternative, try the Maranta in downtown Duitama. It's a 30-room colonial house with gardens, a bar, a restaurant, and nice rooms.

Western Central Region

Giradot

EL PENON
Ave. Kennedy/Vía El Peñén
Phone (83) 26981/2/3
Fax (83) 24221
Telex 47343
Bogotá phone (1) 2560045
Category: Deluxe
Resort, lakeside, 42 rooms & 25 cabins, beach, pool, horseback riding, tennis, casino, water skiing, billiards, ping-pong, paddle boats.
Rates: $56/$73 S/D incl. tax ($120 per cabin). AmEx, Visa, Diners accepted.
Directions: Overlooking a lake, El Peñén, on the outskirts of Giradot, a 7-minute drive from the city center and 132 km southwest of Bogotá (3 hours) via the Bogotá-Cali Highway.

Located on the site of a former *hacienda* overlooking a lake of the same name, the Peñén, which dates from the early 1970's and is well maintained, is a fashionable tropical resort that attracts wealthy Colombians from Bogotá, Cali and Medellín. The major drawing cards of this modern, sprawling complex are its sandy beach with palm trees, a huge L-shaped pool surrounded by sunning chairs, and two excellent clay tennis courts. Guests can also go horseback riding, water skiing, play billiards and ping-pong, or try their luck at the ever-popular casino. On the beach there are swings, see-saws and merry-go-rounds for the children. A number of straw huts provide shelter for those seeking protection from the sun. A good place to sit during the day is the breezy thatched-roof restaurant and adjoining bar. They are a level above the pool, so you can get a good view of swimmers, the lake, and all the action, including the water skiing and paddle boating, which never seem to stop.

Guests have a choice between rooms and cabins. The former are standard in size and located in a modern white building. They have fine carpets, TVs, telephones, piped-in music, air conditioning, long dressing tables, comfortable reading chairs, ample closet space, and tile bathrooms with marble basins and combination baths. There are four types and sizes of cabins, all of which are cement constructions painted white. The furnishings are similar to those in the guest rooms. Most bungalows have two bedrooms, two bathrooms, and a porch, but no kitchenette; unfortunately, however, only some of the porches face the lake. All in all, this tranquil and relaxing establishment, surrounded by trees and flowering bushes, makes a good get-away for the weekend, especially for those coming from Bogotá, as the weather there is often chilly.

HOTEL BACHUE

Carrera 8 No. 18-04, phone (83) 26791/5, Bogotá phone (1) 296-8153; fax (1) 296-8228
Category: A. Modern, downtown, 103 rooms, pool, disco.
Rates: $29/$38 S/D incl. tax; $36/$47 S/D suites. All major credit cards accepted.
Directions: In the heart of Giradot.

The liveliest hotel in Giradot is the Bachué, a modern family-oriented establishment near the heart of town. The action during the day focuses around the pool, which is surrounded by tall ferns, palm trees and usually lots of sunbathers (mostly parents keeping an eye on their children). All 103 rooms face inward towards this central area and have balconies for viewing the activity.

A breezy thatched-roof restaurant, **La Cabana**, is at one end and is a relaxing place to dine or have a drink. Latin instrumental music is usually playing in the background. Selections on the menu include *viudo de capay*, a fish dish which is the chef's recommendation, as well as coq au vin, pepper steak, seafood casserole gratinada, ceviche, banana split, and seven exotic fruit shakes. At night the more formal **El Bosque** restaurant is popular, as is the hotel's disco. The hip ones, however, head for **El León Dorado**, a sidewalk café several blocks away; it's the "in" place for eats, drinks and just hanging out. Alternatively, aim for the **Taberna Quiteña** on the corner of Carrera 10 and Calle 18. It's a small bar with interesting decor and an English-speaking owner – a good place to have a few beers at night.

The guest rooms, usually fully booked October 12-16 during the city's main festival and again during the 15 December-15 February high season, consist of standard units and junior suites. The latter are very popular, especially with families, as the children can sleep on the sofas. These suites have two carpeted rooms, air conditioning, and modern furnishings. The living area is just big enough for two sofas and a minibar, while the bedrooms have color TVs, telephones, comfortable beds, desks, closets, balconies, and modern tile bathrooms with showers. The standard units are similar, but without the living area.

HOTEL TOCAREMA
Carrera 7 No. 20-02
Phone (83) 23914
Bogotá phone (1) 218-1146
Category: B
Grand old hotel, near center, 65 rooms, pool, restaurant.
Rates: $19/$25 S/D incl. 5% tax. All major credit cards.
Directions: A 10-minute walk up a hill from the center, overlooking town.

Perched on a hill overlooking the city, this grand old hotel, which dates from the mid-50's, was completely renovated in the late 80's. It used to have no serious rival in the Giradot area. Today, several newer establishments get top billing, but the Tocarema remains in excellent condition and is the best choice for those who appreciate older operations. The front side of this white three-story structure is lined with palm trees and potted plants and has a wide breezy terrace from one end to the other. The walkway offers excellent views of the city below and is a great place for guests to sit, day or night. A long clean pool with lights for night swimming is directly in front and, fortunately, is well shaded. The sun can be blisteringly hot around noon. Guests can also sit at one of the various covered tables surrounding the pool and order drinks from the nearby bar. In short, the ambience here is quite inviting, which is a major reason the Tocarema remains highly popular with vacationing Colombians on weekends.

The public areas occupy the ground level and are wonderfully breezy, with high ceilings and ubiquitous twirling ceiling fans. The atmosphere is exceedingly casual; ferns and other potted plants wave in the breeze, beautiful tile floors with different hues color each room, and there are a variety of comfortable old-style chairs. If you stroll into the game room you'll find two ping-pong tables and a gorgeous old billiard table. You'll also find a dining room on this floor and, even though it's quite large, well placed section dividers help make the dining areas more intimate.

Spacious hallways upstairs add to the hotel's airy atmosphere. The guest rooms are reasonably attractive and spacious and have red tile floors, floor-to-ceiling curtains, queen-size beds, walk-in closets, telephones, air conditioning, comfortable chairs, porches (but no seating), and old-style bathrooms with fixtures in good working order, including showers.

Alternative: **HOTEL PLAZA CRILLON**
Carrera 24, Melgar, phone (83) 450369
Rates: $18/$25 S/D incl. tax. Most major credit cards are accepted.
Directions: 16 km east of Giradot in the heart of Melgar on the Bogotá-Giradot Highway, 116 km from Bogotá.

There are no decent alternatives to the Tocarema in Giradot, so you may have to go to Melgar (16 km) for a similar class hotel. The Plaza Crillón in Melgar is a two-story, colonial-style hotel with a wooden second-floor balcony and lots of shade trees. It tries to give the appearance of being old but, in fact, dates from around 1970. It features a small kidney-shaped pool, a baby pool, a decent open-air restaurant, and 34 immaculately clean rooms. Although accommodations are a bit small and fairly basic, they do have fans, tile floors, twin beds with fresh sheets, closets, and tiny tile bathrooms with showers.

Medellín

HOTEL POBLADO PLAZA
Carrera 43a No. 4 Sur 75
Phone (4) 246-6093/268-5555
Fax (4) 268-6949
Category: Deluxe
Modern refined hotel, 50 rooms, nice area, pool, sauna, shops.
Rates: $135/$155 S/D incl. tax. All major credit cards.
Directions: On the main drag in the exclusive El Poblado residential area, 10 minutes by taxi to downtown.

The Poblado Plaza, located in Medellín's most fashionable district, has been in operation since 1989. It is the city's newest class act and is an excellent choice for those who prefer a bit of quiet elegance to the energy and exuberance of the Inter-Continental, the hotel's only serious rival. With only 50 rooms, this smart and popular establishment is less than a sixth the size of its competitor, but there's still a lot of activity here, especially on weekends.

The six-story property is attractively located among trees and has an understated off-white exterior. You'll quickly sense the air of modern elegance which this place exudes. The lobby, for example, has marble floors, brass chandeliers, plants in large brass pots, and flowers on the reception desk. Further back is the main sitting area, which is a relatively small room with elegant flowered carpets in pink and gray overtones, leather sofas, Victorian-like chairs, brass-based lamps, a recessed ceiling with a brass chandelier, a gold-leaf framed mirror and, almost always, a large flower arrangement.

The Poblado also has one of the city's best restaurants. The elegant decor – fine wallpaper, plush green and reddish carpeting, fancy chairs with fabric in soft gray and pink, a recessed wood-panelled ceiling, and oil paintings on the walls – matches the quality of the food, which is truly superb. The cuisine is international and the menu features a number of flambé dishes, escargots, shrimp and corn bisque New Orleans style, sea bass Florentine style with spinach and cream sauce, filet mignon, and Irish coffee. There's also a fine pastry cart. As guests dine they can hear the pianist playing in the adjoining bar; his music flows delightfully into all the rooms on the ground floor. They can also look out onto a lawn bordered by flowers; this secluded area is for swimming and sunning and also serves as spill-over space for the numerous parties hosted here by the local elite.

Getting a room at the Poblado can be difficult, so you should definitely reserve in advance. Each unit has queen-size beds with feather pillows, beautiful fabrics, thick carpets, satellite TVs, minibars, large closets, and tiled combination baths.

Alternative: INTER-CONTINENTAL MEDELLIN

Calle 16 No. 28-51, Variante Las Palmas, phone (4) 266-0680/246-4710, fax (4) 266-1548, telex 66685
Rates: $155/$170 S/D incl. 15% tax. All major credit cards are accepted.
Directions: On the outskirts of the Poblado residential section and away from its commercial center, a 10-minute taxi ride to the city center.

Those who want all the amenities of a first-class hotel will most likely prefer the nearby 336-room Inter-Continental. It has an Olympic-size pool, clay tennis courts, a health club, a sauna, a putting green, ping-pong, car rental, a travel agency, numerous shops, a children's playground, and even a small bull ring which is used at fiesta time. One of the chain's most impressive establishments in South America, it holds an unbeatable location on a hillside overlooking the city. Consequently, the accommodations, which are well equipped and nicely decorated, have great views. During the day most guests spend their time around the pool surrounded by palm trees and flowers, or at the **Terraza Bar** overlooking this area. The hotel's fanciest restaurant and bar are on the top floor and offer spectacular views of the city.

HOTEL NUTIBARA

Calle 52A No. 50-46
Phone (4) 511-5511
Fax (4) 231-3713
Telex 66563
Category: A
Old European facade, central location, 226 rooms, pool, full gym, disco, Turkish bath, casino.
Rates: $74/$90 S/D incl. 5% tax. Major credit cards.
Directions: Downtown, facing the main plaza.

The well-maintained and long-established Nutibara is unique in Colombia in terms of its grand old European character. You'll sense it immediately from glancing at the hotel's exterior, a granite facade topped by a fancy curly motif. Overlooking the city's main park and the governor's palace, this graceful 10-story structure, which has a newer similarly styled annex, continues to dominate the city's heart.

The hotel's most appealing feature is its colonial-style café which features a daily buffet and has an open-air section towards the street – similar to a French sidewalk café. A wonderful retreat from the city's hustle and bustle, this outdoor section of the café is completely shaded by trees and tall plants and is clearly an enjoyable spot. The metal garden furniture here is well padded, so it's both attractive and comfortable. Even if you don't stay here, at least visit for drinks or a light meal. The Nutibara also features a more formal restaurant offering international cuisine that is usually good. In addition to its eateries, the hotel has a popular pool and sunning deck on the second floor, a health club, a Turkish bath and full gym on the roof along with a casino and a nightclub.

The rooms in the main building have old-style furnishings in keeping with the rest of the hotel, good quality rugs, fancy fabrics, comfortable reading chairs, well-stocked minibars, satellite TVs on request, air conditioning, good views, and modern tile bathrooms with combination baths. Units in the annex across the street are also quite good, with older furnishings but similar features (TVs, minibars, etc.). A good number of these rooms lack views.

***Alternative:* GRAN HOTEL**
Calle 54 No. 45-92, phone (4) 251-9951, fax (4) 251-6035, telex 65326
Rates: $46/$60 S/D incl. 5% tax. All major credit cards are accepted.
Directions: 4 blocks east of the main plaza, just east of Avenida Jorge Gaitan.

If the Nutibara is full, try the 12-story, 120-room Gran, which caters to business people and has a striking modern facade. The interesting exterior, however, belies the interior, which is singularly ordinary. The lobby, for example, is long and impersonal, with stone flooring and commercial sofas, plus an undistinguished bar. There are, however, a number of amenities: sauna, Turkish bath, travel agency and, best of all, a small roof-top pool with an adjoining bar. And, while the rooms do not have air conditioning, they are standard size and comfortable, with fans, carpets, cable TVs, minibars, reading chairs, desks, ample closet space, and modern tile bathrooms with showers.

HOTEL VERRACRUZ
Carrera 50 No. 54-18, phone (4) 231-5511, fax (4) 231-8881, telex 65307
Category: B. Tower, central, 134 rooms, pool, sauna, travel agency, Turkish bath, barber shop.
Rates: $23/$30 S/D incl. tax. All major credit cards are accepted.
Directions: Downtown 2 blocks behind (north of) the Nutibara.

The competition is stiff among the city's cheaper business-class hotels, most of which are in the center near the Nutibara and have drab run-down exteriors. The Verracruz has the edge in large part because of its attractive lobby and, more important, its top floor, which features a pool, sauna, Turkish bath, bar and restaurant. It's a great place eat and drink, and view the city. Unfortunately, the pool is too small for swimming laps and has no sunning chairs, but it's good for cooling off, especially if you've been in the sauna. You'll undoubtedly find the breezy open-air bar a wonderful place for breakfast while admiring the city below. For other meals you can try the adjoining main restaurant, which serves good food, has a nice informal atmosphere, and affords the same panoramic views.

The hotel's ground floor public areas are quite nice. The lobby has a nice cozy ambience and features stone flooring, Oriental rugs, comfortable old-style chairs, scattered plants, and a TV at the far end. The decor of the rooms could be better, but it at least beats that of the hotel's competitors (ever so slightly!). All units have fans, TVs, telephones, closets, ordinary beds and carpets, and small tile bathrooms with showers. A few of the rooms facing the street also have small balconies.

First Alternative: **HOTEL AMBASSADOR**
Carrera 50 No. 54-50, phone (4) 231-5311, fax (4) 231-5312, telex 65267
Rates: $26/$34 S/D incl. 5% tax. All major credit cards are accepted.
Directions: On the same block as the Verracruz.

The 13-floor, 135-room Ambassador, which is very similar to and affiliated with the nearby Verracruz, has a reasonably presentable lobby and acceptable rooms. Its main attraction is the roof-top pool which, although a bit small, is better than the Verracruz's. It's very popular and has plants surrounding it. On a typical day many guests can be found here, lounging on the sunning chairs surrounding the pool or having a sip at the adjoining bar, which is protected from the sun. The rooms have satellite TVs and carpets, but are otherwise quite ordinary. They feature average beds, plain walls, spartan furnishings, closets, fans, and small bathrooms with marble-top basins and showers.

Second Alternative: **CASA DORADA DEL GRAN HOTEL**
Calle 50 No. 47-25, phone (4) 2455470/0217
Rates: $13/$18 S/D incl. 5% tax.
Directions: 5 blocks south-east of the main plaza in a commercial area.

For a less expensive category C hotel, try the Casa Dorada, which is affiliated with the Gran Hotel. It's a very clean place with a stone floor lobby and a pleasant restaurant which serves good breakfasts. The rooms are small and have unadorned walls, no fans and, in some cases, no windows. In other respects they are fairly decent as they have reasonably comfortable beds, carpets, TVs, telephones, and private tile bathrooms with showers.

Cali

INTER-CONTINENTAL CALI
Avenida Colombia 2-72
Phone (23) 812-186/823-225
Fax (23) 830-219/822-567
Telex 55599
Category: Deluxe
Modern, central, 383 rooms, pool, tennis, health club, small casino, car rental, tennis, travel agency, disco, sauna, Turkish bath.
Rates: $120/$144 S/D incl. tax. All major credit cards.
Directions: Downtown, overlooking La Maria Park & the Cali River.

The city's top address, the Inter-Continental, is the only deluxe hotel in town. But now that Cali has replaced Medellín as the drug capital of Colombia, one wonders how long this will last. In the meantime this is definitely the place to stay for those with big bucks. This hotel has it all –

convention facilities for 1,200 people, an Olympic-size pool, shops galore, a piano bar, a nightclub, a casino, a fully-equipped health club, and a lighted, artificial-grass tennis court. With 370 rooms, the hotel can hardly hope to give much personalized service; still, the staff does a reasonably good job despite, reportedly, occasional gaffes. The huge lobby, with its marble floors, mirrored walls and glass chandeliers, is designed to impress. To find a quiet place to sit down, you'll have to walk towards the rear and into the piano bar – a very comfortable area with plush leather sofas, recessed chandeliers, and carpets.

Further back you'll find a long patio and, beyond, the hotel's huge pool and lawn. This area, which can be quite breezy at night, is by far the nicest place to sit during the day or night, and for this reason there are lots of sunning chairs all around the pool and lawn furniture all along the patio. At lunch and dinner, you can usually find an extensive buffet here. Many guests come just to sit, have a drink, talk, and watch the palm trees waving in the breeze. On special occasions, the lively bar on the patio features music and folkloric entertainment. For dining, however, the locals prefer the more reasonably priced pizzeria inside. Designed to look like a street-side café, it's usually crowded and very lively at meal time.

The artistically decorated, wood-panelled guest rooms are top notch and offer satellite TV, minibars, wide beds, plush bed covers, deluxe carpets, ample furnishings including sofas, plus top quality bathrooms with lots of counter space and combination baths. In sum, the quality of this operation is about what you'd expect of an Inter-Continental hotel. A note of warning: If you plan to be here around Christmas time, be sure to book a room well in advance, as Cali's famous annual fair (with bull fights and all) takes place between December 25 and January 3.

HOTEL EL PENEN

Calle 1 Oeste No. 2-61, phone (23) 834-444/8, fax (23) 892-498
Category: A. Aparthotel, 24 rooms, restaurant, laundry.
Rates: $43/$55 S/D incl. tax. All major credit cards.
Directions: 2 short blocks behind Hotel Dann and 4 short blocks from the Inter-Continental.

Although the security situation in Cali is more relaxed than one might expect considering the city's notorious drug and anti-drug operations, it could change. Regardless, street crime has been a problem for many years, so having a good location is, for many people, critical. The Peñén fills the bill in this regard as it's only two blocks from the Inter-Continental and in about as good an area as you'll find.

Built in 1986, it's a fairly small eight-story operation with 24 top-quality rooms and little else. The accommodations are large, air conditioned and comfortable, with wide beds, attractive pink bedspreads, fine carpets, satellite TVs, telephones, well-stocked minibars, large closets, cushy armchairs for reading, breakfast tables, desks, and tile bathrooms with modern fixtures and showers.

The public areas consist of a small presentable lobby in brick motif with a compact sitting area to one side, and an adjoining restaurant with about eight tables – best for breakfast and snacks rather than full meals. The staff is very professional and, as a result, they get much repeat business. This serves them well, as the Peñén is not well known except with frequent travelers to Cali.

***First Alternative:* HOTEL OBELISCO CALI**

Carrera 1 Oeste No. 4-39, phone (23) 837-420, fax (23) 830-219
Rates: $64/$75 S/D incl. tax. All major credit cards are accepted.
Directions: Severalblocksfrom the Inter-Continental.

If the want a hotel with a pool or sauna and don't mind paying a little more, you'll probably prefer the Obelisco, which is a newer and larger hotel nearby. It features a small pool with an adjoining glassed-in sauna and prides itself on the personal attention given to its guests. All 60 guest rooms have satellite TVs, carpets, air conditioning, matching bedspreads and curtains, and modern baths; the more expensive units also have balconies.

***Second Alternative:* HOTEL ARISTI**

Carrera 9a No. 10-04, phone (23) 822-521, fax (23) 839-697, telex 51154
Rates: $58/$75 S/D incl. tax ($40 for an unrenovated room with fan). Major credit cards are accepted.
Directions: Downtown, 10 blocks from the Inter-Continental and bordering an unsafe area.

The old 10-story Aristi has been recently renovated and may be preferred by those who like older establishments. From the outside this place is not inviting, but inside it's very active, even a bit grand, with a lively high-ceiling lobby that will give you the impression of stepping back into the 1940's. The numerous amenities here, particularly the lovely pool on top and the Turkish bath complex, are major attractions for the mainly Colombian clientele. A beauty parlor, barber shop, and a pre-Colombian art shop are also on the premises. All 169 rooms have satellite TVs, minibars, and tile baths with showers. Only those units which have been renovated have air conditioning, new carpets, new draperies and bedspreads.

PENSION STEIN

Avenida 4a No. 3-33
Phone (23) 614-927/99
Category: B
Stone mansion, near center, 24 rooms, pool, TV room, dining room, English spoken.
Rates: $25/$33 S/D incl. tax; $38/$45 S/D with full board. No credit cards.
Directions: Across the river from the Inter-Continental and 2 blocks further north, in a nice residential area.

If the idea of staying in a magnificent 1940's stone mansion with a swimming pool and a Swiss ambience sounds interesting, by all means book a room here. Enrique Frei, the friendly Swiss-Colombian owner, runs this establishment with gusto and charm; he also speaks English, Spanish, French and German. Years ago he took over the management from his mother, who converted this wonderful house into a hotel around 1960 or so. Enrique's clients are mainly young and middle-aged American and European overland travelers, who hear of this gem by word of mouth. He makes everyone feel at home, so it's a great place to meet other travelers; indeed, you can't avoid them. Every night at 7 p.m. he sounds the dinner bell. The meals, which cost about $5, are served family-style, i.e., you help yourself to what's served. The set menu changes daily. As in all the rooms, the ceilings here have huge exposed wooden beams, and the walls, which are lined with pictures and plates from Switzerland, have wainscoting and attractive wrought iron lighting fixtures.

Mr. Frei can often be found chatting with guests in the lobby, which has an antique Swiss clock behind the small reception desk, a very old telephone on the wall, two leather-back chairs, a sofa, wood-panelled walls and ceilings, and a formal staircase with red carpeting and banisters. A coat of arms over one of the arched doorways and a huge oil painting along the stairway add still more touches of old Europe. When they're not lingering around the dinner table or sunning at the pool, guests tend to use the main sitting room, which is quite elegant with large Oriental carpets, dark wood-panelled walls and ceilings, two luxurious sofas and three high-back chairs in matching material, several fancy Victorian chairs, a Swiss cuckoo clock, an interesting collection of ceramic plates with scenes of different Swiss villages, plus a TV. There's no bar, but you can order drinks at any time of the day and take them wherever.

Guests also have the option of sitting out on the front stone terrace, but the views are blocked by the trees. In fact, the trees add a gentle touch of seclusion. In back there's a small pool surrounded by lots of greenery and, on two sides, by a stone wall. You can sun directly on the grass or on cushions laid out for this purpose.

As for the guest rooms, they should seem almost superfluous at this point in any decision to stay here. Spacious and fine, but not nearly so fancy as the public areas, they have papered walls, old furnishings, bureaus, desks, chairs, fans and private showers. There are only 24 of them, so calling in advance is highly recommended. If you reserve well ahead of time or arrive early in the day, you might even luck out and get the big room in the tower.

HOTEL LA MERCED
Calle 7a No. 1-65
Phone (23) 822-520 or 791-397
Category: B
Colonial exterior, central location, 60 rooms, pool, ping-pong, billiards, sauna, English spoken.

Rates: $16/$21 S/D, plus 5% tax. All major credit cards accepted.
Directions: 2 blocks east of the Inter-Continental and one block off the Cali River.

The Merced's Spanish colonial exterior consists basically of plain white walls with dark wood trim, traditional wooden windows, a second-story veranda, and tile roofing. From this you may think that the hotel's interior atmosphere must be very peaceful. Nothing could be further from the truth. The Merced, which tends to attract a young crowd, is one of the most active hotels in Cali and a great buy. Most appealing are the hotel's numerous facilities, which include a medium-length pool, a sauna, a spacious and popular TV room, and a restaurant. You'll also find a game room with ping-pong and billiard tables, which are in good condition and frequently in use at night. The pool is illuminated for those who like to swim a few laps after the sun goes down. The hotel's location in the heart of town near the Inter-Continental and the Cali River is another drawing card; still another is the friendly, English-speaking staff.

The restaurant's decor is cafeteria-like – metal chairs and matching tables with tablecloths and artificial flowers, bare brown tile floors, overhead fans, and a huge photograph covering almost an entire wall. The meals are reasonably priced and better than the decor might suggest; selections include starters such as Russian salad, also tasty *robablo a la plancha* (braised fish), chicken creole style, beef stroganoff, and *sobrebarriaga a la criolla* (a Colombian beef dish with cheese). The restaurant offers six or so desserts and a selection of wines.

The rooms – spotless, with high ceilings and plain white walls – feature blue wall-to-wall carpeting, large closets, small desks, comfortable beds, and private bathrooms with fairly old fixtures in good working order, including hot-water showers.

***Alternative:* HOTEL RIO CALI**
Avenida Colombia 9-80, phone (23) 803-156/7/8
Rates: $16/$23 S/D incl. tax. All major credit cards are accepted.
Directions: 2 blocks east of La Merced and 5 short blocks east of the Inter-Continental on the same street.

If the others are full and you want a place in the same general area (which is one of the safer districts in this drug-trafficking capital), one old stand-by you could try is the 50-room Río Cali, formerly the Menendez, which is in the center overlooking the Cali River. It's an old-style hotel with a spacious lobby, a large reasonably-priced restaurant which is popular with the locals, and plain high-ceiling rooms. These have fans, telephones, and private tile baths with showers in good working order. Due to good maintenance, the hotel's continuing decay is very slow, and the ambience remains appealing.

Buenaventura

HOTEL ESTACION
Calle 2 No. 1A-08
Phone (23) 23935/6
Category: A
Grand hotel, ocean front, 80 rooms, pool, restaurant, bar.
Rates: $45/$59 S/D incl. tax. All major credit cards.
Directions: In the heart of town, overlooking the water.

This grand old hotel may not be in and of itself enough to make you want to come to this uninteresting port city, but if you're here, it is well worth staying at. Architecturally, it's the most interesting hotel in Colombia. Wonderfully located overlooking the water, this white neoclassical

French structure was built in 1928 by Pablo Emilio Paez, an architect from Bogotá. It was the first commercial building in Buenaventura and was erected at the end of the then new Ferrocarril del Pacífico, facing the railway station – hence the name Estación. As you walk around this charming place you'll notice that virtually all the adornments, from those on the ceilings to those on the balconies, have oceanic themes; huge oyster shells, starfish and other aquatic animals. An interesting feature is the skylight, which bathes the central pentagon area with soft orange sunlight.

Back in 1928, Paez's critics said that this Gothic-inspired building should have been built of stone like most Gothic structures in Europe, but the architect, who adored ornate buildings, reasoned that if the British Parliament could be of brick and cement, so could the Estación. Carefully restored in 1982 to its former glory, the striking hotel retains most of these original details. The restaurant here is the best in the city, as are the ocean-facing rooms. The bowl of fruit that you may find in your room says a lot about the quality of service you're likely to receive here.

Alternative: **HOTEL FELIPE-II**
Carrera 3A No. 2-44, phone (23) 22820

If money considerations are important, your best bet is the Felipe-II. It is nearby in the heart of town and has rooms that cost only a quarter of those at the Estación. They are acceptable and feature air conditioning, TVs, phones and private baths with showers.

Popayán

HOTEL MONASTERIO
Calle 4 No. 10-50
Phone (39) 232-191/6
Fax (39) 243-491
Bogotá phone (1) 256-8182
Bogotá fax (1) 256-8182
Category: A
Former monastery, two stories, 47 rooms, central location, pool, courtyard and restaurant.

Rates: $39/$52 S/D incl. tax. All major credit cards are accepted.
Directions: Downtown, 3 blocks west of the plaza.

It's not often that one gets the opportunity to stay at a 300-year-old former monastery. If you come to Popayán, which is about 150 years older still, you can do just that by checking in at the Hotel Monasterio. The locals in this historic town prize this place and it's the frequent site of wedding receptions. The white two-story tile roof structure has a typical colonial design, but on a grand scale. It has a large inner courtyard lined by arched columns which support a covered walkway. In the center of this is a functioning stone fountain that is surrounded by grass and bushes.

If you continue towards the rear, you'll reach a brick terrace where breakfast is served. As in much of the hotel, the furnishings here have a monastic element about them – simple, mostly wood, and aesthetically pleasing. As you sip your mild Colombian coffee, you can look out over the large lawn towards the oval pool just 100 meters away. It's barely long enough for swimming laps and has numerous chairs around it. On special occasions, meals are served from the thatched-roof hut next to the pool. Further afield you'll find a garden where the hotel grows its own vegetables. You'll also see lots of trees encircling the entire area, which is why everywhere you walk you'll be entertained by the sound of chirping birds.

Returning to the main part of the hotel, you'll find **La Herrería**, the hotel's main restaurant. It's a spacious room with large impressive columns that give it a formal and austere appearance. There's also an open-air reception area here with a sitting room to one side. At night, the latter is about the only area to sit. Comfortable but a bit plain, it has leather sofas and matching chairs, ordinary carpeting, and a TV.

The rooms are unexceptional and somewhat musty. They have small windows, carpets, bureaus, TVs, minibars, phones, closets, and comfortable twin beds. The private bathrooms have old fixtures and showers.

HOTEL CAMINO REAL

Calle 5a No. 5-59
Phone (39) 232-546
Category: B
Colonial house, central, 29 rooms, restaurant and bar.
Rates: $19-$20/$25-$28 S/D incl. tax. All major credit cards are accepted.
Directions: At the south-eastern corner of the main plaza.

Inviting and atmospheric are the words that come to mind when describing this delightful hostel. No hotel in Colombia comes close in terms of the number and variety of objects and knick-knacks on display. In every public room, as well as the hallways and stairwell, you'll find a collection of memorabilia displayed closely together so as to fit them in. You name it, it's here: a large number of fascinating photos and posters of the area surrounding Popayán, antique oil paintings, extensive collections of old irons, sewing machines, saddle stirrups, weights, and bugles.

Because of the friendly atmosphere and good service, the Camino Real, which is one of several of the city's beautiful colonial residences that have been remodeled into hotels, is something of a meeting place for the locals. The feeling here is similar to that in a British pub where people meet, have a few drinks, and exchange gossip. The bar has original wide-board wooden floors, captain's chairs with leather seats, small round tables, several plants, and classical music playing in the background.

What foreigners often remember most is the restaurant, which happens to be the best in town. Of particular note is their huge six-course dinner special – reasonably priced at around $7. You can also eat much more modestly and cheaply. The dining area is small, with the same flooring as the bar, seven attractive tables, and old kerosene lanterns on the walls.

Most of the rooms are upstairs. They're a bit cramped, but are nevertheless quite good. They offer TVs, telephones, plain carpets, ordinary twin beds, small desks, closets, and decent old-looking bathrooms with fixtures in good working order, including hot-water showers. For just a dollar or two extra you can get a slightly larger unit with windows facing the street. From the second-floor hallway (onto which most rooms open) you can admire two courtyards, both of which are full of plants and add still more charm to this home-like establishment.

HOTEL LA PLAZUELA
Calle 5a No. 8-13
Phone (39) 231-084/235-912
Category: B
Colonial house, central, 30 rooms, restaurant and bar.
Rates: $16/$23 S/D incl. tax. All major credit cards.
Directions: On the same street as the Camino Real, 3 blocks to the west.

If the Camino Real is full, don't worry. The Plazuela is just three blocks away and is well maintained. It is very similar in many respects except that the atmosphere, while good, can't quite match that of the Camino Real. Like the latter, it's a remodeled colonial mansion. Much of the updating took place very recently, in 1983, following an earthquake which severely damaged or destroyed many of the city's fine old buildings. The white two-story building is much as it used to be. It features a central stone-floor courtyard and a non-functioning granite fountain surrounded by an arcade of square columns and a walkway onto which most rooms open.

Entering the main lobby you'll see some high-quality water colors by local artists; they line the walls here as well as the hallways. The lobby has an attractive sitting area with carpets and comfortable sofas and chairs. Further along you'll come to the restaurant, which is fairly attractive and has bare brick flooring, wooden tables with captain's chairs, and wrought iron lighting fixtures. There's also a bar in back which is probably the best place to spend time, although its rustic atmosphere can make it seem a bit cold at times. The decor is similar to that of the restaurant and features a fireplace at one end of the room and a brick bar at the other, attractive wooden tables with captain's chairs and long benches with stools.

The rooms are standard size and a good number of them face the street. The plain white walls and the furnishings, which are simple and made of old wood, are appropriate to the character of the building. The units also have new carpets, telephones, TVs on request, old-style lamp fixtures, desks, closets, a few paintings on the walls, and ordinary tile bathrooms with showers.

***First Alternative:* HOSTAL LA CASONA DEL VIRREY**
Calle 4 No. 5-78, phone (39) 231-836
Rates: $16/$21 S/D incl. tax. Credit cards are not accepted.
Directions: In the center, one block from the Camino Real.

If the others are full, try the Casona del Virrey. It's slightly cheaper and likewise in an old colonial house, with a friendly staff and large rooms with hot-water showers.

***Second Alternative:* HOTEL LA ERMITA**
Calle 5a, No. 2-77, phone (39) 231-936
Rates: $11/$16 S/D incl. tax. Visa is accepted.
Directions: On the same street as the Camino Real, 3 blocks to the east.

For a less expensive category C hotel, try the Ermita, which is on the same street as the Camino Real, next to the lovely old Ermita Church. It's an attractive colonial house with clean rooms, private baths with hot-water showers, TV, and excellent breakfasts.

San Agustín

HOTEL YALCONIA
Carrera Parque Arqueologico
Phone (988) 373-001/373-131
Category: A
Modern, outskirts of town, 36 rooms, unheated pool, billiards.
Rates: $23/$31 S/D incl. tax; $25/$34 S/D suites. Major credit cards.
Directions: On edge of town on the road to the park, 1 km from the plaza.

The modern two-story Yalconia, the town's undisputed leading hotel, is on the outskirts and features a large lawn in back with a clean unheated pool. Except during the peak rainy season (June through August) when the skies are gray, this is a wonderful area to spend time and relax; the water is warm enough for swimming then as well.

The best place to relax inside is the main sitting room, which has thick carpets, comfortable modern armchairs, a TV, and a fireplace, which gets put to good use in this cool town at 1,700-meters altitude. The bar, which has a number of tables for drinks and cards, has a second fireplace. The atmosphere is a bit sterile, as it is in the remaining public areas.

The rooms are quite neat with good views, comfortable beds, telephones, and tile bathrooms with hot-water showers. There are no carpets or chairs. If you take one of their single-room "suites," (just 10% more) you get a little more space, carpeting and a terrace. It may be worth the few extra dollars.

HOTEL OSOGUAICO
Carrera Parque Arqueologico, phone (988) 373-069
Category: B. Homey, 30 rooms, restaurant, unheated pool.
Rates: $14/$19 S/D incl. tax. No credit cards.
Directions: 1½ km further out of town on the road to the park, a 35-minute walk from town and 1 km before the park entrance.

If you prefer places with a cozy feel to them and you don't mind being 2.5 km out of town (but near the park), you'll almost certainly prefer the Osoguaico. This single-story white house with bright red trim is run by a delightful German couple. The attractions of being here (aside from the owners) are the low prices and the relaxing area in back, which has a small unheated pool, a nice yard with grass and flowers, and a thatched-roof hut with tables for drinks. The hostel also provides laundry service, a small lobby with TV, and a pleasant dining room offering home cooking. One of their specialties is baked guinea pig, which is a delicacy throughout the Andes.

The rooms, which are reminiscent of those in a cheap European B&B, have a spotless, comfortable appearance, and many of them offer great views. However, they're so cramped that there's not enough room even for a reading chair. The bathrooms are also tiny and are all shared, but they're at least clean and have warm-water showers. Finally, if you'd prefer to camp, you can do that, too. The owners maintain a camping site and charge about $1 a person.

HOTEL COLONIAL

Calle 3a No. 11-54, phone (988) 373-159
Category: C. Colonial building, central, 12 rooms, restaurant, hot-water showers
Rates: $3 per person. No credit cards.
Directions: Downtown, 2 blocks from the park and 1 block from the Coomotor bus station.

The Colonial is a beautiful two-story building near the center and a good place to stay for the money. Just don't expect much of the rooms – they are about as plain as they come and a few don't even have windows. They have simple beds, wooden floors, unadorned walls, bare light bulbs, clean shared bathrooms and, unlike many hotels of this class, hot water day and night.

The best features of the Colonial, besides the friendly manager, are the public areas, in particular the open-air restaurant in back. It's quite pleasant and has an attractive thatched roof. There are tables here for drinking and eating. Food from the bar is quite good and reasonably priced. If you look towards the garden, you may even see some parrots and monkeys. Upstairs on the old wooden balcony you'll find lots of comfortable chairs where you can relax with a cocktail. In short, the Colonial has much to recommend it, despite the rather stark guest rooms.

***Alternative:* HOTEL CENTRAL**
Calle 3a No. 10-32, phone (988) 373-027
Rates: $5/$8 S/D incl. tax ($2/$4 S/D with shared bath). No credit cards.
Directions: Half a block down from the Colonial.

If the Colonial is full or you require a private bath, try the nearby Central. It's an old two-story house with a central courtyard, a dining room with inexpensive meals, and secure parking. The friendly owners speak English and will wash your clothes and even help organize rental horses if you ask. The rooms are very basic, with simple wooden beds, blankets but no sheets, bare light bulbs hanging from the ceiling, and tiny clean private baths with cold-water showers, towels and toilet paper.

Southern Region

Pasto

CHALET GUAMUEZ
Laguna de la Cocha, Pasto
Phone (277) 1 – ask the operator to connect you with the inn
Cables: Chalet Guamuez
Category: A
Rustic lodge, lakeside, 15 rooms and cabins
Rates: $14/$19 S/D incl. tax ($25 for a 6-person cabin). All major credit cards.
Directions: On the western shore of Lake La Cocha, 18 miles (a 45-minute drive) east of Pasto via the paved road to Mocoa and 300 meters or so before the better-marked Hotel Sindamanoy. The taxi fare from Pasto is about $12.

A delightful place to stay a few days in the Pasto area is the Chalet Guamuez, which is a homey retreat in a somewhat remote wooded area overlooking Lake La Cocha. It is less than an hour from Pasto. Resembling a Swiss lodge, this rustic log-cabin-style place has been owned and run since 1965 by a friendly Swiss-German couple, the Sulsers. After talking with Walter and his wife, you'll want to take a walk and admire the establishment from the outside. Strolling to the lake 200 meters away, you'll see gorgeous wildflowers everywhere, as well as the Sulser's extensive garden, which supplies the restaurant with all of its vegetables;

you may even see a few grazing milk-cows here and there. Swimming in the lake, which is 2,860 meters above sea level, is only for the very hearty, as the water temperature is similar to that of the air, which averages around 55°. Not surprisingly, most guests are content with taking a launch out on the lake and fishing!

The main sitting room, which is where everyone spends time, has great views of the lake and a cheerful lodge-like atmosphere. It features wooden walls, old tile floors, comfortable wooden armchairs and sofas with leather seats and backs, and rough all-wood coffee tables. Brightly colored curtains, numerous arrangements of wildflowers, a TV, walls covered with photographs, and a frequently-used red brick fireplace in the center complete the picture. The rustic theme continues into the adjoining restaurant, which has wooden tables and chairs. Meals here are wholesome, but the choices are limited. There are typically four soups, including French onion soup, trout prepared four different ways, some beef dishes such as pepper steak, and four desserts. The food is fine, but what truly stands out is the garden-fresh salads that come with the meals – they're terrific.

The guest rooms are quite charming and half of them have views of the lake. They are standard size and have carpets, wool covers on the beds, heaters, desks, wooden walls, ceilings with exposed beams, and bathrooms with reliable hot-water showers and wooden walls. There are also some log cabins set apart from the main building. These sleep up to six people and those with vans can camp for free. For a memorable experience, stay here.

Alternative: HOTEL SINDAMANOY

Laguna de la Cocha, phone (277) 1609, Pasto phone 235-017/8, Bogotá phone (1) 217-6200
Rates: $31/$40 S/D incl. 5% tax. All major credit cards are accepted.
Directions: About 300 meters beyond the Guamuez, on the same dirt road.

This log-cabin-style lodge, which is part of the German Morales hotel chain along with Hotel Morasurco in Pasto, is attractive on the outside, but inside it lacks the cozy atmosphere of the Guamuez. On the other hand, it is ideally located right at the lake's edge. All 22 rooms have lake views, although only a few have heat. Even when the hotel is full, the bar and nearby sitting room don't seem to attract many guests, probably because of their rather cold and uninviting decor. The restaurant, on the other hand, is well used. Impressive, with a high A-frame ceiling, it offers good meals, including rainbow trout prepared seven different ways – stuffed with herbs, with wine sauce, a la Portuguesa, etc. Whether or not you stay here, you can hire the hotel's boats for excursions on the lake.

Trips include a 10-minute run to Isla de la Chorota nature reserve, which has little wildlife but is interesting for its trees and flora.

HOTEL MORASURCO
Ave. de los Estudiantes
Phone (277) 235-017/8/9
Telex 53737
Bogotá phone (1) 217-6200
Category: A
Modern, residential area, 60 rooms, Turkish bath, ping-pong, billiards, unisex beauty parlor, newsstand, shops.
Rates: $38/$54 S/D incl. tax. All major credit cards are accepted here.
Directions: On the Pan-American Highway to Cali, 2 km from the center on Pasto's northern edge.

Pasto's leading hotel and part of the German Morales chain, the Morasurco is a five-story red brick structure dating from 1970. It is modern looking and well maintained. The main sitting area is a spacious room in the rear overlooking a grassy backyard. There is a children's playground here and hills beyond. It's a pleasant room with lots of natural light, comfortable sofas and chairs, white rugs on parquet floors, and a TV. Check out the two large murals to one side; they are quite colorful and combine successfully both modern and primitive artistic styles in depicting Colombian village life.

The adjoining restaurant is a large area with comfortable armchairs, tables with pink tablecloths, plants to fill up space, numerous modern paintings on the wall, plus a huge 16th-century mural of a port scene with Spanish galleons. For a change of scenery, try **El Chalet Suizo** across the street; it's one of the city's top restaurants.

The guest rooms are fine, but not exceptional. They feature plush wall-to-wall carpets, reading chairs, desks, ample closet space, and tile bathrooms with new-looking fixtures and showers.

Alternative: **CUELLAR'S**
Carrera 23 No. 15-50, phone (277) 230561/232879, fax (277) 238274
Rates: $29/$36 S/D incl. tax. All major credit cards are accepted.
Directions: Downtown on a busy street, several blocks from the central plaza.

This 37-room businessman's hotel is architecturally interesting both inside and out. It serves as an excellent less expensive alternative to Morasurco and has a more convenient downtown location. What's most striking is the four-story atrium lobby, which separates the new section from the old. The facilities include a good restaurant and, most unusual, a 10-lane bowling alley in the basement. The rooms are quite good, with comfortable beds, carpets, small color TVs, desks, and tile bathrooms with showers.

HOTEL SINDAGUA
Calle 20 No. 21B-16
Phone (277) 235-404/230-371
Fax (277) 239-119
Category: B
Modern, central, 33 rooms, sauna, excellent restaurant.
Rates: $13/$16 S/D incl. tax. All major credit cards.
Directions: On a busy street 4 blocks from the main square.

Dating from around 1980, the four-story, centrally located Sindagua is a clear notch above its competitors. There are numerous signs of this all about, from the complimentary cocktail offered to guests upon registering and the fresh roses on all of the dining tables to the general facilities, which include a sauna, exercise bikes, private parking, and one of the city's top restaurants, **El Condal**.

For a category B hotel, the restaurant here is unusually good. Chinese food, including sweet and sour fish, chop suey and superb steamed fish, dominates the menu. But there are many other house specialties, including *cazuela de mariscos* (seafood stew), sea bass in almond sauce, Spanish paella, rainbow trout, various types of ceviche, plus an excellent salad bar and a good wine selection. They also offer a full complement of more ordinary dishes such as roasted chicken or steak. On weekends guests can listen to Javier's organ as they dine. Afterwards, they can retire for a nightcap to the softly-lit, red-carpeted bar adjoining the restaurant.

Compared to the dining area, the rooms are a bit disappointing, showing no decorative imagination whatsoever. Still, they are clean, bright, and in reasonably good condition. They provide most necessities, including ordinary beds with thin bedspreads, slightly frayed industrial carpets, black and white TVs, telephones, simple chairs, natural-wood closets, and tile bathrooms with ordinary fixtures including hot-water showers, but no shower heads.

First Alternative: **HOTEL EL DUQUE**
Calle 17 No. 17-17, phone (277) 237390/236587
Rates: $10/$14 S/D incl. tax. Most major credit cards are accepted.
Directions: In the center, about two blocks from the bus terminals.

The four-story El Duque has newer accommodations and is virtually as good as the Sindagua. A plus is that it's slightly closer to the center. The 19 rooms here are a bit small, but they are neat and have comfortable beds, carpets, color TVs, telephones, large closets, and tile bathrooms with new fixtures and good showers. The hotel is on a noisy street, so try to get a unit towards the rear. There's also an attractive bar/restaurant on the roof with excellent views of the city; it's a great place to have a drink or a bite to eat.

Second Alternative: **HOTEL AMERICANA**
Carrera 22-A No. 15-51, phone (277) 238413/239304
Rates: $9/$13 plus 5% tax. All major credit cards.
Directions: In the center on a quiet street, a block behind the better-known Hotel Cuellar's.

If the others are full, try this three-story, 31-room hotel which opened in 1989. The rooms are tiny and there's no restaurant, but otherwise this new place has much to recommend it. The hotel is well managed by a very friendly staff and the accommodations are spotless. Rooms are furnished with carpets, color TVs, telephones, piped-in music, closets, and private tile bathrooms with new fixtures. There's also a restaurant a block away which will deliver to your room.

Third Alternative: **HOTEL MAYASQUER**
Avenida de las Américas 16-66, phone (277) 235284
Rates: $4/$6 S/D incl. tax. Credit cards are not accepted.
Directions: 2 blocks from the bus terminals, which are between Carreras 18 and 20.

For a less expensive category C hotel, try the Mayasquer, which is up a flight of stairs in a four-story building on a quiet street near the bus station. Run by a friendly lady, Cecilia Zutta, it has rooms with telephones and private baths and a comfortable sitting area with a TV and a coffee machine. If her rooms are all taken, try **HOTEL JUANAMBU** (phone 234970) which is a few meters away at No. 16-40. It is well marked and is similar in many respects to the Mayasquer.

Coastal Region

Cartagena

HOTEL CARIBE

Carrera 1a No. 2-87
Phone (56) 650-155
Fax (56) 653-707
Telex 37811
Category: Deluxe
City's grande dame, 362 rooms, beachfront, pool, tennis, water skiing, parasailing, snorkeling, deep sea fishing, gym, garden, children's play area, bar, restaurant.
Rates: $104-$122/$118-$129 S/D incl. tax ($148-$175/$171-$186 S/D in high season, 12/20-4/30). All major credit cards.
Directions: In the heart of Bocagrande, the major beach area, 2 km from downtown Cartagena and the colonial section.

If you've ever wanted to stay at a grand Mediterranean-style hotel like the Breakers in Palm Beach, but you could never afford it, here's your chance at less than half the price. Built in the 20's and recently remodeled, the Caribe, which is very well maintained, was the first major hotel in the then undeveloped Bocagrande section. The huge entranceway, with its 25-foot ceilings, massive square columns, pink walls, brass lighting fixtures and wicker furnishings, radiates the atmosphere of a grander bygone era. To one side you'll find the **Boler Bar**, a formal high-ceiling bar which is highlighted in front by a huge stained-glass ornament.

During the day, most of the action takes place in back around the long eight-lane pool, which is lined with almost 100 sunning chairs. The surrounding garden has huge coconut palms and various shrubs, plus a small pond, a playground, and several cages with monkeys and some gorgeous parrots. Nearby, you'll find most of the hotel's numerous amenities, including a fully-equipped gym, sauna, jacuzzi, steam room, nursery, clothing shops, beauty parlor, art gallery, travel agency, drug store, jewelry shop, as well as a sports center which offers scuba diving, water skiing, jet skis, and offshore fishing. There is also a cement tennis court nearby and a beach across the street with a private entrance.

Guests have four choices for dining: an open-pit barbecue, a thatched-roof, make-your-own pizzeria, a snack-bar at the beach which serves typical Cartagena food, and the hotel's formal restaurant, the **Don Pedro de Heredia**. Don Pedro's offers over 15 starters, such as spinach cannelloni or crab claws in garlic and gaspacho, and about 30 main dishes, such as baked red snapper, seafood casserole, lobster thermidor, chateaubriand and duck à l'orange. The grilled dishes are best; others are often disappointing.

For really great seafood in Cartagena, try the **Restaurant Capilla del Mar**. It is just four blocks away at Carrera 5 No. 8095 and faces the port. Don't confuse this with the nearby hotel of the same name. Another of the city's most highly regarded restaurants is the **Bodegón de la Candelaria** (phone 647-251), which is in an aged colonial house on Calle de la Damas in the old city. The atmosphere here is unparalleled in Cartagena. Another good choice in the old section of town would be the **Taberna la Quemada** (phone 645-612) on Calle de la Amargura. It's a cozy restored tavern with a maritime atmosphere; the specialty is *pargo a la Quemada* (red snapper). To get to any of these, take one of the horse-drawn carriages stationed just outside the hotel.

Guest rooms in the Caribe's older section are the most atmospheric and many of them overlook the ocean. They have lime green walls, tile floors, satellite TVs, minibars, breakfast tables, cane furnishings, and fine tile bathrooms with wide marble basins, long mirrors, and showers. The newer units in back are similar, but more comfortable and feature modern furnishings, including sofas, large closets, and sliding glass doors opening to private balconies which face the ocean or the lagoon. In sum, if you like grand old hotels, chances are you'll really enjoy this majestic beauty, the granddaddy of them all in Colombia.

Alternative: CARTAGENA HILTON

El Laguito, phone (56) 650-666, fax (56) 650-661, telex 37645
Rates: $155-$190/$177-$240 S/D year round incl. tax. Major credit cards.
Directions: At the tip of Bocagrande peninsula, ½ km beyond the Caribe.

The modern 288-room Hilton, which is a striking Y-shaped building of 10 stories, is about 50% more expensive than the Caribe. It is also a bit isolated, a good 10-minute walk from downtown Bocagrande. Otherwise, it is a good choice, offering slightly better service than the Caribe and a wider array of sports facilities. These include three hard-surface tennis courts, a well-equipped gym, scuba diving, sailboards, small boats, water skiing, jet skis, and a game room with billiards and ping-pong. More important, it's one of only two hotels in Cartagena that have a private beach without a street between it and the hotel (Hotel Las Velas is the other.) There are several restaurants, including one resembling a colonial home, with a central patio and an overhanging balcony. The accommodations, many of which have fine views, are Caribbean-inspired. They have rattan furnishings, light blue and green accents, balconies with views, dressing rooms, and combination baths.

HOTEL LAS VELAS

Calle las Velas No. 1-60, phone (56) 650-000/9, 650-590, fax (56) 650-530, telex 37715
Category: A. 18-story modern highrise, 105 rooms, beachfront, pool, travel agency, laundry.
Rates: $43/$60/$71/$88 S/D/studio/apt incl. tax; $48/$67/$84/$105 high season (12/15-4/20, 6/15-8/31). Minimum 3 nights stay. All major credit cards.
Directions: 2 km from central Cartagena and a 5-minute walk from Bocagrande's commercial center, on the beach between the Caribe and the Hilton.

Constructed in the mid-70's as an apartment building, this 19-story highrise, which is on a quiet street behind the Caribe and near a major shopping mall, is the second of two hotels in Cartagena where you can walk out onto a beach without having to cross a street. All guest rooms have views of the ocean and most have balconies. Add to this that the place is very attractive and prices are much lower than those of the Hilton and Caribe and you have more than enough reasons to book a room here, especially if you're coming to catch a few rays on the shore.

The small bright lobby with formal black and white tile flooring and comfortable wicker furnishings gives an inviting relaxed impression. Further back you'll come to the **Brassiere**, an airy and spacious restaurant with cane furnishings and overhead fans. Just beyond is a garden and a pool which has a small coral island, a slide and is surrounded by sunning chairs. Overlooking this tropical area is a second, more formal restaurant, **La Gavia**, which is popular at night. Selections on the menu include, for starters, shrimp cocktail and sauted squid in garlic and, for a main course, Cartagena seafood casserole, pasta with seafood sauce, Spanish paella, and sweet and sour pork chops.

Beyond the pool you'll find a grass-hut bar area surrounded by palm trees and the beach just beyond, which is attended by hotel lifeguards. Here, parents can relax in the shade with a drink and watch their children building sand castles. The 105 guest rooms consist of 22 small standard units, 45 studios, and 38 apartments. Unless you intend to cook for yourself, the best buys are the studios. They have beds, sofas, matching bedspreads, curtains and sofa covers, satellite TVs, well-stocked mini-bars, large closets, linoleum floors, floor-to-ceiling windows on the ocean side, balconies, and modern tile bathrooms with marble-top basins, wide mirrors, and hot showers. The less expensive standard units are smaller and offer no sofas or balconies. The apartments are larger and have kitchenettes, but no stoves.

***Alternative:* HOTEL SAN PEDRO DE MAJAGUA**
Rosario Island, phone (56) 655-001/654-773, fax (56) 652-745
Rates: $72/$144 S/D incl. tax and all meals.
Directions: The boat trip from Cartagena takes about 2 hours. This can be arranged through the hotel or through a travel agent; price-wise, they're about the same.

For something unusual, consider staying a few days out on Rosario Island. The principal attractions are its beautiful white sand beaches and its coral reefs, which make it a snorkeling and scuba diving paradise. The best place to stay is the Majagua, an Old-World lodge with an appealing French ambience about it. Its restaurant is renowned for the best service and food (most of which is home-grown) of any lodge on the island. Somewhat isolated, it consists of a series of cabins set within extensive gardens, plus a private beach. The main building houses a library with a TV and a terrace bar; at night, the latter seconds as the dining room. Breakfast, on the other hand, is served under giant rubber trees on the lawn overlooking the ocean. Snorkeling, scuba diving, water skiing and sailboarding equipment can all be rented here. The accommodations consist of nine thatched-roof cabins with simple decor, coral walls, bamboo furnishings, hammocks, and terraces overlooking the gardens.

HOTEL CASA GRANDE
Carrera 1a No. 9-128
Phone (56) 653-943/655-309
Category: B
Beachfront cottage, front terrace, 36 rooms, restaurant, English spoken.
Rates: $28/$38 S/D incl. 5% tax; 40% higher with air-conditioning. All major credit cards.
Directions: In Bocagrande, 6 blocks from the center on the beach road & 1½ km from downtown Cartagena.

If a homey beach-front B&B sounds like your cup of tea, head for the Casa Grande, a little-known establishment run by an exceedingly friendly and chatty man, Sergio, formerly of Cali. His clients are about 60% Colombians and 40% foreigners, so there's a good mix here, and he'll make sure you meet other guests.

Some 65 years old, but a hotel only since 1987, this white two-story cottage in barn-red trim has, unlike most beach hotels here, a wonderfully tranquil ambience. It features a tile terrace and gardens in front – perfect for relaxing – and there is a beach just across the street. In the front area, guests can dine outside in the garden, or on the patio, which has a ceiling fan and a bar. There are also armchairs in this area for simply taking a break or reading.

The guest rooms are all in back and vary considerably in configuration. Modest in size and attractively decorated like the rest of the hotel, they have comfortable beds, private baths with hot-water showers, fans, and air conditioning if you're willing to pay substantially more. Unlike most hotels in Cartagena, prices remain the same year round.

***First Alternative:* HOTEL FLAMINGO**

Avenida San Martín 5-85, phone (56) 650-301/656-945

Rates: $24/$31 S/D incl. tax; $28/$40 high season (12/15-4/17, 6/15-8/31). No credit cards.

Directions: In the heart of Bocagrande on the main drag, one block east of Hotel Caribe.

Those who like being in the thick of the action may prefer the well-run three-story Flamingo hotel, located a block from the ocean and in the heart of Bocagrande on the main drag. In front, next to Dunkin Donuts, there's a well-shaded sidewalk café which is great for viewing all the action and is consequently packed with people. There's a restaurant downstairs and a tranquil cement-floor patio in back with various cabañas and shady palm trees – a good area for reading. The beach is just beyond and across the street. Accommodations here are standard size and quite good, with TVs, tile floors and throw rugs, telephones, air conditioning, large closets, and tile bathrooms with cold-water showers.

***Second Alternative:* HOTEL PLAYA**

Avenida San Martín 4-87, phone (56) 650-552

Rates: $18-$24/$26-$31 S/D incl. tax (cheaper units have fans), $24-$26/$29-$33 S/D during high season. Credit cards are not accepted.

Directions: On the same block as the Flamingo.

If the Flamingo is full, try the Playa, several doors down and almost as good, though not as well managed. It has similar quality rooms, with air conditioning and private baths, a pool which is usually too crowded to use, an open-air bar, and a decent restaurant with good breakfasts for about $1. Guests also have the option of saving money by taking a room with a fan and skipping on the air conditioning.

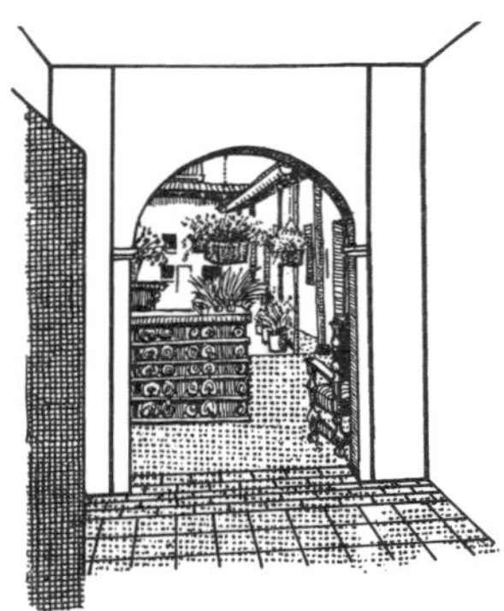

HOSTAL SANTO DOMINGO

Calle Santo Domingo 33-46
Phone (56) 642-268
Category: C
2-story colonial house in town, 12 rooms.
Rates: $12/$21 S/D high season incl. tax (less from 4/1 to 6/14, and 9/1 to 12/14). No credit cards.
Directions: In downtown Cartagena in the old walled section, 1½ blocks from Plaza Bolívar.

If you prefer being downtown in the old city rather than near the beach, the small and tranquil Santo Domingo is an excellent choice. It's hardly luxurious, but the feeling here is one of complete authenticity. Located in the center, this well-run establishment, which in colonial times was a residence, is a bargain. In the off-season prices fall substantially, making it an even better buy. The public areas are quite nice and consist of a narrow tile-floor entranceway leading to a small inviting sitting area with reasonably comfortable chairs and a TV. Further back is a small courtyard, with lots of plants, some chairs for relaxing, and two covered tables. The Santo Domingo has no restaurant, but it does serve cold drinks and coffee.

The accommodations, which have nine-foot ceilings and are all configured differently, are clean but more basic than the public areas would suggest. They have ceiling fans, old cracked tiles on the floor, beds which are a bit narrow but at least don't sag, small windows, closets, exposed light bulbs, and clean private baths with cold-water showers.

Alternative: **HOSTAL BELLAVISTA**
Avenida Santander, phone (56) 654-210
Rates: $8/$10 S/D incl. tax. Credit cards are not accepted.
Directions: On the northern beach road, Avenida Santander, in the direction of the airport, 2 km from downtown Cartagena.

If you'd prefer to be closer to the water and don't mind staying at a place that's somewhat isolated, try the Bellavista. Its a small B&B at Marbella Beach, just two km from downtown Cartagena. Enrique Sedo, the friendly English-speaking owner, helps to give this popular and highly-recommended *hostal* a pleasant, homey atmosphere. The Bellavista features a nice patio, easy access to the beach, and clean, secure rooms with fans and private baths.

PACO'S RESTAURANT

Regardless of what budget you're traveling on, don't miss having at least a drink at Paco's, which is a wonderful bar-restaurant facing Plaza Santo Domingo in the heart of the walled city. It's in a marvelously restored old building and is one of the best upmarket bars in South America. At night, when the ground-level bar is in full swing, Paco's, which often has live musical entertainment, exudes vitality and the romance of another era. If you eat here as well, try their *sifu* (breaded seafood) – a house original. Or ask Nick, the friendly Englishman who runs this place, for other suggestions.

Barranquilla

HOTEL EL PRADO
Carrera 54, No. 70-10
Phone (58) 456-533/340-020
Fax (58) 450-019/451-500
Telex 33448
Bogotá phone (1) 218-1798
Category: Deluxe
Grande dame, Mediterranean style, 268 rooms, pool, tennis, healthclub, sauna, Hertz, business center, shops, beauty parlor, racketball, disco, English spoken.
Rates: $120/$160 S/D incl. tax. All major credit cards.
Directions: 3 km/2 miles from downtown in the city's most posh, residential-commercial area, on a major street with easy access to taxis.

The port city of Barranquilla rates as one of the finest towns in Columbia. Hotel Prado, built in the booming 20's and reminiscent of many of the fine old hotels in Florida of the same era, has the best reputation in town. In 1988, this magnificent Spanish/Caribbean-style structure of three stories (classed as a national monument) was entirely renovated, furnishings and all. So, while the principal facilities are over 60 years old, they remain in top condition.

Casual elegance is the theme throughout. The doorway is outlined in elaborate molding and inlaid columns, and the ground floor French windows are capped with huge blue awnings and separated by wrought iron lighting fixtures and coats of arms. These interesting features give distinction to the otherwise plain beige facade. Inside is breezy and formal – a long corridor, high ceilings, black and white tile floors, two huge wrought iron chandeliers, large French doors, and cane chairs and sofas covered in striped fabric that blends with the wall color. A dozen or so tall palms add a splash of green. The rear gardens are large and tropical – palms extending to the red tile roof, a long pool lined with cushioned lounge chairs, and two clay tennis courts in good condition.

What you'll probably notice first about the older rooms in the main building are the 15-foot ceilings with exposed beams. Rooms are medium size with mini-refrigerators, air conditioning, thick carpeting, satellite TVs, old fashioned closets, and modern tile bathrooms with large mirrors and showers. Only the suites have bathtubs. The service here is good; some of the older staff members have worked here for over 30 years. The hotel's newer accommodations closer to the pool have more modern furnishings and are designed for families.

Of the hotel's four restaurants, the most popular is the moderately priced **La Cabana** next to the pool. You could begin with one of the four starters, such as ever popular *ceviche de camarones* (baby shrimp with onions in lemon sauce), or one of the four soups, such as the cream of asparagus or palm hearts soup. Main dishes include a *cazuela de mariscos* (regional seafood casserole), *sierra marinera* (kingfish glazed with white wine, tomato sauce and seafood), and *chuleta de cerdo currambera* (pork chops currambera style with creole potatoes and corn patties).

On the other side of the pool is a snackbar and pizzeria which reputedly has the best pizza in town. For a more elegant setting there's the **Príncipe Eduardo**, which serves a buffet at noon (except on Wednesdays and Sundays). On those days locals gather for a buffet around the pool, the Sunday one being a *churasqueria* (a wide selection of grilled meats with potatoes). It is regarded as one of the "in" places to go on the Sabbath. On weekend evenings you can salsa away to live music at the hotel's animated nightclub.

HOTEL DANN BARRANQUILLA
Carrera 51B No. 79-246
Phone (58) 450-099
Fax (58) 455-079
Category: A
26-story highrise, 200 rooms, pool, sauna, car rental, hairdresser, parking.
Rates: $70/$91 S/D incl. tax. All major credit cards.
Directions: 2 km further out from the Prado in the city's top residential quarter.

Part of a major nationwide chain, this 26-floor tower is the city's newest major hotel and far better than most of the chain's other establishments. The lobby's marble floors, pale green walls with white trim, thick carpets, subdued lights, attractive wicker furniture with flowered cushions, and judicious use of greenery combine to give it an august air.

If you take an elevator to the top floor, you'll get the best views in Barranquilla of the city and the Magdalena River from the **Bar Mirador** and the adjoining restaurant. The cozy bar, which has plush maroon carpets, cane armchairs with dressy pink and gray striped cushions, numerous plants, and salsa music playing softly in the background, is a good place for a drink as well as just hanging out. The decor of the hotel's main restaurant, which serves fine international fare, is similar. During the day many guests can be found lounging around the pool area below. It has sunning chairs all around, an open-air restaurant, a small thatched-roof bar to one side, and a fountain with water flowing over pebbles that produces a soothing dripping sound.

The accommodations are spacious and reasonably nice with two queen-size beds, fine carpets, bureaus and mirrors in natural wood, flowered curtains and bedspreads, satellite TVs, minibars, air conditioning, and tile baths with showers. Room service is available 24 hours a day and the staff is very professional.

***First Alternative:* HOTEL PUERTA DEL SOL**

Calle 75 No. 41D-79, phone (58) 456-144, fax (58) 455-550, telex 35596
Rates: $75/$100 S/D incl. tax. All major credit cards are accepted.
Directions: 15 blocks from the Dann towards the center.

This modern seven-story hotel, formerly the Cadebia, has taken on a new name since its refurbishment. It's now more popular than ever with the locals and may be preferred to the Dann by some foreign travelers as well. During the day, the center of attention is the V-shaped pool in back which, unfortunately, becomes almost unbearably crowded on weekends. Other amenities include a sauna, car rental, casino, disco, and a beauty parlor. All 110 rooms have double queen-size beds, satellite TVs, minibars, fine carpets, comfortable reading chairs, large closets, and tile bathrooms with marble counters and combination baths.

***Second Alternative:* APARTA-HOTEL EL GOLF**

Carrera 59-B No. 81-158, phone (58) 342-191/342-290, telex 33589
Rates: $23/$33 S/D incl. tax. All major credit cards are accepted.
Directions: A mile beyond Hotel Prado and 3 miles from downtown in a quiet residential area.

The relatively low price of the Golf makes it hard to beat in terms of value for money. The hotel is set in a quiet residential area, Barrio El Golf, not far from the Prado. All 40 rooms here are large, but definitely don't warrant being called suites. Regardless, they are excellent for the price and feature wall-to-wall carpets, air conditioning, well-stocked minibars, reading chairs, desks, double queen-size beds, small color TVs, walk-in closets, and tile bathrooms with modern fixtures and hot-water showers. The hotel's amenities include a restaurant, sauna, beauty parlor, and a pool long enough for swimming laps. If you like places with an active atmosphere, you may not like this modern three-story hotel because it's exceedingly tranquil, with very little going on. The somewhat remote location and poor access to taxis is an even greater drawback and is the main reason why business is slow and prices are low.

HOTEL MAJESTIC
Carrera 53, No 54-41
Phone (58) 320-150/2/4
Fax (58) 413-733
Category: B
Old palatial house with new wing, 46 rooms, pool, English spoken.
Rates: $25/$34 S/D incl. tax. AmEx & Visa.
Directions: 2 km from the center and 15 blocks before Hotel Prado, in a mixed residential-commercial area. Taxis can be found nearby.

For a charming place to stay that costs far less than the city's other major hotels, you can't beat the Majestic. It's a picturesque hotel not far from the Caribe and popular with North Americans. Dating from the 20's and traditional in style, it has a long white porch in front that is lined with Greek columns and fancy railings. On the other side of its white stone wall is a busy street, but once inside this beautiful building you'd never know it. Tranquillity also pervades in back where you'll find a clean pool surrounded by sunning chairs, various coconut palms and other greenery.

The most interesting area of the hotel is the old section, which was formerly a private mansion. The lobby, with its ceiling fans, carpeted floors and various seating arrangements, is comfortable but nothing special. To one side, however, you'll find an elegant column-encircled ballroom, which is a popular place for wedding receptions. On the same side is a long formal dining room with 10 tables. It features 18-foot ceilings, elaborate molding, two glass chandeliers, papered walls, marble-looking Doric columns, tall French doors, fancy tile flooring, Louis XIV-style chairs, air conditioning, and nattily dressed waiters. The bilingual menu includes, for starters, Peruvian ceviche, Mexican-style oyster cocktail, and oxtail soup. The specialties of the house are Cuban-style rice, beef stroganoff, seafood casserole, and grilled jumbo shrimps. A typical meal costs about $8, more with wine. Chilean wines predominate, but for something different ask for a bottle of Cragales – a good but rarely offered table wine from the Cali area.

The accommodations in the newer section are standard size and quite acceptable. They offer two single beds, thick bed covers, small TVs, wall-to-wall carpeting, breakfast tables, leather chairs, large closets, and spotlessly clean bathrooms with long mirrors and tile showers. You may find the hot water supply erratic and the air conditioning a bit weak, but in most other respects this establishment is flawless and, overall, it's highly recommended.

First Alternative: **HOTEL ARENOSA**
Carrera 48 No. 70-136, phone (58) 359-356/450-071
Rates: $19/$24 S/D incl. tax ($23/$28 S/D with air conditioning).
Directions: 10 blocks from Hotel Prado.

This reasonably attractive four-story hotel with a Moorish facade has the great advantage of being in the same vicinity as Hotel Majestic and Hotel El Prado, which is a relatively safe residential/commercial district. All 50 rooms have comfortable beds, TVs, telephones, decent private baths, and fans or air conditioning. There is also a sauna on the premises.

Second Alternative: **HOTEL VICTORIA**
Calle 35 No. 43-140, phone (58) 410-055/410-439
Rates: $8/$10 S/D incl. tax ($11/$14 S/D with air conditioning). No credit cards.
Directions: In the center, 2 blocks from La Costena bus station.

For a less expensive category C hotel your best bet is the large five-story Victoria in the heart of town and in excellent condition for its old age. It features a decent restaurant, elevator, spacious halls, and 55 large rooms with high-ceilings, freshly painted walls, ceiling fans, telephones, dressing mirrors, closets, and clean private baths with all necessities. It's well managed with a friendly staff that has even been known to lend guests money until the morning in cases where they arrive without cash!

Santa Marta

El Rodadero

HOTEL IROTAMA
Km 14, Vía a Barranquilla
Phone (54) 218-021
Fax (54) 218-077
Telex 42475
Bogotá phone (1) 217-4311
Category: Deluxe.
Vacation beach resort, 155 bungalows, pool,sailing, volleyball, horseback riding, tennis, ping-pong, sailboards, children's playground, English spoken.
Rates: $48-$82/$61-$112 S/D incl. tax low season (4/3-6/14, 9/1-12/14); 20% more during high season (minimum stay 1 week then). Children under 4 free, under 9 half-price. All major credit cards.
Directions: On the Caribbean shore, 82 km east of Barranquilla and 14 km west of Santa Marta and beyond El Rodadero.

With bungalows spread over a wide area (some just 75 meters from the water), special activities and tournaments planned every day, and a location well out of town in the shade of waving coconut palms, the Irotama has the ambience of a club as much as a hotel. For family vacations on the beach, it's perfect. Ditto if you're looking for a Club Med environment.

Among the 155 cabins, you have three types to choose from. In all of them the accent is on practicality, not elegance. The more expensive *Bohio* cabins with stone walls and crowned with huge thatched roofs, resemble African huts. From your front patio surrounded by flowers you can breathe the fresh air and admire the ocean. Inside you'll find two air-conditioned rooms, one with a leather sofa bed and two chairs, and a second with two beds, TV, mini-refrigerator, ceiling fans, ample closet space, tile floors and white walls. Bathrooms are big and have two sinks and a shower. With the less expensive cabins you'll get pretty much the same amenities, but they are not as picturesque; some do not have porches and the furnishings are slightly simpler.

The choice of recreation activities is like that offered at a Club Med – tennis (two lighted cement courts), sailing (three Laser-type boats and one catamaran), sailboards, horseback riding, exercise classes, and ping-pong. Alternatively, you can join in one of the daily soccer or volleyball tournaments on the beach. Those with children can leave them with a babysitter or take them to the play area. For meals, there are four restaurants to choose from. Most people opt for the buffet, which has a different theme every night (Chinese, seafood, Columbian, etc.); there's also an à la carte menu. Around 9 p.m. every evening there's a special activity – native dancing groups, bonfires on the beach, dancing contests and the like. If you're looking for a disco, you'll have to take the hotel bus into nearby El Rodadero.

***Alternative:* HOTEL GRAN GALEON**
Km 17, Vía a Barranquilla, phone (56) 240-991, Bogotá fax (91) 288-5110

Situated three km west of the Irotama, the 178-room similarly-priced Galeón is a large new complex with a replica of an old sailing ship to admire. It has several pools, numerous water activities, car rental, and shops – a good place for those with kids perhaps.

HOTEL LA SIERRA
Carrera 1 No. 9-47, El Rodadero
Phone (56) 227-197/227-960
Fax (56) 228-198
Telex 38873
Bogotá phone (1) 217-6200
Bogotá fax (1) 217-3478
Category: A
Modern, beachfront, 74 rooms.
Rates: $45/$58 S/D incl. tax. Major credit cards.
Directions: On beach road in downtown El Rodadero, 10 km west of Santa Marta.

El Rodadero, a small town 10 km west of Santa Marta, is one of Columbia's major Caribbean beach resorts. So you'll definitely want to be lodged in a room overlooking the ocean, preferably with a balcony. The modern 10-story La Sierra, built in the early 70's, provides both, along with a sidewalk café and the ocean just beyond. What's more, rooms are offered at very affordable prices.

What's particularly nice about La Sierra is its location. You can have a drink on a shaded terrace or on your own private balcony, then take a swim in the water. While the modern white exterior is hardly exceptional, the lobby is newly remodeled and attractive.

The rooms, varying in size from small to medium, are bright and spotless, with off-white walls and tile floors, but no rugs. Each comes with a well-stocked mini-refrigerator, a radio alarm clock, TV, air conditioning, a fairly sizable closet and a tiny balcony with one plastic chair. In the tile bathrooms with hot-water showers you'll find a small package with aspirin, Alka-Seltzer, a shoe rag and an antacid pill – a nice but all too rare touch that suggests the management is keener on service than most.

At the **Terraza del Mar** restaurant you have your choice of dining inside with breezy overhead fans or outside on the terrace under the trees with antique-looking lamp posts. The beers seem at the point of freezing – a tip off that the restaurant serves better food than its modest appearance might suggest. You have a choice of nine starters, including a tasty *sopa del chef*, shrimp ceviche (a favorite raw seafood dish along the western coast of South America), and lobster cocktail. For the main course you might try their chateaubriand – thick and juicy with a butter sauce and spices and usually cooked exactly as ordered. Some of the other 17 selections on the English and Spanish menu include *pargo* (red snapper), grilled or in a seafood sauce, a seafood casserole, *róbalo* (haddock) Hong Kong style, plus a selection of chicken and pasta dishes. A typical three-course meal with beer will run you no more than $8. A bottle of their Chilean wine, however, will put the tab up a full $17 more!

The real surprise of the evening was when our table was serenaded by a group of three guitarists – a nightly occurrence. For that, the hotel deserves another star in our opinion!

Alternative: HOTEL TAMACA INN

Carrera 2a No. A 11-98, phone (56) 227-015/227-028, fax (56) 227-202, telex 38879
Rates: $54/$70 S/D incl. tax (about 25% lower in off-season). Major credit cards.
Directions: On the beach, 2 blocks west of Hotel La Sierra.

A very strong competitor of the Sierra hotel is the long-standing Tamacá Inn. It's an aging seven-story structure that still attracts much repeat business, particularly families, because of its pool, its fine service, and a good nearby beach. There are actually two pools – a baby pool and an adult pool with a stream-like fountain flowing into it. Numerous plants and palm trees surround the water, providing relief from the hot sun and a relaxing ambience to boot. And the beach is just a stone's throw away. Other amenities include a casino, an air-conditioned bar for cooling off, and a tropical open-air café with bamboo furniture overlooking the ocean. The accommodations are large, air conditioned, and reasonably attractive. All of them have private baths with hot-water showers. Many of the 82 rooms have ocean views and units on the first two floors feature balconies.

HOTEL PARADOR DE MESTRE
Calle 10 No. 1-13
Phone (56) 228137/8
Category: B
Modern, beachfront, 3 stories, 30 rooms, restaurant, parking.
Rates: $16/$24 S/D incl. tax. All major credit cards.
Directions: Next to La Sierra.

A great place around the corner from La Sierra is the Parador de Mestre, which is well maintained and shares the Sierra's great advantage of being just off the beach. It's a relatively small three-story hotel with a rough white cement exterior. There is a tiny tile-floor terrace at the entrance with several rocking chairs. Upon entering, you'll find a pleasant lobby with modern paintings on the walls, tile floors, cane sofas in light summery colors, a large-screen TV, and plants here and there. Adjoining the lobby is a small restaurant from which you can view the sea.

There are about 30 units, which are all excellent value for the price. They are almost standard size and have comfortable beds, nice tile floors, telephones, rough plastered walls, ample closet space, and attractive new bathrooms with modern fixtures. Many of the rooms have balconies and the more expensive units have air conditioning instead of fans.

First Alternative: **HOTEL EL RODADERO**
Calle 11 No. 1-29, phone (56) 227262
Rates: $19-$20/$27-$29 S/D incl. tax (25% lower in off-season). Major credit cards.
Directions: 2 blocks west of the Parador de Mestre and very near the Tamacá Inn.

If the Parador de Mestre is full, try the Rodadero, which is just two blocks away and very near the beach. It's a long-standing one-story structure that is slowly deteriorating, but has one very nice feature, namely a long pool surrounded by shade trees. Another plus is the manager, Marina Salcedo, who is very helpful and speaks English. The rooms are fairly good, with air conditioning and private baths.

Second Alternative: **HOTEL LA RIVIERA**
Carrera 2a No. 5-42, phone (56) 227666
Rates: $21/$28 S/D incl. tax (25% lower in the off-season). All major credit cards.
Directions: 4 blocks east of the Parador de Mestre and one block inland.

If you'd like to be in the heart of town, try the Riviera. It's a large 81-room hotel with a presentable lobby, a reasonably comfortable TV/sitting room, a decent restaurant, and clean air-conditioned rooms with private baths. It's also conveniently located in the center, only a block from the beach and near lots of good places to eat.

Third Alternative: **HOTEL VALLADOLID**
Carrera 2a No. 5-67, phone (56) 227465
Rates: $14-$16/$19-$21 S/D incl. tax (about 12% lower off-season). Credit cards.
Directions: In the heart of town, 50 meters from the Riviera Hotel.

This category C hotel has a very helpful staff and is in the heart of town, only a block from the water. It has a modern exterior and reasonably attractive public areas including a very presentable lobby and a small restaurant. While the rooms don't measure up to the public areas, they are standard size, clean, and have ceiling fans, tile floors, closets, and private tile baths with cold-water showers.

San Andrés Island

HOTEL AQUARIUM
Avenida Colombia No. 1-19
Phone (811) 23120/26932
Bogotá phone (1) 282-9745
Fax (811) 26174
Telex 40126
Category: Deluxe
Waterfront, 112 suites, scuba, water skiing, sailboarding school, jet skis, kayaks, sailboats, sun deck, shops.
Rates: $97 per suite incl. 15% tax, larger suites up to $168. All major credit cards.
Directions: On the edge of town at the far northeastern end of the beach road (Ave. Colombia), a 10-minute walk to the center.

In operation since the late 1970's, the Aquarium is not just one of the island's top two hotels; it's also a very unusual and striking place. Consisting of 14 round three-story structures, some built right over the water and all connected by a deck-like walkway, it is certainly eye-catching. Naturally the environment is a very breezy one, and from virtually every room you'll feel as if you're right on the water. The main attraction here is scuba diving and sailboarding – it's a paradise for enthusiasts of these sports as the water is crystal clear. Guests can rent all the equipment necessary for these two sports as well as jet skies, water skis, surf kayaks, small sailboats and Hobie Cats. There's a dive shop (the Aquamarina) with certified scuba instructors, and numerous other shops, including a sailboarding school, a motorbike rental shop, and a gift shop.

If all you care about is lying on the sun-drenched shores, the Aquarium may not be the best choice because you must walk five minutes or so to the nearest beach. Most guests looking for sun simply walk out on the main pier and plop down in one of the many sunning chairs there. For a cool drink they need only signal to the waiter from the nearby **Marine Bar**, which has a large number of sailboards stacked alongside, reflecting the sport's great popularity here.

For lunch and dinner you have three choices. The most informal and popular is the **Caballito de Mar** sidewalk café, which serves a dynamite lunch buffet. There's also the more formal **La Barracuda**, which is set inside an angular two-story building facing the sea. It offers good food and fantastic views of the ocean. The fanciest of the three is **La Bruja**, an exotic thatched-roof place over the water designed to resemble a witch's hat. A small cozy place with low lights and predominantly wood and glass decor, it's probably the best restaurant on the island and certainly the most seductive.

The rooms are very breezy and hence need no air conditioning. All are two- or three-room apartments consisting of one or two large bedrooms (each with a bath) and a combined dining room, kitchenette and living area. Each unit has a color TV, refrigerator, overhead fans, bare tile floors, wicker furnishings, modern paintings on the walls and, most important, a balcony with comfortable padded chairs.

***Alternative:* BAHIA MARINA**

Carretera San Luis Km 5, phone (811) 23539/23657, telex 40156
Rates: About $95 per room incl. tax. All major credit cards.
Directions: A 10-minute taxi drive from the airport out on Carretera San Luis.

If you'd prefer a resort with a private beach and you don't mind being out of town, book a room at the Bahía Marina, which is only a 15-minute drive from the center. It was completely renovated in 1993 and upgraded into a luxury resort, but it still has the ambience of a small private club; most important, it's the only hotel with a private beach. It has an ocean-side restaurant and extensive sporting facilities, including an Olympic-size pool and a tennis court. For watersports enthusiasts it offers boats and all necessary gear for scuba diving, sailboarding and deep-sea fishing. The guest rooms, which feature satellite TVs, air conditioning and kitchenettes, are individual cabañas surrounding the pool and are entered through private gardens. To enjoy this delightful place, you'll have to come during the winter season, which is the only time it's open.

HOTEL CASABLANCA

Avenida Colombia No. 3-59
Phone (811) 25950/24115
Fax (811) 26127
Telex 40120
Category: A
Modern, beachfront, central, 55 rooms, pool, satellite TVs.
Rates: $56/$79 S/D incl. 5% tax. All major credit cards.
Directions: Downtown on the beach road near intersection of Colombia and Costa Rica.

Those looking for a well-run hotel in the middle of the action and near a good beach should consider the Casablanca. It features a swimming pool, air-conditioned rooms with terraces and some ocean views, satellite TVs, and a good restaurant. It's right in the thick of things, directly across the street from a clean popular beach and a three-minute walk from the very heart of this free port, which is a shopper's paradise.

When you register for a room in their cool lobby, you'll sense very quickly that this place is well managed. The cane sofas and armchairs here have plush cushions in soft purple colors, and the wonderful beach-scene paintings and flowers on the tables add a nice decorative touch. Outside, the pool, which has lots of sunning chairs and is surrounded by grass, palm trees, flowers and other greenery, is the center of attention. It's a relaxing balmy area, and most of the rooms look out onto it. If you take a first-floor unit in this pointed two-story structure, your room is likely to have a shaded terrace facing the pool. Most rooms on the second floor afford a good view of the sea.

The hotel's restaurant, which serves very good continental dishes, has one side facing the pool and another facing the street and ocean; the latter section, rather like a glassed-in sidewalk café, is one of the best places in town for people-watching. The accommodations are spacious and well appointed with natural wood furnishings, tile floors (no rugs), satellite TVs with video players, wide beds, air conditioning, minibars, comfortable armchairs, ample closet space, and modern bathrooms with showers.

Alternative: HOTEL EL ISLENO

Avenida de la Playa No. 5-117, phone (811) 23990/1/2, fax (811) 23126, telex 40128
Rates: $44/$59 S/D incl. 5% tax ($107/$200 S/D incl. tax and full board). Major credit cards are accepted.
Directions: On the edge of town near the airport, at the opposite end of the beach road from Hotel Aquarium and a 10-minute walk to the center.

Those looking for less crowded beaches and/or rooms with a guaranteed view of the sea are likely to prefer the Isleño, which is away from the center. This well-managed beach-front hotel has three floors containing 52 units. It's attractively set in a palm grove across the street from the beach; all the rooms have balconies facing the ocean. A traditional favorite of US tour groups, it's understandably quite popular and often fully booked. The Isleño is a good choice for sports-minded travelers, as both sailboards and sailboats can be rented here and there are four tennis courts to boot. The hotel also features an attractive restaurant with good food and a cozy bar on an open veranda with captain's chairs. The rooms are air conditioned and have standard appointments, TVs, telephones, minibars, and baths with hot-water showers.

HOTEL BAHIA SARDINA

Avenida Colombia No. 4-24, phone (811) 23793/23587, fax (811) 24363
Category: A-B. Modern, beach, 43 rooms, pool, restaurant.
Rates: \$25/\$34 S/D incl. 5% tax, \$53/room with balcony (slightly less in the low season). All major credit cards.
Directions: On the beach road near downtown, between hotels Casablanca and El Isleño.

For a beach-front hotel at half the price of either the Casablanca or the Isleño, a good choice would be the Bahía Sardina, which is between the two. Open since 1985, this new-looking four-story establishment features a stylish lobby, a small pool, and air conditioned rooms, half of which face the ocean. Try to get a unit facing the sea, as the views enhance them considerably. They have color TVs, spotless tile floors, cane furnishings, breakfast tables, thick bedspreads, telephones, and bathrooms with new fixtures including hot-water showers. The more expensive "salons" have balconies facing the ocean.

One sign of the hotel's good management and service is the lobby, which is breezy, well maintained, and nicely decorated with comfortable cane sofas and armchairs, textured wallpaper, wood-panelled ceilings, and various plants at one end. Flanking this area is a neat but fairly sterile-looking bar/restaurant. It's okay for breakfast, but for lunch and dinner you should consider walking towards the center and looking for an interesting eatery, such as the reasonably-priced **Sea Food House** facing Parque Bolívar. Bahía Sardina offers a pool, but it's so tiny that only small children would enjoy it.

HOTEL MOLINO DE VIENTO
Ave. Colombia No. 3-111
Phone (811) 26442
Telex 40118
Category: B
Central, beachfront, 6 rooms.
Rates: $45 incl. tax, $24/$33 S/D low season (2/16-6/14, 9/1-12/14). All major credit cards.
Directions: Next door to Hotel Casablanca.

For a cozy place in the center facing a beach, try the Molino de Viento. There are only six rooms, all quite attractive, with nice gray carpets, minibars, air conditioning, twin beds (one of which is queen size), thick bedspreads, natural wood furnishings, and small tile baths with showers. Five of the six units have balconies facing the ocean. All the city's action passes just below – a major plus of this tiny establishment.

The public facilities include a small second-floor sitting area with cane furnishings, a TV, a tiny lobby, and a very cozy, almost cave-like restaurant. It looks plush and is air conditioned. There are nicely covered tables, shining glassware, and wooden walls. Most important, the manager, Franco Pierleoni, is very friendly and helps immensely in making this place special.

First Alternative: **HOTEL GALAXIA**
Avenida Colon, phone (811) 23013/26057, telex 40161
Rates: $18-$21/$23-$30 S/D incl. 5% tax; $9-$12/$18-$21 S/D low season (2/16-6/14, 9/1-12/14). Most major credit cards are accepted.
Directions: In the heart of town, one block behind the Molino de Viento.

The nearby 50-room Galaxia is far inferior, but not bad at all for the lower price. It's only a block from the beach used by Casablanca and Molino de Viento. The rooms are fairly small, but very neat. They have narrow but comfortable beds, new-looking tile floors, freshly painted walls, fans, telephones, closets, and private tile bathrooms with cold saltwater showers. The restaurant here isn't so bad either.

Second Alternative: **HOTEL HERNANDO HENRY**
Avenida de las Américas No. 4-84, phone (811) 26416/23416
Rates: $10/$19 S/D incl. 5% tax, lower in the off-season. No credit cards.
Directions: 3 blocks from the airport towards downtown, 2 blocks behind Hotel Bahía Sardina.

For a less expensive category C hotel, try the Hernando Henry, a modern-looking four-story hotel near the beach. Run by Ada and Hernando Henry, it is tops in its price range and has a presentable lobby, a good restaurant, and rooms with fans and balconies. It's also only two blocks from both the ocean and the heart of town. If it's full, which is often the case, first try the similarly-priced **HOTEL COLISEO** (phone 23330), which is two blocks away at Carrera 5 No. 1-59, 20 meters behind the well-known Hotel Cacique Toné. Another option is **HOTEL MEDITERRANEO** (phone 26722), which is nearby on Avenida Los Libertadores, between the Hernando Henry and the Cacique Toné.

Ecuador

In recent years the most popular tourist destination in the western half of South America has been Ecuador, which benefits from having a year-round mild climate, the lowest prices in South America, and one of the lowest crime rates on the continent. Ecuador also has a good number of the charming hotels that were formerly *haciendas* or colonial residences. Price-wise, most of them are incredible deals.

The country's star attraction is the Galapagos Islands. Rather than staying at hotels on the islands, most travelers go on one of the many charter boats that make week-long trips around the islands. They vary in size from eight berths to 90 berths, the smaller vessels generally being less luxurious but more personable, with fewer tourists to ruin the tranquil ambience and the viewing of truly incredible wildlife. It's also possible to stay at hotels and take day trips. The main advantage of this is that you get a better feeling for life on the islands; the big disadvantage is that you see far fewer animals.

Most travelers to Ecuador arrive by plane at Quito, which is 2,850 meters/9,350 feet above sea level and the second highest capital city in the world, exceeded only by La Paz, Bolivia. As you're descending towards the airport, the huge cone-shaped mountain you'll see in the distance is Cotopaxi, the country's second highest volcano. Ecuador has 10 major snow-peaked volcanoes, all quite accessible by road. Climbing them is one of the country's major attractions. Quito itself is usually described as charming and quiet – charming because of the numerous colonial buildings in the old "centro," (which is no longer the commercial heart of the city) and quiet because the streets seem to be rolled up at night.

Two great advantages of traveling around Ecuador are that there are good roads everywhere (except in the jungle) and the distances are relatively short. The hottest tourist spot outside Quito is Otavalo, which is a two-hour trip north via the Pan American Highway. Every Saturday morning until around 1 p.m., there's a huge market near the center of town where local Indians sell their crafts, most notably their weavings. On the way here you'll pass the equator, which is marked by three features: a globe, the country's third highest volcano (Cayambe), and Hostería Cusín, an old *hacienda* that is now one of the most delightful hotels in the country. A short distance further north you'll pass Cotacachi, the main center for leather goods, and Ibarra, where you can catch a funky, crowded train, which is really a bus on tracks, to the coast. This memorable all-day trip is only for the truly adventurous, however.

Traveling south from Quito you'll pass Cotopaxi and La Ciénega, which is one of the country's oldest *haciendas* and now a hotel. Further south are Saquisili – famous for its traditional Thursday market – Latacunga, and Baños, which is the country's major hot springs resort and a popular year-round destination for both travelers and vacationing Ecuadorians. Nearby is Riobamba, where on a clear day you can see Chimborazo, the country's highest volcano. Not far from Riobamba you can hop a ride on an old coal-burning train to the coast. This is a trip no one should miss; just don't be surprised if a derailing adds a few hours to your journey!

Further south still you'll come to Cuenca which is full of old colonial buildings and is considered the country's most beautiful city. Most travelers to Cuenca take in a side-trip to Ingapirca, the site of the country's major Inca ruins. Much further south you'll come to Vilcabamba, which is located in a more temperate zone and is a popular trekking and horseback riding spot. Some years back this area became world famous for the large number of centenarians residing here.

Ecuador is not known for its beaches. The most popular coastal resort is Salinas, which tends to be overcrowded on weekends by natives of nearby Guayaquil. This latter city, which is a port and the country's largest metropolis, is not attractive except along the waterfront, but it is definitely vibrant. Travelers looking for uncrowded beaches would do well heading further north to tiny Montañita, which is the country's major surfing beach, and to Puerto Rico, where a unique ecological tourist hostel called

Alandaluz is located. Because of the proximity of the beaches near Esmeraldas, Quitenos tend to prefer them, especially Atacames, which is unfortunately known for its pickpockets, or Same, which is better. En route to this area you'll pass through Santo Domingo de los Colorados, a famous bird-watching center also noted for its natives, the colorfully painted but fast disappearing Colorado Indians.

Ecuador's other principal attraction is the Amazon jungle. The country's best jungle lodge is La Selva, located a few hours downriver from Coca, which in turn is accessible by plane from Quito. The rainforests here contain far more wildlife than those around Misahualli (mee-sah-wah-YEE), but the lodges downriver of this latter village cost about half as much and are more accessible (six hours by vehicle from Quito to Misahualli and by motorized canoe from there to the lodges). In short, Ecuador packs more into its small area than just about any country in the world, which is why it's such a hot destination point for travelers.

Quito

HOTEL ORO VERDE
Ave. 12 de Octubre 1820
Phone (2) 566-497
Fax (2) 569-189
Telex 21017
Category: Deluxe
Modern highrise, 241 rooms, pool, gym, sauna, steambath, squash, racketball, medical center, travel agency, business center, casino, shops.
Rates: $160/$198 S/D incl. tax. Major credit cards.
Directions: Near the center, some 12 blocks north of the US Embassy and about 17 blocks from Hotel Colón.

The city's leading hotel is the new Oro Verde, which has been a smash hit since it opened in 1990, despite its high prices. With only about half the accommodations of its principal competitor, Hotel Colón, this sleek, 14-story, two-tower complex has, unquestionably, the best restaurants of any hotel in the city. Also, the large array of facilities here ensure the hotel's status as a five-star establishment by Ecuadorian standards; they include a heated indoor-outdoor pool, a small gym with aerobics classes, squash and racketball courts, a sauna and Turkish bath, a business center, and a casino.

The hotel's lobby is the most elegant and spacious in Quito. It features shiny marble floors, two-story ceilings, chandeliers, walls lined with rough pink granite combined with textured linen fabric, comfortable sofas, and fine antique furnishings. Adjoining the lobby is **La Cafeteria Quito** which is attractively decorated with lots of brass trimming and is the most popular restaurant here. For lunch you may want to come early as the buffet, which is moderately priced, typically attracts an overflow crowd of hotel guests and locals, and getting a seat can be a problem. This bistro-like restaurant also serves the best breakfasts and the most tempting desserts in town. To the rear of the hotel is the elegant **Le Gourmet**, which, as the name suggests, is one of the finest and most expensive French restaurants in the city.

Even though the accommodations are luxurious and nicely decorated, they are slightly smaller than standard and may seem somewhat cramped, especially those with two queen-size beds. In other respects, however, the rooms are excellent and have everything you'd expect and more – cable TVs with many English-language stations, well-stocked minibars, international direct dial telephones, deep blue carpets, fine modern art by local artists, spacious closets, breakfast tables, and combination baths with hair dryers, personal toiletries, and second telephones. Most important, the service – despite the hotel's large size – is superb. That's because the staff, which prides itself on its Swiss management, is the most professionally trained in Quito. In short, for good service, great food, and a wide array of facilities, the Oro Verde is unbeatable.

HOTEL COLON INTERNATIONAL

Avenida Amazonas y Patria, phone (2) 560-666, fax (2) 563-903, telex 22542
Category: Deluxe. Modern, central, 420 rooms, pool, gym, sauna, steam bath, hot tub, car rental, hairdressers, disco, casino, shops, travel agency.
Rates: $106-$139/$125-$158. All major credit cards.
Directions: At the southern end of Amazonas, across from Parque El Ejido.

The huge 20-story Colón, which occupies an entire city block, is the major landmark in Quito's commercial district and represents the very heart thereof. Located on the city's principal commercial street, Amazonas, it is just a few blocks from, seemingly, everything. For example, the city's top handicraft shops, La Bodega and Galeria Latina, are just three blocks to the north. The location is unbeatable. Moreover, while the Oro Verde may outrank the Colón, the latter is less expensive and a better buy. For both reasons, the long-standing Colón continues to do a booming business and remains the most vibrant and active hotel in town.

With some 20 shops in the arcade you could easily spend an entire morning just shopping. A renowned local artist, Olga Fish, has a store here, plus there's a good bookstore with many publications in English. The hotel's pool is a bit small and disappointing, but the health club is first rate. There are also lots of places to hang out, the best being the quiet Reading Room, which features a selection of some 20 newspapers from around the world, along with plush leather sofas and chairs, English fox hunting prints on the walls, wood-panelled walls, and brass chandeliers. Others prefer the peaceful sitting area around the hotel's dramatic six-meter-high fountain or the more active glass-bubble-top bar adjoining the lobby and overlooking Amazonas, Quito's Fifth Avenue. The Colón offers numerous good restaurants to choose from, but none of them are outstanding. The hotel's moderately priced Sunday brunch at **La Rotisserie**, on the other hand, is famous and attracts large crowds, including many locals. The ever-popular 24-hour coffee shop is one of the very few places in town for a late-night snack.

The accommodations, most of which are standard size and in the hotel's massive L-shaped section, are lacking in local color except for native art on the walls, but all have views of the city as well as queen-size beds, cable TVs, fine carpets, spacious closets, and large tiled bathrooms with combination baths.

HOSTAL LOS ALPES
Calle Tamayo 233
Phone (2) 561-110/128
Category: A
Cozy inn, 24 rooms, restaurant, laundry.
Rates: $35/$53 S/D incl. tax. All major credit cards.
Directions: Downtown, 1 block behind the US Embassy.

Of all the hotels in South America that could be described as "cozy inns," none is finer than Los Alpes, one of most popular establishments in Quito. It's a comfortable three-story establishment with a large hedge and a small yard and porch in front and an alpine ambience inside. The occupancy rate hovers around 99% year round; consequently, getting a room without a reservation is purely a stroke of good luck.

Claudio Facchinei, the multilingual Italian owner/manager who has lived most of his life in South America, is the principal reason for the hotel's phenomenal success. Over the years patrons from around the world have shown their appreciation by sending Don Claudio ceramic plates from their homes, which he and his Ecuadorian wife have proudly mounted on the walls in the restaurant and other public areas. They are both avid golfers; if you go upstairs you can see the 60-odd trophies that they have won over the years. You'll also find a glassed-in greenhouse on this level that is warmed by the morning sun and has lots of plants and several swing chairs – perfect for reading during the day. Walking around downstairs you'll see assorted pots, interesting local paintings, a large green tapestry that was a gift of Olga Fish (a world-famous local artist of German descent), an antique upright piano, an old record player, local newspapers, and English-language paperbacks and magazines.

There are two main sitting rooms, both with white walls, beamed ceilings, comfortable tooled-leather furniture, and local crafts displayed here and there. In the evening the cozy one with a fireplace is most popular. There's always a crackling fire then, making it the perfect place for drinks and quiet conversation. Pisco sours, which are made from a Peruvian grape brandy, are the specialty here and they're outstanding, even by the highest Peruvian standards. Adjoining this area is the dining room, which serves very good reasonably-priced meals, including a few local specialties. Try their Ecuadorian soups; they're particularly good.

The accommodations are inviting and well maintained, with colorfully papered walls, carpets, exposed-beam ceilings, ample closet space, bureaus, black and white TVs, and spacious tile bathrooms with showers and a fairly reliable supply of hot water. The main complaints are that they're a bit small and have no work tables, and those on the third floor suffer from poor water pressure. As for the service, the English-speaking staff here is friendly and professional and attempts to cater to guests' individual needs. This is one reason why Los Alpes gets so much repeat business.

First Alternative: **HOSTAL VILLANTIGUA**
Calle Jorge Washington 237 y Tamayo, phone (2) 234-018, fax (2) 545-663
Rates: $45/$60 S/D incl. tax. Most major credit cards are accepted.
Directions: Around the corner from Los Alpes.

If Los Alpes is full or if you like places with a colonial ambience, try this new hostel nearby. It's a restored old house furnished with antiques.

Second Alternate: **CHALET SUISSE**
Calle Victoria y Calama, phone (2) 562-700, fax (2) 563-966, telex 22766
Rates: $53-$72/$66-$83 S/D incl. 20% tax. All major credit cards are accepted.
Directions: 6 blocks north of Hotel Colón along Ave. Amazonas and 1 block east.

If you prefer places with more amenities and don't mind paying a little extra, check the Chalet Suisse. It's an eight-story Swiss-owned operation that is well managed and has a rustic Swiss ambience. The lobby features knotty-pine walls, wrought iron lighting fixtures, beamed ceiling, deer heads on the walls, and old Swiss bells over the reception desk. The hotel's facilities include an excellent but expensive restaurant, a sauna, a whirlpool, a jazz bar, and a casino. If these are unimportant, then you're likely to find Chalet Suisse over-priced. Even if you don't stay here, the cozy restaurant, which is heated by a roaring fire in the center, is a good place to dine. Fondue (four kinds), raclette, wienerschnitzel, baked Alaska, and crepes suzettes are all specialties. The accommodations have wall heaters and are quite comfortable, with deep pile carpets, wood-panelled walls, bottled water, TVs, large closets, and carpeted combination baths with telephones, marble sinks, and bidets. There's same-day laundry service as well, and the check-out time is a very decent 3 p.m.

Third Alternative: **HOTEL AMBASSADOR**
Ave 9 de Octubre 1052 y Colon, phone (2) 561-777, 562-074, fax (2) 503-712
Rates: $23/$28 S/D incl. tax. All major credit cards are accepted.
Directions: Several blocks from Chalet Suisse, it's 7 blocks north of Hotel Colón along the main drag, Avenida Amazonas, and 1 block west.

A good and much less expensive alternative to the Chalet Suisse is the Ambassador, which was completely renovated in 1988. It's a two-story white structure with a restaurant, bar, travel agency, and 40 guest rooms. The public areas consist of a small presentable lobby, three sitting rooms, a small bar, and a restaurant. The cozy and inviting sitting areas, which are relaxing and good places to spend time, have stone fireplaces, rugs, and comfortable chairs. Only one of them has a TV. The restaurant is also quite attractive, with lots of plants, carpets, 10 or so tables, and reasonably-priced meals. The guest rooms are standard size and feature old-style furnishings, twin beds which are almost queen size, TVs, soft brown carpets, and standard size bathrooms with showers and long counters.

Fourth Alternative: **AMARANTA INTERNATIONAL HOTEL**
Calle Leónidas Plaza 194 y Jorge Washington, phone (2) 560-586
Rates: $36 per suite incl. 20% tax. All major credit cards are accepted.
Directions: 1 block behind (west of) Los Alpes and the US Embassy.

If all you care about is the room and you'll be staying more than a day or two, you should check this eight-story, all-suites aparthotel, just a block from Los Alpes and the US Embassy. All 20 suites have wall-to-wall carpeting, color TVs, comfortable sofas, combination dining-working tables, fully-equipped kitchenettes (with well-stocked refrigerators), comfortable bedrooms with queen-size beds, ample closet space, and modern tile bathrooms with combination baths. There's also a restaurant on the premises and laundry service and room service are both available.

RESIDENCIALCARRION
Calle Carrión 1250 y Versalles, phone (2) 234-620
Category: B. B&B, central, 22 rooms, restaurant, bar.
Rates: $8/$12 S/D incl. 20% tax. All major credit cards.
Directions: Near the center and Santa Clara market, next to an OCEPA (handicrafts) outlet.

If you like B&Bs, check the Carrión. It has a comfortable ambience and seems to attract more than its fair share of interesting independent travelers. Only five blocks from the heart of the modern commercial district, this two-story structure, which has a lawn, shrubbery and swings in front, looks more like a house than a hotel. Inside, it features a small lobby, a dining room, and three bright sitting rooms. These cozy sitting rooms are a good place to meet other travelers. Each is carpeted and has lots of comfortable armchairs and sofas; one also has a stone fireplace and a TV.

The accommodations are more than adequate, but are modest in size and sparsely furnished. They have double beds, telephones, tables, wooden chairs, and blue tile bathrooms with modern facilities including showers and long mirrors. Chances are you'll appreciate the young staff too, as their friendly exhuberance and helpful attitude more than compensate for what they lack in professional training. For a chance at one of the rooms you should plan to arrive early as they fill up fast.

EMBASSY HOTEL
Ave. Wilson 441 y 6 de Diciembre
Phone (2) 566-990
Fax (2) 563-192
Telex 21181
Category: B
Modern, central, 60 rooms, restaurant, travel agency.
Rates: $22/$24 S/D incl. 20% tax. All major credit cards.
Directions: From Hotel Colón it's 2 blocks east on Patria, then 7 blocks north on Ave. 6 de Diciembre and 1 block west on Wilson.

For the money, you can't go wrong at the long-standing and ever-popular Embassy Hotel, which is almost always full. In part because of the French management here, it is especially popular with the French and other Europeans.

The three-story motel-like structure is totally uninspired throughout and the staff is lax; nevertheless, the hotel attracts a very loyal clientele due to its location and surprisingly good restaurant. The lobby has unattractive and somewhat worn vinyl seating, wooden floors, postered walls, and moderately loud music. There is also a travel agency here.

The accommodations are similarly uninspired, but they are reasonably comfortable and offer queen-size beds, wooden floors covered with small green rugs, unadorned white walls, light-wood desks with mirrors, several wooden chairs, and small tile bathrooms with ordinary fixtures including showers but no counter space. Rental TVs are also available. For just a bit more money you can get a two-room suite with a fireplace and heating.

The worst feature of the Embassy is that there's no place to sit other than in the noisy, sterile lobby. The best feature is its restaurant, which is plain, but serves very good food, even by French standards, at exceedingly reasonable prices. Among the selections are coq au vin, French onion soup, duck à l'orange, chicken in curry sauce, chateaubriand, stuffed avocados, grilled jumbo shrimp, crepes suzettes, and omelettes flambés. The three-course menu of the day is much less exotic and costs only $3 with coffee and tax. And all of this is served with home-made French bread.

First Alternative: **RESIDENCIA CUMBRES**
Calle Baquedano 148 y Ave 6 de Diciembre, phone (2) 562-538/702, fax (2) 562-702
Rates: $18/$23 S/D incl. breakfast & tax. Credit cards are not accepted.
Directions: Behind (south of) Hotel Embassy, on the same block, but with a different street entrance.

If the Embassy is full (often the case), try the Cumbres, directly to the rear and an excellent unheralded alternative. Usually full by noon, it's a modern three-story building with 19 guest rooms, a cozy TV room, a spacious sitting room, antique furnishings, rugs, and a fireplace. Included in the price of a room is a huge full English breakfast.

The accommodations are a bit small, but they're spotless and bright with attractive wooden floors, throw rugs, single beds, good lighting, work desks, and modern tile bathrooms with showers and a reliable supply of hot water.

Second Alternative: **POSADA DEL MAPLE**
Calle Rodriguez 148 y 6 de Diciembre, phone (2) 544-507/237-375
Rates: $11/$17 S/D ($13/$19 with shared bath) incl. tax and full breakfast. MasterCard & Visa accepted.
Directions: From Ave. Patria, go 10 blocks north on 6 de Diciembre (3 blocks past the Emabassy Hotel turn-off), then ½ block west on Rodríguez.

If having access to cooking facilities is important, you may prefer this new hostel. It runs in the same price range if you take a room with shared bath. It has a warm atmosphere and a very friendly staff and attracts primarily international travelers.

***Third Alternative:* RESIDENCIAL MARSELLA**
Calle Los Rios 2035 y Castro, phone (2) 515-884
Rates: $4/$8 S/D incl. tax. Credit cards are not accepted.
Directions: 1 block east of, and up the hill from, Parque La Alameda, which is approximately the dividing line between the old section (the *centro*) and the new commercial section of Quito.

The Marsella is a good category C hotel that may well be the best option for those spending equal time in both the old and new sections of town. This family-run place, which is very popular with backpackers and fills up fast during the day, is a four-story building with one particularly nice feature – a terrace on top with fine views of Pinchincha and other surrounding mountains. You'll find several chairs and tables there for relaxing and taking in the views. The hostel has no restaurant, but the small guest rooms are clean and feature wooden floors and shared baths with relatively new fixtures. There is hot water in the morning until around noon. Units on the top floor are best because of the views. For double the price you can have a carpeted room with a private bath. This hostel also offers laundry service and free space for storing luggage.

***Fourth Alternative:* LA CASONA DE MARIO**
Calle Andalucia 213 y Galacia, phone (2) 230-129/544-036
Rates: $6/$12 S/D incl. tax. Credit cards are not accepted.
Directions: From the US Embassy, go 7 blocks north on Ave. 12 de Octubre, then 2 blocks east on Madrid and ½ block north on Andalucia.

For a category C hotel in the newer section of town where much of the commerce is now centered, try this great new place. Run by friendly Mario Tautasso, it's a comfortable two-story colonial house in a quiet neighborhood. La Casona offers eight guest rooms, a relaxing living room, a fully-stocked kitchen, laundry facilities, stored luggage space and a nice yard. The rooms are shared unless you reserve a double and the communal baths have hot-water showers.

Northern Highlands Region

Otavalo & Cotacachi

HACIENDA CUSIN
Lago de San Pablo
Phone (2) 105 (Operator Otavalo); 920-207 (IATEL) ask for hotel
Quito phone (2) 440-672
Category: A
Ex-*hacienda*, 24 rooms, horseback riding, squash, tennis, restaurant, bar, conference facilities.
Rates: $40 per room incl. tax; $30 per room for local residents (2 nights minimum). All major credit cards.
Directions: The hotel is about 8 km southeast of Otavalo near Lake San Pablo. Coming from Quito, about 10 km before Otavalo you'll see the lake. Continue several km and take the first paved road to your right (which circles the lake) and follow the signs (about 1 km). Note: The junction on the main highway is easy to miss as is the hotel's small sign there, so look carefully.

If you were to have just one place to stay in Ecuador, this would be it. The Cusín (cou-SEEN) is a beautiful centuries-old ex-*hacienda* near Lake San Pablo. It earns this top rating in part because of the delightful English owners, Nick and Barbara Millhouse, who have run this place since 1990, and Marsha, the friendly manager. Filling the inn on weekends is never a problem, but during the week business here, as elsewhere in the area, is slow. To take up the slack they have upgraded the facilities so as to make this charming place suitable for use as an educational center, which is Nick's as yet unrealized dream. As a result, the guest rooms are now very nicely furnished and the amenities include new squash and tennis courts, both of which are in excellent condition. There are also horses for all riding levels and arranged guided trips that include visits to the Colombian-owned rose farm next door and to the homes of some Otavalo weavers.

Even if you're not interested in the hotel's sports facilities you're sure to enjoy its beautiful shaded grounds, with flowers everywhere and hummingbirds here and there. Inside the hotel's main building, which dates back to 1602, you'll find an inviting, cozy sitting room with high ceilings, parquet floors, carpets, an old fireplace that's virtually always lighted at night, about five comfortable, heavy armchairs, a huge antique tapestry, some old religious oil paintings, a turn-of-the-century telephone that still operates, and some ornately carved chests, tables and chairs.

Further back you'll find the dining room, which features high ceilings, wooden floors, a fireplace, old tables and colonial-era paintings. Meals are served family style, meaning you get no choice other than what is put on the table. Thankfully, they're quite good and wholesome. Breakfast and other meals cost around $3 and $8, respectively. Also adjoining the sitting room is a cozy bar with cedar panelling, carpets, a fireplace that puts out considerable heat, comfortable armchairs, round card tables and an ever-popular dart board. This bar is wonderful; it usually becomes very animated on weekends after dinner. As a result, it's also the best place by far for meeting other travelers.

The guest rooms are all charming and each is furnished and configured differently. All have antique furnishings, wooden floors with rugs, meter-thick walls, beds with firm mattresses and lots of blankets, comfortable reading chairs, and small bathrooms with old fixtures. There are hot-water showers. If you plan to visit on a weekend, reservations should be made well in advance, as the Cusín is always fully booked at that time of the week. Ask for a room with a fireplace as temperatures drop significantly at night. Be warned: If you hear someone walking around in the middle of the night and the floors squeaking, don't worry – it's just one of the ghosts, of which there are apparently several!

HOSTERIA LA MIRAGE

Cotacachi
Phone (2) 915-237
Category: A
Ex-*hacienda*, 15 rooms.
Pool, tennis, exercise room, sauna, zoo.
Rates: $23/$30-$38 S/D incl. tax. All major credit cards.
Directions: In Cotacachi on town's western edge, 12 km beyond Otavalo.

If you like animals, the chances are that you'll love the well-managed Danish-run Mirage. Staying here is like being on a farm. Fortunately, the 13 macaws, four toucans, two great danes and the doberman are in cages or fenced in. The remaining animals – at last count there were four pheasants, four guinea hens, eight llamas, five horses, one peacock, and various ducks, sheep, goats, and chickens – meander freely about the grounds. Children love this place and adults seem to like it even more. Athletically-inclined travelers can choose from a variety of activities, including horseback riding, tennis, swimming in a 20-foot solar-heated pool, and exercising in a gym with a sauna. To play tennis, however, you'll probably have to shoo away the llamas from the court. They love to lie there!

In spite of these facilities, most guests – largely foreign travelers and expatriates – come to relax and enjoy the views of nearby snow-peaked Cotacachi Volcano. They are attracted by the hotel's picturesque buildings, the fantastic guest rooms, the fine restaurant, and the extensive grounds. Walking around, you'll find a sizeable vegetable garden that supplies the restaurant with fresh produce. On weekends the dining room attracts overflow crowds at lunch time. It is quite attractive and has antique furnishings, high wooden ceilings, pale pink curtains, Danish plates on the walls, plants, roses on all the tables and, most considerate, a waiting area with sofas and a fireplace. Guests can feast on duck à l'orange, shrimp in wine sauce, steamed sea bass, homemade soups and ice cream, and Ecuadorian specialties such as *locro* (potato soup) and *empanadas de morochi* with hot tomato sauce (turnovers filled with meat). The bar has elegant antique furnishings, several oil portraits, and a fireplace that's almost always lighted.

The hotel's best feature is its wonderfully romantic guest rooms. Each one is unique, but they all have antique furnishings, European prints on the walls, tile floors, fireplaces, matching bedspreads and curtains, breakfast tables, and tile bathrooms with showers. Some units also have porches. The beds are magnificent and no two are alike; some are intricately carved wooden beds with canopies, while others are made of brass. Just don't forget to order breakfast in bed!

CABANAS DEL LAGO
Lago de San Pablo
Phone (2) 435-936
Category: A-B
Lakeside, rustic, 10 cabins and 10 rooms, miniature golf, riding, water skiing, boats.
Rates: $16/$20 S/D cabins incl. tax ($12/$17 for rooms); less for residents. All major credit cards.
Directions: On the same road as the Cusín but 4 km further around the lake.

Located at the foot of Imbabura Volcano and on the edge of Lake San Pablo, this rustic lodge is popular with both Ecuadorians and foreigners. Most people come just for a meal at the lakeside restaurant. The principal drawing cards are the unbeatable views of the lake, which comes right up to the building, and the good food, especially the braised dishes – chicken, sea bass, trout and shrimp. Other selections include T-Bone steak, several delicious Ecuadorian soups, an economical three-course special for only about $1.50, some fancy desserts, and a good selection of Chilean wines. People are also attracted by the informality here. The knotty-pine walls and exposed-beam ceilings, long wooden tables with benches, straw-roof bar, and stuffed birds, deer heads and animal skins covering the walls combine to create a charming rustic atmosphere. For entertainment, guests have lots to choose from – row boats, paddle boats, water skiing, horseback riding, and miniature golf.

The lodge consists of two long brick buildings plus a number of cabins. In the center is an imaginative miniature golf course with animals all around. These include two scarlet macaws, various small birds in cages, monkeys, a partridge, and several peacocks strolling around freely. The best units are the cabins; they have two small rooms with bunk beds, brick fireplaces (wood is delivered nightly), red checkered curtains, front porches with chairs and views of the lake, sheepskin rugs, uncomfortable sofas made of twine, brick walls, and tiny bathrooms with hot water in the morning and evening.

***Alternative*: HOTEL YAMOR CONTINENTAL**

Panamericana Norte, Otavalo, phone (2) 920-451/982
Rates: $12/$16 S/D incl. tax; Visa and MasterCard are accepted.
Directions: On the northern (Ibarra) side of town on the Pan-American Highway, a 10- to 15-minute walk northeast of the market.

This modern 55-room establishment, which dates from 1978, has an attractive exterior and formidable grounds. The facilities, the most extensive of any hotel in town, include a volleyball court, a pool, a tennis court, a small zoo, and two restaurants. Note that the pool, which is clean and open to the public for about $1 a person, is only for the brave. The water is unheated and usually quite chilly. In addition, the tennis court is barely usable, and the zoo, home to several ducks in a small pond and some caged monkeys and macaws, is a bit pitiful. The guest rooms, on the other hand, are sizable and quite attractive. They have golden carpets, comfortable beds, TVs for rent, desks, wardrobes, and tile bathrooms with double sinks and hot-water showers.

HOTEL OTAVALO
Calle Roca 504 y Montalvo
Phone (2) 920-416
Category: B
Old-fashioned, 50 rooms, restaurant, bar.
Rates: $6/$10 S/D incl. tax; $4/$8 S/D with shared bath. All major credit cards.
Directions: One block east of Otavalo's central plaza.

For years this old-fashioned hotel has been been a favorite of foreign travelers on modest budgets. There are other hotels that are better buys and offer a more personal touch perhaps, but those who have a weakness for places with interesting interiors and the ambience of a bygone era are likely to prefer the Otavalo. The plain exterior gives little clue of what you'll find inside. As you enter, you'll immediately notice the wonderful wide-board floors and the bold arches on the first and second floors, surrounding the central area, with a skylight above and wrought iron lighting fixtures on the walls. On both floors you'll find lots of potted plants and cushioned lawn chairs to relax in. There are several elegant antique sofas near the reception desk on the first floor, plus a cozy carpeted sitting room with comfortable chairs and sofas.

The most popular hang-out is the **Golden Eagle Coffee Shop** on the ground floor. Even if you don't take a room at the hotel, come for a drink or a snack; hamburgers, hot dogs and not-so-good pizza by the slice. Their superb homemade ice cream and pies rival those of the Shanandoa at the market. The room itself, which seems more like an authentic centuries-old bar, is simply marvelous and features the original wood flooring, papered walls, round tables with captain's chairs, and copper chandeliers. The main restaurant upstairs is more formal, with a stone fireplace, glass chandelier, and red wallpaper. The menu offers *pollo nevado* (white chicken) and *corvina al plátino* (sea bass with plantains), plus some fancy desserts.

The accommodations in the main building are of modest size with high ceilings, carpeted floors, plain furnishings and unadorned walls, beds with slightly sagging mattresses, and old-style high-ceiling bathrooms with old fixtures in good working order. The cheaper rooms have shared baths and no outside windows, while units in the newer annex across the street are clean, but slightly noisy and less atmospheric.

When you're in town at the Plaza de Panchos, stop by **the Shanandoa**, an extremely popular tiny café overlooking the plaza; it serves the best apple, blackberry and blueberry pies à la mode in South America. If you're in town on a Friday evening you can get one hot out of the oven.

Alternative: **HOTEL RIVIERA Y SUCRE**
Calle Moreno y Roca.
Rates: $4/$8 S/D incl. tax. Credit cards are not accepted.
Directions: Around the corner from Hotel Otavalo.

This popular long-standing hotel, which is a large old house with a courtyard, can't quite match the Hotel Otavalo in terms of architectural interest, but the friendly Belgian lady who runs this place gives it a more personable, relaxed atmosphere. She's an expert on the area and can give you all sorts of tips on where to go and how to get there. She also speaks four languages – Spanish, English, French and Dutch. The *hostal*, which has clean rooms with hot-water showers, features a book exchange, ping-pong, a garden, and a cafeteria noted for its breakfasts.

Ibarra

HOSTERIA SAN FRANCISCO
Chachimbiro, Imbabura
Phone (2) 920-387 (Hacienda Pinsaqui)
Category: A-B
Ex-*hacienda*, 8 rooms, pool, tennis, horseback riding, restaurant.
Rates: $12/$16 S/D incl. tax. Diners Club card.
Directions: Go 22 km past (north of) Ibarra on the Pan-Am Hwy, then turn left for Salinas & Tumbabiro; it's 8 km past Tumbabiro.

Since 1987 this lovely old and relatively-unknown *hacienda* has been operating as a hotel. It's just a 45-minute drive from Ibarra, but the location is sufficiently remote (a three-hour drive from Quito) that few people seem to know of this gem. The setting is idyllic and the picturesque countryside here is perfect for hiking, horseback riding, and mountain biking. In addition, the hostel has its own pool which, though not very large, can be quite refreshing after a day's outing. There are horses for riding and a tennis court for which rackets and balls are supplied. An added plus is that the Chachimbiro thermal baths are just three km away. The hotel's dining room is a long, bright room with one window monopolizing an entire wall, pine furniture, and an enormous welcoming fireplace. Most important, the food, which is mainly traditional Ecuadorian fare, is delicious. The pine motif is repeated in the bedrooms, which are furnished with large beds or bunk beds and solid chests of drawers. In combination with white-washed walls and stone-flagged floors, the effect is one of pleasant airy simplicity. In short, this place has all the ingredients of a marvelous undiscovered hideaway, with lots of activities to pass the time.

HOSTERIA CHORLAVI
Panamericana Sur Km 4
Phone (2) 950-777/952-775
Quito phone (2) 522-703
Category: A
Ex-*hacienda,* 48 rooms, pool, tennis, playground, steam bath, sauna, squash.
Rates: $22/$30 S/D incl. tax. All major credit cards.
Directions: On the southern outskirts of Ibarra, 111 km north of Quito & 20 km beyond (north of) Otavalo.

One of the best-known hotels in the highlands is the Chorlaví, an historic *hacienda* more than 150 years old that has been operating as a hotel since 1973. Always busy on weekends, the hotel is famous in large part because of its restaurant, always packed with tourists from the market in Otavalo on Saturdays at lunch time. The *parrillada* (barbecue buffet) served then (and again at Sunday lunch) is simply great, especially the homemade bread. There's always a group of musicians playing away in the courtyard and the whole day is very festive. A good way to start off the celebrations is with a *llamaranda*, a vodka-Campari-fruit drink that will knock your socks off. Take it easy!

The three-room restaurant is quite attractive, with wooden-beam ceilings, colorful tablecloths and all sorts of kitchen ware, pottery, old sewing machines and some 50 antique irons as decoration. On weekends, however, the best place to eat is the courtyard, which is lined with potted plants. One of the specialties of the house is *trucha de Zuleta a la Chorlaví* (a specialty trout dish); their *copa Chorlaví* ice cream sundae is also a knock out.

At night the best place to spend time is the main sitting room, which has antique sofas and chairs in formal red-flowered material, old paintings, a fireplace, a moose head, a color TV, and exposed-beam ceilings. There's a bar next door. A walk around the grounds during the day can be quite fun. There are lots of trees, fig bushes, and flowering bougainvilleas, as well as an old foot bridge and, on clear days, views of the nearby volcanoes. The facilities include a reasonably long unheated pool, a sauna, a Turkish bath, a play area for kids, an excellent squash court, and a tennis court in virtually unplayable condition. On special occasions there are also cockfights.

The accommodations are fine, but don't quite meet the standards of the hotel's public areas. They are standard size with wooden floors, throw rugs, beam ceilings, heavy colonial furniture, old poster beds, colorful bedspreads, telephones, wardrobes, and tile bathrooms with ordinary fixtures and showers but no counter space. Units in the newer annex are also attractively furnished but they are less atmospheric.

HOSTERIA RANCHO DE CAROLINA
Panamericana Sur Km 4
Phone (2) 953-215
Category: A-B
Ex-*hacienda*, 9 rooms, restaurant, bar, patio.
Rates: $18/$24 S/D incl. tax. Visa & MasterCard.
Directions: On the dirt entrance road to Chorlaví.

If the Chorlaví is full, your best alternative in the area is the Rancho de Carolina next door. It's a small place with only nine guest rooms, but the hostel is quite comfortable. During the day the nicest place to sit is the central patio. It has a glass roof to keep the area warm and is filled with the sound of trickling water from a small stone fountain. There are a number of chairs here for reading and relaxing. The inn's restaurant, which features bright checkered tablecloths, opens onto this area. This helps to create a feeling of spaciousness. At night most guests use the sitting room. It has comfortable antique chairs, oriental rugs, and exposed-beam ceilings. An alternative is the small adjoining bar, which features an unusual lighting fixture made of baskets and reed.

The best accommodations are the suites. They offer fireplaces and very comfortable furnishings. The standard units are much smaller, with plain white walls, comfortable beds and reading chairs, throw rugs, closets, and tile baths with showers.

HOSTAL EL EJECUTIVO
Carrera Bolívar 9-69
Phone (2) 952-575
Category: B
4-story hotel, 16 rooms, restaurant.
Rates: \$7/\$12 S/D incl. tax. No credit cards.
Directions: Downtown, 3 blocks north of the railway station.

For an inexpensive hotel near the center of town, check the Ejecutivo; it's reasonably attractive and not bad for the price. The location is convenient, especially if you'll be going in the wee hours of the morning to buy your ticket for the train to San Lorenzo. If you can avoid having to deal with the unfriendly managing lady, your stay here might even be a pleasant one. On the ground floor you'll find a cafeteria where you can get breakfast, plus a somewhat inviting sitting room with several comfortable sofas and chairs. The accommodations are fairly small, but they're spotless, freshly painted, and the beds are fairly new. In addition, the private tile bathrooms are quite adequate, with modern fixtures and showers.

As an aside, talking with low-budget travelers, you'll soon find that most of them are in Ibarra only to catch the early train to San Lorenzo on the coast. Don't miss this trip; it's likely to be your most memorable experience in Ecuador. The train is really a bus on tracks; parts of the route are so steep that the driver drops sand on the tracks to ensure traction. The trip takes about nine hours if all goes well and up to twice as long if not. The tracks follow the Mira River for much of the way, at times clinging to cliffs high above the river. They wind through the most highly bio-diverse area of the country, from dry sierra forests to wet tropics. Along the way you pass through numerous villages and no fewer than 52 tunnels. Riding on top and ducking these tunnels is half the fun, but you must at least start the trip in your seat. Just squeezing onto the train is a major accomplishment. For more details, see the South American Explorers Club in Quito.

Alternative: **HOTEL IMBABURA**
Calle Miguel Oviedo 9-33, Ibarra
Rates: $2/$4 S/D incl. tax.
Directions: 3½ blocks west of the railway station.

If you're looking for dirt cheap accommodations and like places with character, head for the old Imbabura. It's a wonderful old two-story house that has an attractive central courtyard with a fountain in the middle, balconies all around upstairs, and a dining room with one long table. The prices here are unbeatable, but the rooms are very basic and have shared baths.

Central Highlands Region

Latacunga

HOSTERIA LA CIENEGA
Panamericana Sur Km 72
Phone (2) 801-622/800-740
Quito phone (2) 549-126
Quito telex 2224
Category: A
Old ex-*hacienda*, 28 rooms, cold pool, horseback riding, shops.
Rates: $19/$23 S/D incl. tax. All major credit cards.
Directions: 72 km south of Quito on the Pan-American Hwy., a few km beyond Cotopaxi Park, 18 km before Latacunga, and 1 km off road. Look for sign/arched gate.

If a prize were given for the most picturesque hotel in Ecuador, surely the winner would be La Ciénega. It is a popular destination for tourist groups and is located outside Quito near Cotopaxi, Ecuador's second highest volcano. This manorial house, which was constructed in the mid-1600's, is one of the oldest privately-owned properties in Ecuador. Back then it was "truly an earthly paradise, large paved patios, artistic fountain, perfumed gardens, singularly formed lanterns, large windows... The rooms on the lower floor were adorned with famous paintings, silks and finely finished furniture..." (from *The Marquis of La Ciénega* by Eduardo Paredes Ortega in La Gaceta, 7/2/81).

Today, this old *hacienda* is much the same, in large part because it has remained the property of a single family. The grounds, however, have been reduced from many square miles to just 34 acres.

The most impressive feature of the hotel is its 150-meter-long entrance way, which is lined with tall eucalyptus trees. The formal white facade is topped by a bell tower and seems Dutch in inspiration, while the rear of the main building faces a beautiful flower garden that has a fountain in the middle. To one side you'll find the estate's small private chapel and, to the other side, a long freezing-cold pool that's more for viewing than swimming. Just beyond the pool is a field that offers fantastic views of Cotopaxi, especially during the early morning and late afternoon when the volcano is not shrouded in clouds. And to the rear of the hotel you'll find an artisan shop, the *hacienda's* stables and, still further, a pond. If you take one of the horses for a ride, you'll get a good view of the surrounding farm land.

Some of the hotel's public rooms are quite grand, especially the main sitting room, carpeted and furnished with very formal antiques, glass chandeliers, fancy red draperies, and three oil portraits of family members. The restaurant too is quite attractive, with wide-board flooring, cupboards with fine antique chinaware, wrought iron lighting fixtures, old paintings, and stone fireplaces which usually have roaring fires at night. There are four dining rooms in all. They are rarely full except at lunch time on Thursdays, which is market day in nearby Saquisili, and sometimes on weekends when the *hacienda* is fully booked. The four-course set menu costs about $4; the food is quite good, but nothing to write home about. A typical meal might consist of *locro* (Ecuadorian potato soup), chicken with mushrooms, a salad, ice cream cake, and Ecuadorian-grown coffee. Afterwards, you can have a nightcap at the hotel's cozy bar.

The size and configuration of the accommodations vary considerably but, most important, they are all warm, with two-meter-thick walls in the main building and effective space heaters. They also have carpets, comfortable beds with piles of blankets, bottled mineral water, wrought iron ceiling lights, old drawings on the walls, plain wooden desks with mirrors, walk-in closets, and tile bathrooms with old fixtures in good working order. The showers have a supply of hot water in the mornings and evenings.

HOSTERI RUMIPAMBA DE LAS ROSAS

Panamericana Sur Km 100, Salcedo
Phone (2) 726-128 or 726-306
Telex 2249
Category: A
Rustic lodge, 34 rooms, heated pool, zoo, ping-pong, horseback riding, tennis, playground, shops, gardens, restaurant, entertainment.
Rates: $16-$21/$21-$26 S/D incl. tax. All major credit cards.
Directions: 10 km south of Latacunga, entering Salcedo.

Rumipamba has the most playful ambience of any hotel in Ecuador. It has a small zoo (deer, llama, macaws, monkeys, doves, chickens, peacocks, and eagle-like aguilas), free-roaming rabbits, large duck pond, horses for riding, grass soccer field, basketball and tennis courts, playground, huge outdoor chess board, three excellent ping-pong tables, and a heated kidney-shaped pool with sunning chairs. Children think this place is marvelous. Just roaming around the extensive grounds and through the hotel's antique shop can be a lot of fun.

Most people are only familiar with the restaurant; it's the most popular one in the highlands between Quito and Cuenca, which says a lot about the quality of the food and the attractiveness of the setting. So at lunch time on weekends expect it to be packed. Meals here are quite good: chicken roasted or in herb sauce or baked sea bass, to name a couple. On Sunday the meals are exceptional, starting with a truly incredible breakfast buffet and continuing with a lunch buffet, which is extremely popular and always accompanied by a live orchestra. If you stop for a meal, check the patio behind the dining area; it has a water fountain and rustic tables and chairs made of logs – perfect for drinks.

One of the hotel's most appealing features is its charming, rustic decor. The restaurant, for example, features dark red tile flooring, white walls with dark wooden wainscoting, exposed beams, wooden carvings on the walls, and all-wood chairs and tables. The accommodations are equally attractive. The "superiors," which are the best and most spacious, are decorated with antique irons, guns and cowboy chaps on the walls and have natural wood furnishings. They have comfortable single beds with thick woolen blankets, carpeted floors, heating, wrought iron lamps, telephones, and tile baths with showers and plenty of hot water. The standard units have similar decor, but they're a bit small. All in all, it's a great place for families, or for lovers seeking a weekend hideaway.

Alternative: **HOTEL ESTAMBUL**
Calle Belisario Quevedo 7340 y Salcedo, Latacunga, phone (2) 800-354
Rates: $3/$5 S/D incl. tax. Credit cards are not accepted.
Directions: In downtown Latacunga, 1 block northwest of the main square.

Among the cheap category C hotels, the pickings in this area are slim. The best buy is the friendly Estambul in Latacunga. Extremely basic and priced accordingly, it is set around an attractive courtyard and is clean, safe, and quiet, with a balcony on the roof and parking in the rear. The management can make arrangements for trips to Cotopaxi Volcano as well. Although the Estambul is hardly special, it's sometimes full of backpackers headed for Cotopaxi or, on Thursdays, to the traditional market nearby at Squisili. So call ahead.

Baños

HOTEL VILLA GERTRUDIS
Avenida Montalvo 2075
Phone (2) 740-441/2
Category: A
Home-like, 12 rooms, private restaurant.
Rates: $41/$80 S/D incl. tax and 2 meals (50% less for nationals). No credit cards.
Directions: 3 blocks south of town plaza & 3 blocks west of the baths.

If the idea of a peaceful Swiss inn sounds appealing, check out the Villa Gertrudis. Run by Marcelo Torres, it's the best managed hotel in town and the only top-tier hotel that is geared mainly to foreigners, the older set, and those without children. Similar in style to Los Alpes in Quito and inspired by a European inn, this charming two-story establishment is homey and exceedingly tranquil. It has a pleasant staff seemingly as old as the building itself, which was built by Germans over 50 years ago. On weekends, Marcelo is usually here, but during the week the old caretaker rules.

Guests can hang out in the sitting room or the restaurant; they both have sturdy no-nonsense furnishings. The restaurant in particular is a bit spartan, with bare wide-board floors, and wooden tables and chairs, but the food, which consists of mostly continental fare, is quite good and wholesome. Since most choose to have breakfast and dinner here, lunch can be at one of the city's many restaurants. The long-standing **Café Alemán**, which is one of the city's most popular meeting places and only a block away, would be an excellent choice.

Outside, the hostel, which is surrounded by grass and hedges, is quite attractive, but the open spaces are too small for walking around. The guest rooms, which are standard size, are also quite nice, with wide-board flooring, throw rugs, comfortable armchairs for relaxing, beds with thick comforters, and combination tile baths with old fixtures in excellent working order. If you're coming to Baños on a weekend, be sure to reserve in advance. Otherwise your chances of getting a room will be slim.

Alternative: **HOTEL SANGAY**
Plazoleta Isidro Ayora 101, phone (2) 740-490/740-056, fax (2) 562-497, Quito phone (2) 432-066, Quito fax (2) 432-622
Rates: $22/$32 S/D rooms with tax and breakfast ($30/$40 S/D cabins), 50% less for residents. All major credit cards are accepted.
Directions: On the southeastern side of town directly across the street from the main baths.

Facing the main baths in town, the 60-room three-story Sangay rates the most stars of any hotel in town and is better for families or those who like hotels with a livelier ambience or numerous facilities. In the main building there's a good restaurant, a travel agency and a game room with ping-pong, while in back the hotel features a hot-water pool and a grassy area with a playground, also a cement tennis court, squash court, gym, sauna and steam bath. The guest rooms have color TVs and private baths, and there is a choice between a room in the main building or, much better, a cabin in back.

HOTEL PALACE
Avenida Montalvo 20-03
Phone (2) 740-470
Category: B
Old hotel next to baths, 30 rooms, pool, restaurant, bar.
Rates: $9/$13 S/D incl. tax; $13/$26 S/D incl. tax & 2 meals. All major credit cards.
Directions: On southeastern side of town next to the main baths.

For the low price, choice location and good vibes, it's hard to beat the wonderful old Palace. Attracting mainly middle-class Ecuadorian families, it's a well-maintained, old-fashioned hotel with a genuine, comfortable feeling, a friendly staff, and the ambience of a bygone era. The restaurant, reputedly quite good, has old wooden flooring, natural wood wainscoting, long draperies, lots of hanging potted plants, colorful modern paintings, and dining tables with flowers. Adjoining this is an inviting bar with a color TV, comfortable sofas and armchairs, a bar with wooden stools, a natural-wood ceiling, and lots of sunlight.

In back there's a a shallow kidney-shaped pool with lights for swimming at night and clean water from the same source that fills the baths. You'll also find some screeching macaws in under-sized cages, several tables with awnings, lots of benches, trees and flowers, a children's playground with swings and see-saws. There's a bar with a TV and natural wood furnishings and a popular game room with a billiard table, ping-pong, and a dart board.

The guest rooms have neither TVs nor telephones, but they are spotlessly clean. Still, the accommodations don't quite match the standards of the hotel's public areas. They are quite plain, with wooden floors, throw rugs, simple queen-size beds with lumpy mattresses, and small tile private baths with aging fixtures, including showers, in good working order. In sum, for an older place with an authentic Ecuadorian ambience, book a room here.

First Alternative: **CASA NAHUAZO**
Vía al Salado, phone (2) 740-315
Rates: $8/$12 incl. tax and breakfast. Credit cards are not accepted.
Directions: On the southwestern edge of town on the road to the El Salado baths, which are only several minutes walk away.

This quiet country house on the edge of town is run by a friendly ex-Peace Corps volunteer who is also in the business of offering professional travel assistance for trips to nearby areas. Catering mainly to gringos and the younger set, this friendly, laid-back B&B is very relaxing, with a comfortable living room and guest rooms with hot-water baths. An additional feature is that it's only a few steps from the Salado baths. On clear days, which are extremely rare in this area, the hostel affords excellent views of Tungurahua volcano.

Second Alternative: **CAFE CULTURA**
Avenida Montalvo y Calle Santa Clara, phone (2) 740-419
Rates: $7/$14 S/D incl. tax. No credit cards are accepted.
Directions: On Montalvo, a block west of the baths and Hotel Palace.

If you'd rather be in town and the idea of a quaint colonial-style house with a balcony and a garden sounds appealing, you may prefer a room at this popular café. Better known as a restaurant, it's a cozy and hospitable Danish-run establishment which is very near the baths and serves vegetarian food and excellent breakfasts; don't miss their pancakes. However, it's closed Thursdays and there are only four units, so call in advance or come early in the day.

Riobamba

HOSTERIA LA ANDALUZA
Panamericana Sur Km 183, phone (2) 904-223/243
Category: A. Traditional *hacienda* style, 16 rooms, restaurant, horses.
Rates: $22/$28 incl. tax (double if paid in dollars or US credit cards). Major credit cards.
Directions: On PanAm Hwy., 16 km north of Riobamba.

Chimborazo, the country's tallest volcano, is often so shrouded in clouds that for weeks on end its snowy slopes are not visible. When they do appear, however, the views thereof are superb from Andaluza, which is at the foot of the volcano and may be the country's highest hotel above sea level. Tungurahua and Altar are easily viewable from here as well.

The hotel was built in 1988, but the traditional-style architecture makes it seem much older. The attractive exterior, for example, has plain white walls, dark wood trim, a red tile roof, an arched walkway leading to the entrance, and flowers all around. In a similar vein, the two dining rooms feature a large stone fireplace, exposed beams, terra-cotta tile floors, paned windows, high ceilings and oil portraits. At lunch time on Sundays, which is the restaurant's big day, there are usually overflow crowds, mostly locals from Riobamba.

Besides dining, the main activity here for those who are fit is hiking; the *hostaría* can make àrrangements for renting horses as well. And on special occasions, which is a choice time to visit, the small bull ring in back comes into action. Accommodations are in a two-story, horseshoe-shaped structure behind the restaurant that has a large courtyard in the center. The rooms are standard size and have fine maroon carpets, queen-size beds with thick blankets, wrought iron lighting fixtures, well-used fireplaces, space heaters, wood-beam ceilings, comfortable reading chairs, oil portraits on the walls, and modern tile bathrooms with showers.

HOTEL EL GALPON
Argentinos y Zambrano
Phone (2) 960-981
Category: A
Modern, near center, pool, sauna, casino, disco.
Rates: $25/$32 S/D incl. tax. All major credit cards.
Directions: 1½ km from downtown on a hill overlooking the city.

If the Andaluza is full or you need a hotel in town, your best bet by far among similarly-classed hotels is the Galpón, an architecturally interesting concrete structure on a hill overlooking the city. In terms of ambience, it cannot begin to compete with the Andaluza and the atmosphere here is a bit cold. However, the Galpón is a modern well-maintained establishment with far more amenities, including a heated pool, sauna, casino, disco, and a decent restaurant with panoramic views of the city. The accommodations have TVs, carpets, private baths, and many have good views of the city as well.

Alternative: **HOTEL LOS SHIRIS**
Avenida 10 de Agosto y Rocafuerte 2160, phone (2) 960-323
Rates: $6/$9 S/D incl. tax.
Directions: 1 block east of the railway station and 5 blocks south of the main plaza.

The city's mid-range hotels are a sorry lot. For a category B-C hotel, however, Los Shiris is a reasonably good buy and conveniently located near the center. The rooms are quite good and nicely furnished, plus the staff is friendly and there's a good restaurant to boot.

Second Alternative: **HOTEL METRO**
Calle Borja y Lavalle, phone (2) 961-714
Rates: $3/$5 incl. tax. Credit cards are not accepted.
Directions: On Borja, at the entrance to the railway yards.

A majestic hotel from the golden era of the railroads, the Metro is now run-down, but it's a good choice for those on a very low budget who like traditional places with an old-timey atmosphere. Inside, the rooms all have their original wood paneling and the stairways their original banisters. The accommodations are quite large, with heavy furnishings and beds that are reasonably comfortable.

Cuenca

HOTEL ORO VERDE (La Laguna)
Ave. Ordóñez Lasso
Phone (7) 831-200
Fax (7) 832-849
Telex 48554
Category: Deluxe
Modern highrise, lake, on city outskirts, 79 rooms, pool, playground, restaurant, sauna, steam bath, tiny gym, access to tennis and golf.
Rates: $75/$84 S/D incl. tax. All major credit cards.
Directions: On Tomembamba River, 2 km east of center.

Now part of the prestigious Oro Verde chain, also known as La Laguna, this is the city's only deluxe establishment with lots of amenities likely to fill the bill if you want a modern hotel. The facilites include a heated modest-size outdoor pool, a tiny poorly-equipped gym with several different exercise machines and little else, a sauna, a Turkish bath, a playground, a disco, and access to golf and tennis. Fishing and hunting outings can also be arranged. The hotel's best feature, however, is its 100-meter-long, man-made lake which has a grassy bank, a large family of ducks, and rental boats for rowing around – perfect for kids and lovers. An added feature is that the hotel overlooks the Tomembamba River, which runs alongside the property and is set against a mountain backdrop. For some travelers, however, the location on the outskirts of town is a major drawback.

As you dine from the hotel's main three-room restaurant, you can gaze out onto the lake and river. The food, which is mainly French, is the best in town and also the most expensive. Among the numerous selections are Alaskan sea bass stuffed with shrimp, seafood casserole, sole stuffed with lobster mousse, filet of beef Normandy, Zurich-style veal, and seafood fricassee with puff pastry. There's also a comfortably furnished bar and a cheaper restaurant serving local Ecuadorian fare.

When booking a room, guests have a choice between those in the hotel's 14-floor tower and those in a long, three-story brick structure on concrete piers alongside the lake. Attractively furnished and reasonably spacious, they all have marble-top tables, plush carpets, telephones, heaters, color TVs, comfortable reading chairs, papered walls, large closets, and marble-floored combination baths with long mirrors and lots of counter space. In short, if you're looking for a hotel with a host of amenities or top quality accommodations, stay here.

HOTEL CRESPO
Calle Larga 793
Phone (7) 827-857
Fax (7) 834-677
Category: A
Converted old mansion, central, 29 rooms, restaurant and bar.
Rates: $25-$27/$32-$38 S/D incl. tax; $13/$17 in annex. All major credit cards.
Directions: 4 blocks south of main plaza.

With block after block of colonial-era buildings, Cuenca is the country's most picturesque city. Part of the fun of visiting here is staying in one of these charming old structures, a number of which have been converted into hotels. While the long-standing Crespo, which is a lovely and dramatic remodeling of an early 20th-century, three-story mansion, now has strong competition from some similar establishments. Daniel Kuperman, a Frenchman, has run this place since 1970 and done a marvelous job in preserving the building's traditional flavor.

Each floor has a cozy sitting area with a fireplace, comfortable sofas and chairs, carpeted floors, antique lamps, paintings, plants, and English-language magazines. As you climb the old wooden staircase, sunlight filtering through the colorful top-floor skylight will light your way.

The spacious high-ceiling guest rooms are delightful. They are carpeted, heated and have waist-high wood paneling, long mirrors, wood and chrome furnishings, bottled water, TVs with movies, telephones, free standing closets and small tile bathrooms with showers only. The hot water supply, however, is not 100% reliable. Ask for a unit on the second floor as they have the highest ceilings or, if you don't mind paying a bit more, one facing the river, as they have the best views. Crespo is the best choice among the low-budget establishments.

Many people stop by the Crespo just for a meal. The restaurant here may not be the best in town, but it is one of the more atmospheric. It boasts antique wood-and-glass chandeliers, high-back wooden chairs, carpeted floors, ceiling-to-floor gold curtains, and service with a flair. The bilingual menu offers many interesting selections including, for starters, caviar, snails and sherry consomme and, as main courses, a delicious French-style rabbit dish, Alsacian-style leg of lamb, roast duck a l'orange, steamed trout and seafood casserole. For dessert, their chocolate mousse and strawberries in fresh cream are unbeatable. The Crespo remains an excellent choice. Its friendly and efficient English-speaking staff and considerate 2 p.m. check-out time are icing on the cake.

***First Alternative:* HOTEL INCA REAL**
Avenida General Torres 8-40 y Sucre, phone (7) 823-636/825-571
Rates: $16/$20 S/D incl. tax. Most major credit cards are accepted.
Directions: 2 blocks west of the main plaza.

An excellent alternative, closer to the center and cheaper to boot, is the Inca Real, which is a charming old mansion dating from 1820. It has recently been renovated and turned into a very nice hotel. One of the best features is that all 30 rooms surround a glass-covered courtyard, of which there are three; another is that the staff here is very friendly. Accommodations are quiet and comfortable. There are telephones and modern private baths, plus a good restaurant and bar.

***Second Alternative:* HOTEL INTERNACIONAL**
Calle Benigno Malo 1015 y Gran Colombia, phone (7) 824-348
Rates: $18/$23 S/D incl. tax, children under 12 free. Visa, MasterCard & Diners.
Directions: 1 block north of the main plaza.

The exterior of this stately three-story hotel is ornate, architecturally interesting and eye-catching, with white walls, numerous little balconies, pink, baby-blue and burgundy trim, plus giant hanging ferns. The structure dates from the early 1930's. An unusual feature of the accommodations is their beautifully painted high ceilings, which vary from room to room. They have balconies, gray carpets, telephones, free mineral water on the tables, bathrooms with hot-water showers and, in some units, TVs. The bright and airy restaurant on the second floor of this pretty colonial house has the same high ceilings and colorful white, blue and pink trim, as well as numerous tall windows. The food is quite good, especially the American breakfasts, which cost about $1.75 and are good value. There's also an extensive dinner menu, which includes sea bass, shrimp and trout dishes, filet mignon, beef and various pastas; most main courses cost around $3 plus tax.

***Third Alternative:* GRAN HOTEL**
Avenida General Torres 9-70, phone (7) 831-934
Rates: $8/$11 S/D incl. tax.
Directions: In the center, 1 block north of the Inca Real.

For a cheaper category C hotel, try the charming old Gran, which has lots of character and is just a block away from the Inca. It features a beautiful courtyard and a good restaurant. In addition, the rooms are clean and they have hot water and private baths. This establishment also offers a laundry service.

Around Cuenca

Vilcabamba

HOSTERIA UZHUPUD
Capulispambalures, Azuay
Phone (7) 821-853/828-840
Fax (7) 832-849
Telex 48582
Category: A
Sprawling *hacienda* resort, 1 hour from Cuenca, 49 rooms, pool, volleyball, steam bath, tennis, craft shops, ping-pong, horseback riding.
Rates: $20/$25 S/D incl. tax. All major credit cards.
Directions: The hotel is 34 km northeast of Cuenca and 16 km northwest of Gualaceo. Take the Pan-American Highway north towards Azogues for 18 km where you'll come to a 3-way intersection. Take the paved road eastward towards Gualaceo. After about 8 km you'll come to a fork. The road to your right, which is the main route, continues to Gualaceo, while the left one leads about 8 km to the hotel.

An hour's drive from Cuenca is the Paute Valley, a drier, sunnier and lower-elevated area than Cuenca. Located here is the sprawling, Spanish-style former estate called Uzhupud. It is an extremely popular weekend retreat for wealthy Ecuadorians looking for an escape from the Cuenca's cloudy, chilly weather. Foreign tourists also like it here because of the warm climate. For many, a principal attraction is the pool, which is far larger and warmer than any in Cuenca. Other visitors are attracted by this brick resort's unique atmosphere, which resembles that of a Spanish-style pueblo in miniature. There are numerous buildings here, including a chapel and several artisan shops. There's also a sugar cane mill, orchids, grazing llamas, a small zoo, and extensive gardens with colorful flowers.

Opened in 1981, this estate looks entirely new and has a wide assortment of activities to attract weekenders, including well-maintained tennis and volleyball courts, an under-sized grass soccer field, horseback riding in the hills, a small pond for boating, a playground, ping-pong, a sauna and a steam bath. The pool, however, is where most guests gather and the bar there is very popular. You don't have to book a room to use the pool; it's free if you dine here.

Despite all these attractions, the reason most people come here on the weekends is to eat, either at the Saturday barbecue or for the Sunday buffet, when a traditional Ecuadorian band provides entertainment; the cost of either is about $6. The decor of the main restaurant, La Bella Terraza, is the same as that found throughout the hotel – red tile floors, exposed-beam ceilings, antique brass lighting fixtures, rustic all-wood furnishings, and plain white walls with local decorations here and there.

Most people come only for the day. If you stay overnight you'll find that the accommodations are standard size and quite attractive, with carpets, TVs, beamed ceilings, telephones, piped-in music, brass lighting fixtures over the beds, comfortable reading chairs, flowered bedspreads, wooden bureaus, and top-quality combination baths with modern fixtures. All of them also have good views of the surrounding hills.

First Alternative: **HOSTAL MADRE TIERRA**
Vilcabamba, mailing address: c/o Jaime Mendoza, Box 354, Loja
Rates: $8 per person incl. meals and tax. Credit cards are not accepted.
Directions: 2 km north of Vilcabamba, off the highway to Loja. By bus, it's an all-day trip south from Cuenca; 6 hours Cuenca-Loja (6 departures/day) and 1½ hours Loja-Vilcabamba (departures every hour).

This lovely and highly-recommended place, run by the Mendoza family, caters primarily to low-budget gringo travelers in search of a beautiful, peaceful setting in a temperate climate. (The climate in Vilcabamba, which is only about half as high above sea level as Quito, is perfect.) There are individual cabins with clean shared baths and a host of activities to choose from – horseback riding, sunbathing, taking steam baths and special mud treatments, bird watching, orchid collecting, and Spanish language training. The Mendozas, who speak English and French, can provide you with details for hiking in the area; the Mandango Mountain Trail is particularly beautiful. A final major attraction is their vegetarian home-style meals, made fresh with organic home-grown crops.

Second Alternative: **CABANAS RIO YAMBALA**
Vilcabamba
Rates: $5 per person incl. tax, about $8 with meals; credit cards are not accepted.
Directions: 4 km east of Vilcabamba. For a taxi/camioneta, ask at Señora Carpio's place on the main square in Vilcabamba.

Situated in the upper end of the Vilcabamba Valley, this place is similar to Madre Tierra and equally friendly. It has the great advantage of being near a river where you can swim in crystal clear water and sunbathe on sun-warmed rocks. In addition, there are horses for rent (with or without guides) for trekking and camping in nearby Podocarpus National Park. All the gear you'll need (tents, sleeping bags and food) is available, too. There are cooking facilities for those who wish to prepare their own meals and the owners will even do the shopping for you! Alternatively, try some of their cooking, which is mainly vegetarian fare. Rooms offer shared hot showers, and there is both a laundry service and massages available.

Coastal Region

Guayaquil

HOTEL ORO VERDE
9 de Octubre y Garcí a Moreno
Phone (4) 327-999
Fax (4) 329-350
Telex 43744
USA phone (800) 223-6800
Category: Deluxe
Modern highrise, 191 rooms, pool, sauna, small gym, shops, car rental, casino, access to tennis & golf.

Rates: $160-$168/$200-$208 S/D incl. tax. All major credit cards are accepted.
Directions: Downtown, 10 blocks west of the center.

Travelers who appreciate good food are in for a real treat if they stay at the Oro Verde. It's the city's leading hotel and offers probably the best restaurant in Ecuador – **Le Gourmet**, a cozy dining room with about 15 tables. While there are three other restaurants, including a popular, reasonably-priced, street-side cafe, this fancy French restaurant is what really shines. The theme is one of total elegance – a huge crystal chandelier, fine well-framed reproductions on the walls, two-layer tablecloths, black-vested waiters, white porcelain chain, silverware, comfortable armchairs in soft colors, fine carpeting, candles, and classical music. For starters, you might have a bouillabaisse, artichoke hearts with quail eggs and caviar, or a fabulous lobster bisque. This will be followed by sherbet and the main course. Selections include sea bass with caviar in white wine sauce, stuffed chicken breast with spinach, and lobster thermidor. The dessert tray also looks fabulous.

The hotel itself is a sleek eight-story concrete and glass building. It houses a small uninspired but busy lobby with marble floors and glass chandeliers. The facilities include a pool in back with lots of sunning chairs and an adjoining bar, a sauna and a small gym with a professional instructor, a car rental agency, several shops, a popular piano bar, and a gaily decorated casino, which does a booming business at night.

Accommodations are attractive, if not particularly imaginative, and the efficient Swiss management ensures they're well maintained. They have queen-size beds with floral bedspreads, brass lamps, modern paintings, fine carpets, spacious closets, radios, cable TVs with English-language channels, modern tile combination baths, and 24-hour room service.

HOTEL CONTINENTAL
Calle Chile y 10 de Agosto, phone (4) 329-270, fax (4) 325-454, telex 43799, USA phone (800) 333-1212
Category: Deluxe. Modern lowrise, 91 rooms.
Rates: $120-$126/$144 S/D incl. tax. All major credit cards.
Directions: In the heart of town facing Parque Bolívar.

The modern seven-story Continental boasts the best service of any hotel in the city. It is the type of hotel where, if you leave your room for 1-2 hours, the staff will come in and straighten it up during your brief absence, even providing fresh towels in the bathroom. It's hardly surprising, therefore, that the Continental also has the most loyal clientele of any establishment here. An additional attraction is the hotel's elegant, award-winning restaurant, which serves truly outstanding international food, mostly French. It is, however, quite expensive by Ecuadorian standards. There are two other options; a popular café, offering local fare at more reasonable prices and a 24-hour cafeteria. Another attraction of the Continental is its popular nightclub, the **Music Hall**, which is one of the city's hotspots. Every night there's a floor show and a different lead singer, including the country's top recording artists.

Most clients are foreigners on business; facilities for them include various conference rooms and a business service center. Hertz and several shops are also on the premises. This ultra-modern white buildings is also, from an architectural standpoint, one of the city's most intriguing structures. The covered driveway, however, is a bit awkward, and the small marble-floor lobby is stark and totally uninspired.

The accommodations are standard size and have modern furnishings, including queen-size beds with attractive floral bedspreads, plush golden carpets, cable TVs with many English channels, air conditioning, desks, modern paintings, blinds, ample storage space, and small marble-floor bathrooms with hairdryers, wide counters and mirrors, and tile combination baths. About half the units face Parque Bolívar across the street. Don't fail to take a stroll around that shady park, as it's renowned for its lizards, which are impressively large and run about freely.

***Alternative:* GRAND HOTEL GUAYAQUIL**

Calle Boyacá 1600 y 10 de Agosto, phone (4) 329-690, fax (4) 327-251, telex 3394, USA phone (800) 327-3573
Rates: $118/$126 S/D incl. 20% tax. All major credit cards are accepted.
Directions: In the heart of town, 2 blocks west of Hotel Continental and behind the cathedral.

For the money, this older but well-maintained 181-room hotel in the center is a better buy. This five-story hotel is oriented to a North American clientele, including airline personnel, and the facilities here are quite impressive. It has a pool in a lush garden with a 10-meter waterfall and a sun deck, several restaurants, a sports complex with squash courts, a well-equipped weight room, a sauna and a steam bath. The large guest rooms come with cable TVs, carpeting, coffee makers, and small tiled baths with showers or tubs, but no counter space. Even if you don't stay here, you can come to use the pool for $2.

PALACE HOTEL

Calle Chile 214 y Luque, phone (4) 511-080/321-080, fax (4) 322-887, telex 43435
Category: A. Refurbished older hotel, central, 92 rooms, restaurant, travel agency, fax-telex service.
Rates: $54/$72 S/D incl. 20% tax. All major credit cards are accepted.
Directions: 3 blocks north of Hotel Continental.

Completely refurbished in 1990, the old Palace has regained its former glory and then some, making it unquestionably the best mid-range hotel in Guayaquil. In its seedier days it was a hangout for English-speaking expatriates, but now business people predominate as it represents exceptionally good value to them. As you enter the small sophisticated lobby, you'll be struck by the original massive columns that dominate the room. This area is now air conditioned and very attractively furnished with wicker sofas and chairs, plus a large pale mural on the wall. Adjoining the lobby is a brightly decorated, 24-hour café offering a full menu, modern furnishings, white tile floors and fancy windows. Very chic, with an inviting atmosphere, this corner café is quite popular, especially as a meeting place and for drinks. There's also a more formal dining room, a bar, a travel agency and a small business center with fax and telex service.

The rooms, which were also completely renovated, have comfortable modern furniture and carpets, large closets, color TVs, air conditioning, minibars and combination tile bathrooms with marble counters and bidets.

HOTEL PLAZA
Calle Chile 414 y Ballén
Phone (4) 327-140
Telex 42694
Category: B
Modern lowrise, 48 rooms, restaurant, bar.
Rates: $30-$36/$43 S/D incl. tax (50% less for residents). All major credit cards.
Directions: Downtown next to Parque Bolívar, between Hotels Palace/Continental.

Among the economy hotels, the Plaza, which continues to be well maintained and often fully booked, stands out as having the best rooms and overall ambience. The entrance is through a small functional lobby with linoleum flooring. On the same level you'll find an attractive restaurant which is an excellent breakfast spot and features, among other things, a relatively expensive buffet lunch and dinner. Guests also have the choice of using the ground floor coffee shop at the Hotel Doral next door.

The rooms are a good buy as foreigners are usually allowed to pay in sucres, which comes out to half the dollar rate. Check-out time is a very liberal 3 p.m. The rooms, some of which have park views, are medium size with two single beds, small black and white TVs, minibars, air conditioning, linoleum flooring, large mirrors, roomy closets, telephones, and tile bathrooms with hot-water showers, small sinks and no counter space. The two-room, three-person suites are a bargain. For only 20% more, you get a larger unit with a color TV, sofa, carpeting and queen-size beds.

First Alternative: **HOTEL DORAL**
Calle Chile 402 y Aguirre, phone (4) 327-175.
Rates: $18 per room incl. tax ($36 if paid in dollars). Most major credit cards.
Directions: Next door to the Plaza.

If the Plaza is full, try the eight-story, 63-room Doral next door. Despite its presentable exterior, this very similar establishment is more run-down and not as good a buy. It is, however, well located and has a popular sidewalk coffee shop that's open to 11 p.m.

Second Alternative: **RESIDENCIAL METROPOLITANA**
Calle Victor Mañuel Rendó nl20 y Panamá, phone (4) 305-250/1
Rates: $5/$8 S/D incl. tax. Credit cards are not accepted.
Directions: Downtown, 1 block west of the river, very near Parque Pedro Carbo.

For a much cheaper category C in the heart of the city, it's hard to beat the old Metropolitana, which is poorly marked in a decaying old building near the river. The place is very clean and well maintained and there's laundry service, too. It's very popular and almost always full. There are only about 15 guest rooms, so if you don't stop by very early in the day, your chances of getting one will be very slim. All the rooms are on the 4th floor and are quite large. They have beds that sag a bit and shared baths with hot-water showers. Except when there's a water shortage, which happens now and then, this place rates a "best buy." There's no restaurant but, as the Metropolitana is in the heart of the commercial district, finding a place to eat is never a problem, even late at night.

Salinas & Beaches To The North

HOTEL SAMARINA
Vía Salinas-La Libertad
Phone (4) 785-167
Quito phone (2) 457-337 (Hotel República)
Category: A
Beachfront location, 53 rooms, pool, restaurant, beach, hairdresser, shops.
Rates: $24/$30 S/D incl. tax and air conditioning; 15% less during the off-season (May-Nov). All major credit cards.
Directions: 4 km from Salinas on the beach road to La Libertad.

For a major beach resort, Salinas has a surprisingly bad array of hotels. For those attracted primarily by the beach, the Samarina is the best choice. For those with small children it appears to be the only good choice. While the service is no better than adequate, the Samarina has been and may still be the only hotel with an adjoining private beach. While the beach itself is quite small, it is a hundred times more tranquil than the long one in the heart of Salinas (four km away), which is often crowded and littered with trash. This modern complex also has an excellent, clean pool long enough for swimming laps, plus a baby pool. Both are surrounded by lots of relaxing lounge chairs and tables with straw roofs. There is a bar nearby and a decent restaurant overlooking the pool and ocean. Because of these key attributes, the Samarina has become extremely popular with Colombians, who drive several days just to get here. Most bring their families and relatives during the peak months of December and January.

The accommodations are standard size with non-skid tile flooring, two to four single beds, plain walls, no-frills curtains, breakfast tables, comfortable chairs, ample closet space, adequate lighting, and combination tile baths. Most important, they all are breezy, with views of the ocean except for the bungalows, which are in back and not recommended unless you must have a bigger unit and/or air conditioning.

First Alternative: **PUNTA CARNERO INN**

Punta Carnero, Salinas, phone (4) 785-450/785-377

Rates: $28/$34 S/D with air conditioning incl. tax ($20/$26 S/D with fan). All major credit cards.

Directions: At the southern shore of Santa Elena peninsula, 8 km south of La Libertad and a 20-minute drive from Salinas (12 km).

If you're more interested in the views than the beach, you'll probably prefer the Punta Carnero. Well outside of Salinas, this better-known establishment, which dates from the 1960's, is noted for its spectacular location on a bluff overlooking the ocean; the breezes are strong and the views are spectacular. The beach is a good walk from the hotel and the water here is much rougher, with a stronger undertow – not an ideal choice. There is, however, a children's playground, plus a tennis court and a game room with billiards and ping-pong. The pool here is just long enough for doing laps, but has only a few sunning chairs. The best feature is that all 43 rooms have wonderful ocean views and many have balconies as well.

Second Alternative: **HOTEL MIRAMAR**

Le Malecón, Salinas, phone (2) 772596

Rates: $40/$60 S/D incl. tax. All major credit cards are accepted.

Directions: In the heart of Salinas on the main beach road.

Those who prefer being in the thick of things or who are without a car should check the Miramar, which is more expensive and rated as the city's top hotel. For some people the lively atmosphere is a drawing card; for others it's a detraction. Regardless, the service suffers from the constant activity. The pool here is particularly nice, with lots of sunning chairs and surrounded by greenery; the city's public beach is just across the street and often very crowded. Most of the guest rooms have air conditioning and some higher up in this four-story structure have balconies.

ALANDALUZ
Puerto Rico-Puerto López
Pto López phone (4) 604-173
Quito phone (2) 450-992
Category: B
Rustic, beachfront hostel with ecological focus, 8 rooms, 2 cabins, camping, beach, restaurant, bar, volleyball, horseback riding, excursions.
Rates: $12-$14 per person incl. 3 meals & taxes. No credit cards are accepted.
Directions: The complex is just south of Puerto Rico, which is mid-way between Salinas and Jipijapa (85 km north of Salinas, 31 km north of Manglaralto, 12 km south of Puerto López, and 78 km southwest of Jipijapa). The nearest airports are at Manta and Portoviejo, to which there are flights on small planes from Avióneta Terminal at Guayaquil airport and daily flights on TAME from Quito. There are frequent buses from Guayaquil, Manta and Portoviejo to Jipijapa, where you can catch a local CITM bus to the hotel. They follow the Jipijapa-Libertad/Salinas coastal route, leaving in either direction every 45 minutes. From Jipijapa, they reach Puerto Rico and the Alandaluz, which is 50 meters off the highway, about 1½ hours later. From Libertad, the trip is slightly longer. Alternatively, hire a taxi; from Manta or Portoviejo they cost about $25.

Built in 1990, this unique French-run "ecological tourist center" is located on one of Ecuador's least developed beaches. It has been described as a bamboo palace. Set among flowers and organic gardens, the creatively constructed complex is made entirely of natural materials and decorated with abundant plants and shell mobiles. The center is unique in South America in that it's dedicated to exploring ecologically viable strategies for living, including organic agriculture and appropriate technology. For entertainment, guests can enjoy the center's secluded beach, volleyball or horseback riding. Alternatively, they can join one of the tours to either a pre-Incan museum, the small islands off the coast, or to nearby Machalillo Park, which has lovely beaches and is an excellent spot for bird watching.

Due to the convergence offshore of two ocean currents, the area enjoys a rare climate that's pleasantly cooler than that of other lowland regions and is also quite dry. For these reasons too, a wide variety of fruits, vegetables and flowers can be cultivated here. All the center's organically-grown produce is for guests and staff consumption.

Entering the breezy central thatched-roof building one comes into a popular communal eating area. The beach side has numerous hammocks, while the inland side has a fireplace. In the cooler season, nightly after-dinner fires are a feature of this area. Set menus are served at fixed hours; they are a combination of creative vegetarian dishes, fish or poultry. Seafood and pineapple pizzas are a specialty, as are the home-grown salads and home-baked bread and cookies.

Architecturally, the construction of the center is delightful – children love the loft rooms! Units sleeping two to five persons are rustic and offer views of the ocean or the gardens; washrooms with "ecological latrines" are set apart. There are also areas for camping. Due to the many steps and sandy paths, the Alandaluz is not suitable for the disabled.

***Alternative:* RINCON DE AMIGOS**

Montañita

Rates: $2 per person.

Directions: 67 km north of Salinas, 3 km north of Manglaralto, and 28 km before (south of) Alandaluz. Look for the hotel's sign as you head north beyond Montañita.

The best surfing in Ecuador is at Montañita, so young surfers from Guayaquil head here on weekends year round. Most of them camp or stay at the Rincón de Amigos, an extremely basic place right on the beach. The accommodations are nothing more than very simple bamboo cabins; the best ones face the ocean and have patios with hammocks.

What really makes this place special are the owners; Ned, a friendly Irish chap, and Gabriela, his Ecuadorian wife. They serve delicious meals in a breezy open-air restaurant on the sand, and there's always music playing and someone interesting to chat to at the bar.

This surfing hangout is a haven for Peace Corps volunteers as well; they come mainly for the good times and relaxing ambience. For the young at heart, this is the hippest place on the Ecuadorian coast. It's still not overflowing with visitors because the surfing waves are what's special, not the beach.

Esmeraldas & Atacames-Same

CLUB CASABLANCA
Vía Atacames-Same
Phone (2) 713-298
Quito phone (2) 554-933/4, or 235-110 (Wagon-Lits)
Quito fax (2) 554-933
Category: Deluxe
Beach, 38 rooms, pool, fishing, racketball, jet skis, scuba, sailboards, horseback riding, tennis, billiards.
Rates: $55-$76 per room incl. tax. Reservations required. Major credit cards.
Directions: At Same beach, 42 km west of Esmeraldas, (17 km beyond Atacames).

The only deluxe hotel along the northern coast is the Casablanca, which opened in 1989 and is about a $15 taxi ride from Esmeraldas airport. It's a private club open only to members, but foreign travelers and diplomats are also readily accepted. Advance reservations are required; you cannot simply show up at the door. This white Moorish-style complex, which sprawls over a wide area along a secluded beach outside Same (SAH-may) village, is quite attractive architecturally. As you approach the Casablanca from the highway you'll see a series of connecting domed structures surrounded by white sand and palm trees; the atmosphere is that of a north African village in an oasis.

Those athletically inclined take note: the sports facilities here are unequaled anywhere else in the country. The club's four tennis courts (two of clay) are of tournament quality and are located away from the ocean and behind the buildings so as to reduce the effect of the ocean breeze. Guests can also go water skiing, jet skiing, sailboarding, offshore fishing, horseback riding and snorkeling. And since volleyball is the national sport, there's a court for that and, as if that weren't enough, two racketball courts to boot. Those less sports-oriented can lie or walk on the Casablanca's beautiful private beach, which extends for miles. Many guests choose to hang around the long pool, which is in the center of the complex and surrounded by sunning chairs, with a popular bar to the side. Children usually head for the game room, which offers billiards and ping-pong tables. Meals here are quite good, but a little expensive by Ecuadorian standards. Their *parrillada* (grilled meat buffet-style), for example, is excellent, but costs about $10 a person.

About half of the guest rooms face the ocean. The standard accommodations are quite attractive and breezy, but a bit small and underfurnished. They have overhead fans, minibars, terra-cotta floor tiles, white plaster walls, modern baths, and patios with lounge chairs. They do not have TVs, telephones or reading chairs. There are also some larger two-story suites with two or more bedrooms.

HOSTERIA LA PRADERA
Vía Atacames, Esmeraldas, phone (2) 712-946, 714-031, telex 27550, Quito phone (2) 240-853, 245-816
Category: A. Modern, 66 rooms, pool, volleyball, tennis, restaurant.
Rates: $17/$22 room/cabin incl. tax. All major credit cards.
Directions: On the northern outskirts of Esmeraldas, just off the Atacames Highway and 7½ km from the city center.

Esmeraldas is not a city anyone would choose just to visit; beach lovers, for example, all head northwest to Atacames (25 km) or slightly further to Same. However, if you must stay in Esmeraldas and you're looking for the best hotel in town, check in at La Pradera. It's a modern single-story establishment just off the road with some excellent sports facilities, including a competitive-length pool, a tennis court in good condition, a soccer field and a volleyball court. Unfortunately, however, the beach is a good ways away.

The rooms, which are of modest size, have air conditioning, tile floors, comfortable beds, and modern tile bathrooms with showers. Unfortunately, they lack telephones, reading chairs and carpets. The cabins, of which there are several sizes, are better. Those that sleep four people have two air-conditioned bedrooms with baths, plus a living area with an overhead fan, sofas and matching chairs. The atmosphere throughout this place, however, is a bit sterile, which is why the only foreigners staying here are usually on business.

Alternative: **APART-HOTEL ESMERALDAS**
Avenida de la Libertad 407 y Ramon Tello, Esmeraldas, phone (2) 713-713

If you're looking just for a room in Esmeraldas and don't care about having a host of amenities, try the Apart-Hotel instead. It's closer to the center of town than La Pradera and has a good restaurant. It also offers better-quality rooms that feature air conditioning, TVs and minibars. The cost of staying here is slightly less than the Pradera.

CABANAS EL ACANTILADO
Vía Atacames-Same
Quito phone (2) 235-034.
Category: B
Beachfront, rustic, 14 rooms, 30 cabins, restaurant.
Rates: $10/$14 rooms/cabins incl. tax, more in peak season (Dec-Mar and July-Sept). Diners Club card is accepted.
Directions: Just beyond Same near the Casablanca. Take Esmeraldas-Same bus.

For an inexpensive, relaxing beach vacation with a cottage of your own, it's hard to beat the Acantilado. The young and friendly Ecuadorian couple who run this place help give it a special laid-back atmosphere. The English-speaking husband is an artist and will gladly show you his work. The complex is on a bluff overlooking the ocean, with flowers everywhere. You can walk down an easy path to the beach, which is narrow but sandy and safe. It has virtually no undertow and, unlike Atacames beach (where no hotels are recommended), few reported muggings.

The owners run an excellent restaurant, which is the only public facility here and a good place to get to know the owners and other guests. Seafood selections dominate the menu and most are in the $2.50-$3 range, with grilled freshwater shrimp at $4 being the most expensive. The larger cabins have kitchenettes with stoves, refrigerators and lots of utensils, so cooking yourself is possible. The cheapest units are the rooms, but the nicest by far are the cabins. The latter have comfortable beds, fans, picnic-style tables with benches, refrigerators, private decks overlooking the ocean with chairs and hammocks, private baths with cold-water showers, and fresh linens. All in all, this place is a delightful rustic retreat and quite secluded to boot. Call in advance, as it's often full on weekends, especially during the winter months, which is the high season here.

Alternative: **CENTRO TURISTICO MANILA**
Same beach, Quito phone (2) 554-933/235-110 (Wagon-Lits Tourismo)
Rates: $20 per cabin incl. tax, less during the off-season.
Directions: At Same beach, 17 km beyond Atacames.

If the Acantilado is full, try the Manila, which is in Same, not far away. It's run by two Italian families and the restaurant is noted for its fine cuisine, which is mostly Italian. The complex consists of eight separate cabins set right on the beach, each with one double bed, two single beds, and a decent bathroom with a cold shower and a flush toilet. The beach here is long and, except for several other cabana hotels nearby, relatively deserted.

Santo Domingo

HOTEL ZARACAY
Vía Quito Km 1.5
Phone (2) 750-023/316
Fax (2) 754-875
Category: A
Thatched-roof, multi-unit hotel with gardens, 50 rooms, pool, casino, tennis.
Rates: $18/$27 S/D incl. tax. All major credit cards.
Directions: On the eastern outskirts of town on the highway to Quito.

The city's top hotel is the Zaracay, an attractive place consisting of a series of white cement, thatched-roof structures covered with flowering vines. The setting – a large shady lawn with numerous palm trees and flowers everywhere – is also quite nice.

The most inviting area is the main restaurant, which is an open-air, thatched-roof building with tile flooring, lots of ferns hanging from the rafters, bamboo walls, tables, and comfortable armchairs. Breakfast is served in a separate cafeteria; its decor, however, is plain and boring. Further back you'll find a pool just long enough for doing laps, sunning chairs, and a poorly-maintained cement tennis court in barely playable condition. At night, most of the action centers around the hotel's casino, which features roulette and other games.

The accommodations are fine and almost standard size, with fans, color TVs, piped-in music, twin beds with good mattresses, bare tile floors, comfortable cane armchairs, glass-top breakfast tables, large closets, desks, and modern tile bathrooms with showers. As the hotel is often full, especially on weekends, advance reservations are advisable.

First Alternative: **HOTEL TINALANDIA**
Vía Quito Km 16.5
Rates: $40/$75 S/D with tax and all meals. All major credit cards are accepted.
Directions: Coming from Santo Domingo and heading inland towards Quito, you'll find a tiny, easily-missed sign at Km 16.5 pointing down a dirt road to your right that leads to the hotel.

The well-known Tinalandia is renowned as being one of the best places in Ecuador for bird watching. The variety is impressive; over 150 species have been recorded here. Consequently, most of the guests are foreign bird watchers; indeed, very few of them come to Ecuador without spending at least a few days here. On weekends, the Tinalandia's private golf course, which overlooks the Toachi Valley, attracts golfers from Quito and elsewhere.

Doña Tina, the friendly lady who runs this small, comfortable place, has an interesting background. She's a former Russian countess who had to flee France in the 1930's with her husband who had killed a rival in a duel. The French government awarded them this estate, where she has lived ever since. Today, the place is a bit run-down, but the bungalows are still quite decent (though hardly luxurious) and have private baths. In addition, Doña Tina continues to serve the best home-style meals around.

Second Alternative: **HOSTERIA LA HACIENDA**
Vía Esmeraldas Km 13
Rates: $18/$26 S/D incl. tax. All major credit cards are accepted.
Directions: On the Santo Domingo-Esmeraldas Highway, 13 km from Santo Domingo.

If you don't mind being 13 km from Santo Domingo, an excellent choice would be the 20-room Hacienda. The accommodations are very clean and comfortable, and the private baths have lots of hot water. There's also a pool and a small zoo.

Even if you don't stay here, consider stopping for a meal, as the restaurant here is superb. The shrimp ceviche comes in an ice cream soda glass and is chock-full of tiny tasty shrimp and lots of pepper. Their steak and shrimp brochettes and lunch-time salad bar, which has lots of cooked vegetables but no greens, are also tasty.

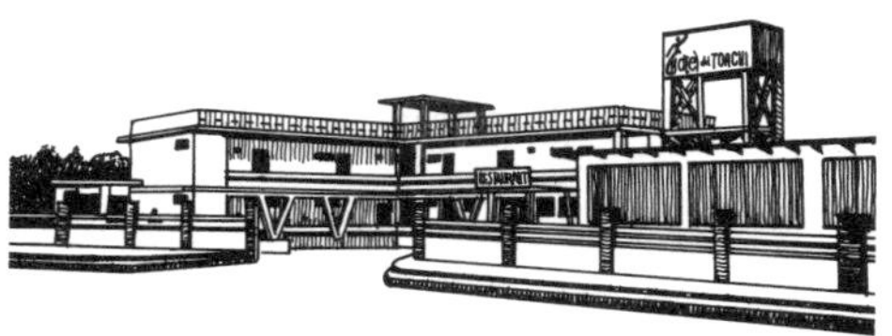

HOTEL DEL TOACHI
Vía Quito Km 1.2
Phone (2) 754-688 to 90
Category: B
Modern motel, 35 rooms, pool, restaurant.
Rates: $8/$11 S/D incl. tax. All major credit cards.
Directions: On the same road as the Zaracay, 300 meters closer to center.

If all you care about is having a room or pool, the less expensive Toachi, just down the road from the Zaracay, would be a good choice. It's an ordinary-looking three-story motel with a sizeable pool in back; the water is often slightly greenish, but in general it seems clean enough for swimming. There's a surprisingly decent and inviting restaurant with tile flooring, attractive tables, and comfortable armchairs.

The accommodations, which are plain, spartan and of modest size, have comfortable beds, but no fans or air conditioning. They have linoleum flooring, telephones, rental TVs, desks, and unadorned walls. The private tile bathrooms are small and a bit run-down, but the facilities, which include hot-water showers, are in good working order.

First Alternative: **HOTEL LA SIESTA**
Avenida Quito 606 y Guayaquil, phone (2) 751-860/751-013
Rates: $5/$9 S/D incl. tax; credit cards are not accepted.
Directions: About half-way between the Toachi and the central plaza, which is a 10-minute walk away.

If the Toachi is full or you'd rather be closer to the center, try the Siesta. It's a single-story motel with a reasonably attractive exterior and a fairly good restaurant; the accommodations, however, are quite plain.

Second Alternative: **HOSTAL EJECUTIVO**
Avenida 29 de Mayo 520 y Latacunga, phone (2) 751-943
Rates: $1.50/$3.00 S/D incl. tax; credit cards are not accepted.
Directions: 3½ blocks from the central plaza on the main drag (29 de Mayo) through town.

For a cheaper category C hotel, try the Ejecutivo, which is nothing special, but probably the best in its class. It's a modern four-story hotel with a presentable lobby, small clean rooms, and private tile bathrooms with cold-water showers. Ask for an inside unit; they are not as noisy.

Amazon Basin Region

Coca & Misahualli

LA SELVA
90 km downriver from Coca
Quito: Ave 6 de Diciembre 2816
Quito phone (2) 550-995; fax (2) 567-297
Category: Deluxe

Rustic lodge with 16 cabins, restaurant, bar, observation tower, excursions, generator.

Rates: $465 per person incl. Quito-Coca air fare in 3-night/4-day all-inclusive package. $110/person each day extra. Resident rate is 50% less. All major credit cards are accepted.

Directions: 3 hours down the Napo River in the hotel's motorized canoe from Coca, which is a 30-minute flight from Quito.

The country's most luxurious jungle hotel is unquestionably La Selva, which won the world's highest ecotourism award in 1992 and has been described by *Playboy Magazine* as "the Holy Grail of resorts for anyone seeking the ultimate jungle experience." Beautifully situated on a lake the color of root beer in the thick of the Amazon rainforests, this brainchild of Eric Schwartz, the American owner, features a 34-meter observation tower. There is also a butterfly farm; one of the more intriguing species is a completely transparent butterfly.

The lodge itself consists of two large, stilted thatched-roof buildings made from palm parts, plus 16 cozy similarly-constructed cabins. The latter have bedrooms with two single beds, private baths with cold showers, and shady porches with rattan lounge chairs. Kerosene lanterns and mosquito nets are provided (although you may notice remarkably few mosquitoes). The setting is incredibly beautiful, complete with Tarzan vines and terrific swimming spots. The dining room and bar, which are candle-lit at night, offer good views of the lake, and the buffet-style breakfasts and dinners are remarkably good, especially the desserts, warm homemade bread, and locally made jams.

Because the lodge is buried so deeply in the jungle, you'll see a much greater variety of fauna in this area than in the region downriver of

Misahualli, where most other jungle hotels are located. This alone is reason enough to bite the bullet and pay the much higher price. La Selva's most prized assets are its guides, such as José, who are natives of the area and can identify virtually every animal and plant in these forests. For bird watchers in particular, these guides are invaluable as they can spot birds among the profusion of plant life that would otherwise be missed – even by experts. They have also helped establish some outstanding wildlife-sighting records here. Birds you are likely to see include macaws, screaming pihas, nunbirds, piping guans, horned screamers, hoatzins, black-capped donacobius, greater anis, tiger herons, cinnamon attilas, and multi-banded aracari.

Every morning, afternoon and night, trekking-canoe excursions are offered to guests. There is also a special week-long program called the Light Brigade, which provides the opportunity of getting even deeper into the rainforests. Each afternoon after walking through the forests, trekkers arrive at a new campsite where tents, food on the fire and cold drinks await them. In addition, you can improvise your own excursions, either by foot or in a canoe. If you bring your own camping gear, you can paddle a canoe downriver and camp on an island. One of the hotel's motorized boats can be reserved to pick you up the next morning. In short, you can make your visit as adventurous or as relaxing as you desire.

Part of the adventure is simply returning to civilization. To catch the morning flight back to Quito, guests must leave around 3 a.m. The whole trip involves several hours of travel in the pitch-black dark, beginning with a peaceful 15-minute canoe trip across Garzacocha (Heron Lake) and hiking almost a km through the forests to get to the Napo. The next stage is a four-hour upriver trip on a seven-meter motorized dugout canoe. In sum, every aspect of a visit to La Selva is memorable, so save your money and splurge on a trip here.

Alternative: IMUYA CAMP

Cuyabena Natural Preserve, Quito phone (2) 464-780, Quito fax (2) 464-702 (Metropolitan Touring)
Rates: $600 per person for 4 nights all-inclusive (meals, air fare, park fee, tax); all major credit cards are accepted.
Directions: Access is by small charter plane.

If you want real adventure, going even deeper into the Amazon rainforests, consider Imuya Camp, which is in the Cuyabena Natural Preserve near the Colombian border. You cannot get any further into the forests than this. Run by Metropolitan Touring and hardly luxurious, the lodge here is much more basic and smaller, with 10 double rooms and shared baths. Most of the touring is done by canoe, which is a quieter and thus better way to spot animals and birds. However, there are also walking treks through the rainforests, including ones at night, looking for caiman. They can be easily spotted by their eyes which glow from the reflection of a flashlight).

LA CASA DEL SUIZO
11 km downstream of Misahualli
Quito phone (2) 544-600 (Hotel Quito travel agency)
Category: A
Swiss-run lodge, 10 cabins, restaurant, bar, excursions.
Rates: $56/$88 S/D incl. tax, 3 meals and tours. Prior payment is required in Quito. All major credit cards accepted.

Directions: From Tena (a 5-hour drive from Quito) continue 5 km south on the Puyo road to Puerto Napo and cross the Napo River, then take your first left after the bridge and continue 25 km eastward along the river's southern bank to the Cabañas Alinahui and, 2 km further, to a ferry spot called La Punta. Here, you'll be met by the hotel's canoe. It's a 3-km/10-minute trip downstream to Ahuano, which is on the river's northern bank and is where you can find the hotel.

If you're using public transportation, take the two-hour Tena-Ahuano bus in Tena and ask to be dropped off at La Punta. Alternatively, you could take a collectivo (community bus) from Tena or Puerto Napo eastward to Misahualli, which is accessible via a road along the river's northern bank starting at Pt. Napo (17 km), and take a canoe from there. The river trip from Misahualli is longer (11 km/45 minutes), but not too much more expensive if you take a public canoe. There are, however, only one or two a day to Ahuano and chartering one (typically $30) can be quite expensive.

The friendliest of the jungle lodges in the Misahualli area is the Casa del Suizo. If you're in luck, you'll be there when the affable Swiss owner is around. He's very conservation-minded and has started a small animal sanctuary here. If you're interested in the area's ecology, he's the man to talk to. He's knowledgeable about the animals and the rainforests, and has a head full of other interesting bits of information as well.

Besides its pleasant ambience and ecological focus, the lodge has a number of other good features. The best is that you can sit on your porch (or in the hotel's public areas) and view the river, a feature none of the other lodges along the Napo have. In addition, the meals here are slightly better and the mosquitoes seem less bothersome. It's also the only jungle hotel with electricity (until 10 p.m.), but for those seeking a wilderness experience this is not necessarily a plus. This thatched-roof complex is quite attractive, with a number of buildings, including several cabins. These are set up the hill and connected to the main buildings by a wooden walkaway.

What you'll remember most about the Casa del Suizo is one of their truly unique jungle trips. After breakfast you'll go by canoe up the Napo to Pusuno, where you'll start a five-hour jungle hike, crossing small rivers and hiking up and down hills, ending back at the Napo. Shortly thereafter, a canoe will pull up with your lunch and about six balsa logs. Having eaten, you and the other guests will build a raft with these logs and float for an hour down the Napo back to the lodge. Believe me, riding down the river at the equator on a raft held together with six logs and holding about eight people is something never to forget. Even though the current is strong, you can slide off the raft and float along at the same pace for as long as you want. It's as good as anything Huckleberry Finn could have experienced!

CABANAS ALINAHUI
8 km downstream of Misahualli
Quito: Ave. Eloy Alfaro 28-54
Quito phone (2) 448-439
Category: A
Rustic lodge, 6 cabins, restaurant, bar, excursions.
Rates: $59/$118 S/D incl. tax, 3 meals and tours. Prior payment in Quito. Most major credit cards are accepted.
Directions: See directions for La Casa del Suizo. Accessible by car, the lodge is 2 km before La Punta, on the same river bank. Travelers without cars have the same options as those given for the Suizo.

Some three km closer to Misahualli is the Alinahui, which adjoins a cattle ranch and has been a jungle resort since the mid-1980's. It's the only lodge in this area that is directly accessible by car – a big advantage for those with vehicles. The attractive complex has a spacious shady lawn, six thatched-roof cabins on stilts, each with two bedrooms and four single beds, plus a main lodge on stilts. The dark wooden cabins are fairly attractive and have screened windows and private baths. The English-speaking couple who run this place are friendly and the meals they provide are quite adequate. Margarita, the Cuban manager, has collected orchids from the surrounding area and grows them here, while Peter

Schenkel, her German husband, has collected and, unfortunately, caged a few jungle animals, mostly monkeys.

One complaint occasionally heard of the Alinahui is that the service, which is usually okay, often suffers on weekends when the hotel is full. So coming during the week or bringing snacks and drinks (in case they run out) may be a good idea. Another complaint is that you cannot see the river from any of the buildings; you must take a short walk to the edge of the nearby bluff or down to the river itself, which is just below. In other respects, however, the Alinahui is quite good. Moreover, they provide a full range of excursions, including walks through the rainforests with Spanish-speaking guides, gold panning with the natives, horseback riding, and visits to traditional healers and local artisans. As on all trips in this area, you'll see few animals on your walks, but the flora can be fascinating and, if you go far enough away from the river, about as diverse as that around La Selva.

***Alternative:* HOTEL JAGUAR**
25 km (1½ hours) downstream of Misahualli, Quito phone (2) 239-400/237-726 (Calle Ramírez Dávalos 653 y Versalles)
Rates: $16/$32 S/D (double this at the expatriate rate) incl. tax & 3 meals. Credit cards are not accepted and their exchange rate for US dollars is poor so bring sucres.

If money is your major concern, try the older 10-room Jaguar, which is geared to Ecuadorians and definitely inferior, but not bad for the money. Indeed, the cheapest way by far is simply to show up at their door and, without even asking, they'll probably charge you the resident rate (which is half that for foreigners). It's not quite as attractive as the others and the meals are poorer (soup, rice and potatoes, fried chicken, fruit), but the staff is friendly. Their jungle tours are similar to those of other hotels and the views of the river from the main building (not the guest rooms), which sits on a cliff above the river, are almost as good as those from the Suizo. There's also a generator that produces just enough electricity to power lights for the restaurant and bar. A major problem is that the only public canoes which go this far downriver leave at 11 a.m. and chartering one costs $30. Getting here, however, is half the fun.

EL PAISANO
Misahualli, Quito phone (2) 522-220 (Explorer Tours at Lizardo García 613 y Reina Victoria)
Category: C. Rustic, 10 rooms, restaurant.
Rates: $2/$4 S/D incl. tax. No credit cards.
Directions: 1 block north of the main plaza.

The cheapest way to explore the Amazon basin is to go to Misahualli and arrange treks from there, avoiding the jungle lodges altogether. Since 1983 when it opened, the best place to stay and eat in Misahualli (pop. 1,000) has been the friendly Paisano, which has 10 very spartan but clean rooms with screens, hammocks outside in the garden, and clean shared bathrooms. Their relaxing open-air restaurant with long wooden tables serves vegetarian cuisine, and their breakfasts are outstanding, especially the banana pancakes. If this popular meeting place is full, try José and Cristina's newer establishment, **EL ALBERGUE ESPANOL**. It is nearby and slightly more expensive than the Paisano. The guest rooms have private baths and there are a few large family rooms that sleep six.

Either place can serve as your base camp for planning one-day to all-week trips into the rainforests and hooking up with other travelers to share costs. Travel agencies that arrange such trips are located all over town. However, a bad guide, of which there are many, is guaranteed to turn your adventure into a nightmare. So be smart and, before coming here, drop by the South American Explorers Club in Quito at Calle Toledo 1254 (phone 2-566-076); they have all the information you'll ever need, including a list of recommended guides. Become a member while you're at it; membership costs only $30 and offers many benefits, including use of the clubhouse and library.

The Galapagos Islands

HOTEL GALAPAGOS
Puerto Ayora, Isla Santa Cruz
Quito phone (2) 464-780 (Metropolitan Touring)
Quito fax (2) 464-702 (Same)
Category: A
Waterfront, modern, 14 rooms, restaurant, bar, laundry.
Rates: $46/$79 S/D incl. tax (30% off for residents). MasterCard, travelers checks.
Directions: On the eastern edge of Pt Ayora, Santa Cruz, a 10-minute walk from center, near Darwin Research Center.

The great majority of visitors to the Galapagos tour the islands by boat and use the boat for their accommodations. If you choose instead to stay at a hotel and take day trips, Hotel Galapagos is by far the best place to book a room. In operation since 1961, it was for many years the only hotel in the Galapagos. Built by the present owner, Jack Nelson, and his father, it's the only American-run hotel in Ecuador. Not surprisingly, about 40% of the clientele here is American. Jack and his wife, who are extremely friendly, have done a superb job in creating a welcoming ambience. The bar, for instance, is self-service (if no one is around) and based on the honor system. The meals, which are quite good and feature produce from the hotel's farm, are all served family-style and at set times and prices – $6 for lunch and $9 for dinner.

A great place to spend time is the main living area, which has a very breezy laid-back atmosphere – reed mats covering the floors, leather chairs from Cuenca, a large colorful batik with a fish theme behind the bar, lights set in driftwood, hammocks, the remains of a sperm whale hanging from the ceiling, maps of the island and interesting paintings on the walls, classical music playing in the background, plants here and there, a sunken sitting area with a chessboard, lots of English-language magazines and books, and a long glass wall for viewing the harbor, which is less than 50 meters away.

You'll find lots of greenery surrounding the main building, which helps hide the fact that it's a rather plain, uninteresting structure. Most important, the hotel boasts its own water system and emergency electrical generator, something almost none of the town's other establishments offer. As a result, the hot water supply, while not overly abundant, is at least reliable, and there's always fresh drinking water in the guest rooms. The accommodations consist of various bungalows spaced over five acres of natural garden overlooking Academy Bay. They have standard size rooms with reed mats covering the floors, comfortable beds, closets, local paintings and tapestries on the walls, tile bathrooms with showers, and windows that face the harbor and catch the ocean breeze. In short, this inn has all the makings of a delightful retreat, and if you ask Jack or his wife, they can arrange for sailing, snorkeling, scuba diving, horseback trips into the highlands and the tortoise reserve, or day trips to other islands.

***First Alternative:* HOTEL DELFIN**

Puerto Ayora, Isla Santa Cruz, Quito phone (2) 464-780 (Metropolitan Touring), Quito fax (2) 464-702 (Same).

Rates: $39/$53 S/D incl. tax; MasterCard and travelers checks are accepted.

Directions: On the outskirts of Puerto Ayora, at the opposite side of the port from Hotel Galapagos. You must take a 200-meter ride by boat from the city dock to get there.

If Hotel Galapagos is full, your best alternative is the Delfín. Built in 1977, the Delfín is owned by a German family, the Sievers, who have lived here since the 1960's and also operate the 10-person yacht, *The*

Beagle. The hotel, which is rather isolated from town and can only be reached by boat, is located in a mangrove swamp and consists of several wooden structures connected by an elevated wooden walkway. The architecture is much more striking than that of the Hotel Galapagos, but the Delfín lacks the latter's warm ambience. The main lounge is a large modern room with high ceilings, wooden floors, and several reasonably comfortable sitting areas. It's attractive enough, but the atmosphere is a bit cold and not particularly relaxing. The same is true of the restaurant. It is housed in an interesting circular building with windows all around, but it has linoleum flooring and plain furniture. Similarly, the 16 guest rooms, which have fans, twin single beds, carpets, and bathrooms with cold-water showers, are fine, but nothing special.

Second Alternative: **HOTEL LAS NINFAS**
Puerto Ayora, Isla Santa Cruz, Guayaquil phone (4) 321-756 (Ninfas Tour)
Rates: \$13/\$20 S/D incl. tax. Visa and MasterCard are accepted.
Directions: In the heart of town, 1 block north of the city dock.

For cheaper accommodations, try Las Ninfas. It's a popular place that is conveniently located, with a garden, a good restaurant, and 24 guest rooms. There are fans and cold-water showers. The hotel also has its own boat and charges very reasonable rates for day trips.

Third Alternative: **RESIDENCIA LOS AMIGOS**
Avenida Darwin, Puerto Ayora, Isla Santa Cruz
Rates: \$5/\$10 S/D incl. tax. Credit cards are not accepted.
Directions: 3 blocks east of the city dock, next to the TAME office on the main drag.

For cheaper accommodations still, try the Amigos, which is also conveniently located in town. Run by Sra. Rosa Rosera, this small, friendly establishment has large breezy rooms with shared baths, laundry facilities, and a homey ambience.

Peru

Few countries in the world can match Peru in terms of historical and cultural diversity and, certainly in South America, it is unbeatable in this respect. Peru is where the most famous Indian group in South America, the Incas, established their stronghold. Less appreciated, perhaps, is the fact that there were a number of other extremely important Indian groups here that predated the Incas by many centuries, including the Moche, the Chimu, the Chavin, and the Nazca. Today, travelers to Peru can see evidence of all of these civilizations: the Inca in and around Cuzco, including Machu Picchu; the Moche and the Chimu in the north around Trujillo and particularly at Chan-Chan; the Chavin south of Huaraz, and the Nazca in the south around Nazca.

Peru is a land of contrast. Virtually the entire coast of the country is sand desert, a freak of nature caused by the Humboldt Current, which runs northward from Antarctica along the South American coast. Two of the country's major cities are close to the coast, including Lima in the middle and Trujillo in the north. Because of this cold current, the rains that would otherwise fall on the coastal area, fall not far away in the sea. That is why Lima is covered with dreary gray clouds from April through December, but receives virtually no rain. When it does rain in Lima it's front-page news. It causes major damage to buildings which, for the most part, aren't constructed to withstand the rain.

Downtown Lima has deteriorated so much in recent years that most travelers stay in Miraflores, one of the city's ritzy suburbs. There is more going on there at night than in downtown Lima which, like central areas of many other cities worldwide these days, has a reputation for thieves. Lima remains, however, a vibrant, interesting city, with numerous museums, an opera house (the season is September), wonderful restaurants (mostly in Miraflores), and bars (most notably in Barranco), where local musicians perform.

Several hours south of Lima along the desert coast you'll come to Paracas, which is most famous for the Ballestas Islands offshore, often referred to as the "Poor Man's Galapagos." Thousands of sea birds flock to the mammoth rocks there and, as a result, you can see an amazing number of sea birds in a small area. Nearby in Pisco and, further south in Ica, is the country's wine producing area; the dry climate is perfect for growing grapes. Try a bottle of Tacama or Ocucaje, the two major brands. Still further south is Nazca, where the mysterious centuries-old Nazca lines can be seen. The best views of these enormous lines that stretch for miles are gained from one of the small aircraft that flies over them. Further south still, at the foot of volcano El Misti, is Arequipa, certainly the cleanest city in Peru and the country's second largest. Its year-round, spring-time weather makes it a favorite with travelers.

As you proceed inland, you'll soon be in the Andes. The highest and most famous range, Cordillera Blanca, is second in height only to the Himalayas. It is in the area around Huaraz, which is a day's drive north of Lima and a Mecca for mountain climbers and trekkers. Still further inland is the country's major attraction for travelers – Cuzco and the famous Incan ruins at Machu Picchu nearby. Cuzco is a marvelous town and small enough to cover on foot; a trip to Peru without going there is almost unthinkable. The valley, which extends from Cuzco towards Machu Picchu, is known as the Sacred Valley of the Incas. It is a wonderful place for trekking and has several famous Indian markets as well as Incan ruins. You can easily spend weeks in the region around Cuzco and never run out of things to do. A day's train ride south of Cuzco brings you to Puno, which borders Lake Titicaca, the world's highest navigable lake. This is also the coldest area in Peru; the average temperature in Puno is 47°F. Travelers can take a boat to one of the islands in the lake and stay overnight with Indian families, then head overland or by steamer to Bolivia.

For birdwatchers, the biggest draw is clearly the Amazon Basin. The rainforests around Puerto Maldonado, which is east of Cuzco by plane, are by far the most impressive, notably Manu Park and the smaller

Tambopata Wildlife Reserve. These two parks are preserving the most pristine rainforest areas in the world, so it's no wonder that the variety of bird life is truly incomparable. Both are set up to receive visitors and, while getting to them is not cheap, a trip to either one would be unforgettable. Finally, there's Iquitos, the largest city in Peru on the Amazon River. From there on down, the river is enormous. The whole region is well prepared for receiving visitors and provides a unique opportunity for adventure travel in this country.

Lima

GRAN HOTEL BOLIVAR
Lima-downtown
Plaza San Martín
Phone (14) 27-6400/45-7743
Fax (14) 33-8626
Telex 25201
Category: Deluxe
Elegant, Lima's grande dame, downtown, 300 rooms, sauna, newsstand, barbershop.
Rates: $74/$86 incl. 23% tax, children up to 10 free. All major credit cards.
Directions: In the heart of old Lima overlooking Plaza San Martín.

With the exception of some truly magnificent hotels in Buenos Aires, the Gran Hotel Bolívar is in a league of its own among hotels in South America's capital cities. None can match this aging beauty, Lima's grande dame, in evoking the spirit of the old world. The entrance lobby is spectacular – 20-foot ceilings with deep recessed panels, marble floors, a huge chandelier, two old-style elevators in brass, wood and glass, and a formal staircase with blue and gold carpeting leading to the mezzanine.

Even more impressive, however, is the adjoining Rotunda, a 50-foot-diameter room lined by Greek columns and glass chandeliers, with a piano in the middle. Afternoon tea here is a long-standing tradition, not to be missed even if you stay elsewhere. From one of the many elegant sitting areas with antique furnishings you can gaze up at the massive, floral-design, stained-glass dome and wonder whether you're not really in Europe.

At the rear of the Rotunda you will find the reading room, another spacious, two-story area with panelled ceiling, square fluted columns, antique furnishings, old rugs, a glass chandelier in the center, and a large fireplace with an oil portrait just above. During tea time, classical and pop tunes from the Rotunda fill this otherwise tranquil area.

There are two dining areas to choose from. The most popular at lunch time is the **Bar Inglés**, an English-style grill. The fare here, mostly English, is standard and very reasonably priced. Their pisco sours are reputedly the best in town. At night, the posh, modern and much more expensive **Bar Bolívar** comes alive, especially when there's a *show folklorico.*

When reserving a room, ask for one on the third or fourth floor. Their ceilings are higher and the furnishings, mostly antiques, are far more elegant than those on the fifth and sixth floors, which are comfortable and more modern, but smaller and less atmospheric. The massive windows, parquet floors, plush throw rugs and traditional appointments on the third and fourth floors all help to make a night here truly memorable. Moreover, you won't lack for modern conveniences such as TVs, air conditioning and first-rate bathrooms.

With all this and such reasonable prices, you'd think getting a room here would be nigh impossible. To the contrary, the Bolívar, which faces the city's main plaza, suffers greatly these days from being in the city center, a decaying area notorious for pickpockets. At night, Miraflores, the main restaurant area, is the best place to be, not the dark and seemingly deserted downtown area. Miraflores is only a 15-minute taxi ride away; still, most travelers prefer one of that suburb's modern, less exotic establishments.

MIRAFLORES CESAR'S HOTEL
Lima-Miraflores
Ave. La Paz 463
Phone (14) 44-1212
Fax (14) 44-4440
Telex 21348
Category: Deluxe
Modern highrise, downtown Miraflores, 150 rooms, pool, panoramic bar, small gym, sauna, Turkish bath.
Rates: $117/$121 S/D incl. 23% tax. Major credit cards.
Directions: In the fashionable "El Suche" area of Miraflores with lots of restaurants and shops nearby, 3 blocks off the main plaza.

Lima's leading hotel, the modern 18-floor Cesar's, has been a Miraflores "institution" from the moment it was built in the late 1970's. This posh suburb is a hive of activity. Shops, restaurants, hotels and nightclubs are everywhere, making the location, three blocks off the central plaza in Miraflores, ideal. For business people, staying at Cesar's is a mark of distinction and for some, perhaps, the sine qua non of a successful trip.

What is most appealing about Cesar's is the successful blend of its ultra-modern architecture, particularly the angular brown stucco and glass facade, with antique furnishings in the public areas. Compared to the bold and unusual exterior, the lobby and adjoining 24-hour tea room seem rather ordinary. There's some original art on the wall and the lobby, marble floored of course, is usually bustling with activity. The hotel is almost always full.

If the entrance area seems a bit cold, head for the ever-popular 18th floor bar, which is a great place to spend time. Even non-guests should stop here to take advantage of the fabulous views of Miraflores and the ocean. The museum-quality, pre-Colombian art on this floor is alone worth the trip. There's also an attractive restaurant, **La Azotea**, which has the same panoramic views, as well as a different buffet every day for lunch and dinner. The hotel's best restaurant is the posh, award-winning **El Lucumo**, which has a French-speaking maitre'd and serves superb French meals, including smoked trout, roast duck in orange sauce and crèpes suzette. Afterwards, you can have a nightcap in the plush, cozy **Bar Estación**, which has a 1912 train as part of its decor, along with etched windows and leather chairs.

The rooms here have virtually every amenity that you'd expect from a capital city's top hotel – satellite TVs, minibars, large closets, thick carpets, comfortable reading chairs, queen-size beds, scales, hair driers and marble sinks in the large white-tile bathrooms. They even have cassette players. The hotel also sports a small pool, a sauna and Turkish bath, and a health club with four exercise machines. What attracts visitors most to Cesar's is its service, which is probably tops among the city's elite hotels.

***First Alternative:* HOTEL EL CONDADO**

Calle Alcanfores 465, Miraflores, phone (14) 44-3614, fax (14) 44-1981
Rates: $92/$98-$111 S/D incl. 23% tax. All major credit cards are accepted.
Directions: One block south of Cesar's.

One of the most popular hotels in Miraflores, especially with tourists, is the 75-room Condado. It's a good choice if you like places with a warm and lively ambience. The public areas, which have an abundance of plants and plush leather chairs, exude a feeling of coziness, while the dining area and ever-popular piano bar are even more attractive and relaxing, with exposed-beam ceilings, wrought iron chandeliers, leather armchairs and carpets. There's no pool, but the Condado does have a book shop, a travel agency, and a solarium on top with sunning chairs. The rooms are large, modern and comfortable, with carpets, satellite TVs, minibars, breakfast tables, hair driers on request, and two-room, carpeted bathrooms with marble counters and combination baths. Rooms in the newer six-story section across the street all have jacuzzis.

***Second Alternative:* HOTEL MARIA ANGOLA**
Ave. La Paz 610, Miraflores, phone (14) 44-1280, fax (14) 46-2860, telex 21380
Rates: $74/$86 S/D incl. 23% tax. All major credit cards are accepted.
Directions: A block south of Cesar's.

A contemporary highrise designed by a well-known architect, the quiet, 67-room Maria Angola is in the heart of Miraflores and attracts mainly business people. It features a small pool, sauna, an English-speaking staff and **Los Faisanes**, one of the loveliest and most expensive French restaurants in town. It has an untarnished reputation and is always candle lit. Maria Angola offers 24-hour fax and telex, 24-hour room service, same-day laundry, secretarial service, and an elegant but sparse marble lobby. The luxurious and ultra-modern rooms are as nice as Cesar's, but almost a third less expensive. This hotel is, understandably, very popular with business people and corporate rates are readily offered. If personalized service is a top priority, don't fail to check this frequently overlooked gem.

***Third Alternative:* EL PUEBLO RESORT & CONVENTION HOTEL**
Km 11.2 Carretera Central, Santa Clara, phone (14) 94-1616/46-6396, telex 25402
Rates: $80/$92 S/D incl. 23% tax, $129 incl. tax for a family-size bungalow. All major credit cards are accepted.
Directions: In the sunny foothills of Santa Clara just outside Lima on the Carretera Central leading east from Lima, about 45 minutes by taxi from Lima or Miraflores. For those without wheels, there's a shuttle bus which leaves for downtown Lima three or four times daily.

If you find the gray skies of Lima simply too depressing, you may prefer El Pueblo, a unique village-like resort on the outskirts of town with 205 units and an English-speaking staff. It's a popular site for conventions and, on the weekends, attracts Peruvians, expatriates and an occasional foreign tourist because of the virtually guaranteed sunny skies of Santa Clara. Constructed in 1975 to resemble a Peruvian village, there's a main square, a bakery, a bar, a stone church (popular for marriages), stores, numerous white stone buildings with balconies and gardens everywhere. Most impressive is the array of sporting facilities which include tennis, squash and racketball courts, two bowling alleys, billiard and ping-pong tables, a large gym and sauna and, most popular, a large pool and an 18-hole golf course. If you're here with a family, you could rent one of the house-like bungalows; they sleep four to six people and have kitchens and fireplaces. You may want to avoid May and June. They are the slow months and it's slightly cloudier then.

HOTEL JOSE ANTONIO

Lima-Miraflores, Ave. 28 de Julio 398, phone (14) 45-6870/45-7743, fax (14) 46-8295
Category: A. Modern, 8 stories, 56 rooms, restaurant, bar.
Rates: $47/$54 incl. 18% tax. All major credit cards.
Directions: On a major side street 7 blocks south of the main plaza in Miraflores, a 10-minute walk therefrom.

Among the city's mid-class hotels, the one with the most sparkle and class these days is the ultra modern José Antonio, which has become increasingly popular with tourists and business people and is wooing clients away from similarly-priced competitors like the nearby Grand Hotel Miraflores. The hotel's eight-story concrete and glass exterior, lined with waving flags, is definitely impressive. The enormous glass entrance doors lead into an imposing high-ceilinged lobby, with stone floors, several intimate sitting areas and lots of potted plants, which add a bit of warmth. Rooms at the San Antonio are, at best, medium size, the lighting is not as bright as might be expected, and the eye-catching carpets are, perhaps, a little too bright blue. Otherwise, however, the furnishings are in good taste and the rooms, like the rest of the hotel, are spotless. Each has a small breakfast table with an arrangement of flowers on top, large closets, piped-in music, a free TV on request, potted plants and tile bathrooms, most with showers rather than baths. Only a few of the rooms are air conditioned, but in cloudy Lima this is not a problem for most guests.

Visitors have several choices when it comes to relaxing, including the lobby and the adjoining piano bar which is very cozy and club-like, with leather stools and heads of various wild animals decorating the walls. There is also a large salon featuring a semi-circular brick fireplace and parquet floors covered with animal skins. The bar and salon lead into the hotel's only restaurant, which is very attractive and has an eye-catching ceiling with wood moldings and a large window for viewing the tranquil residential neighborhood. All this, combined with a pleasant professional staff, make the San Antonio tops in its category.

First Alternative: HOTEL ARIOSTO

Ave. La Paz 769, Miraflores, phone (14) 44-1414/6, fax (14) 44-3955, telex 21195
Rates: $35/$45 S/D incl. tax and breakfast. All major credit cards are accepted.
Directions: Two blocks south of Cesar's on the same street.

Price-wise, the seven-story, 72-room Ariosto is a better deal than the José Antonio. Don't let the ugly, bulky and plain exterior deter you from checking it out. Inside, the hotel is quite attractive, with a warm atmosphere in the public areas. Most people gather in the large rambling lounge, which has a mixture of traditional Peruvian and modern furnishings, stone pillars, ceiling fans, brick floors with carpeting and plants everywhere. My favorite nook, however, is the central, open-air patio, which is shaded by two trees and has a number of chairs for reading and drinks, with potted plants all around. The rooms, only a few of which have air conditioning, are adequate but nothing special, with throw rugs, a single wicker or leather reading chair, telephones, TVs for rent, and tiny tile bathrooms, some with showers and others with combination baths. The hotel's amenities include a very good restaurant and bar, 24-hour room service, laundry service, a travel agency, and free parking.

Second Alternative: EL DORAL HOTEL

Ave. José Pardo 486, phone (14) 47-6305/47-3233, fax (14) 46-8344
Rates: $34/$41 S/D incl. tax. All major credit cards are accepted.
Directions: In downtown Miraflores on a principal thoroughfare next to the landmark Hotel Pardo, 3 blocks west of the central plaza.

If having a pool is important, you may prefer the 37-room Doral, which has a small pool and restaurant on top, but no other public areas except for a miniscule lobby. The rooms are all suites, but are not particularly spacious. The typical unit has a small carpeted bedroom in the rear and a tiny sitting room in front, with two reading chairs and a kitchenette. The latter has an unstocked minibar, stools and a sink, but is otherwise useless, as it lacks kitchenware. Only the top floor rooms have air conditioning.

HOSTAL BEECH

Lima-San Isidro
Calle los Libertadores 165
Phone (14) 40-5595/42-8713
Fax (14) 42-8716
Category: B
B&B, American-run, 25 rooms, garden, laundry, home-like, TV room, English spoken.
Rates: $26/$36 S/D incl. tax/breakfast (reductions after 1st night). All major credit cards.
Directions: A 20-minute ride from downtown old Lima in the heart of San Isidro, the city's most elegant residential area, and a 5-minute taxi ride from downtown Miraflores. The *hostal* is a stone's throw from the huge Camino Real Shopping Center.

In operation since 1957 and recommended by virtually every guide to South America, this tranquil hotel, run by North American Jim Plunkett, is in the heart of exclusive San Isidro and wins hands down in terms of service among Lima's many B&Bs. The Peruvian staff is amiable, English-speaking and gives you the impression of having been here since the *hostal* opened. In fine British tradition, they serve tea promptly every day at 4 p.m. (it comes with the room price).

And even if you'll be arriving late in the evening, they will hold your room if you reserve in advance and let them know your arrival hour. Without a reservation, you seriously risk being turned away, as this peaceful place is often full.

The *hostal's* exterior is plain and not remarkable but does have the redeeming feature of facing a small park. Inside, you'll feel completely at home. The multi-room sitting area resembles more that of a private house than a hotel. There are a number of comfortable chairs and sofas, throw rugs, a fireplace and an attractive stone wall, recent magazines for reading, a TV and a good view of the rear garden. That area is a good place to soak up some rays during the day, or you can sit on the adjoining veranda and enjoy the delightful green scenery. In the mornings, many guests enjoy sipping their coffee here and listening to the cooing pigeons. Alternatively, you can eat inside at the bar/restaurant, which has an attractive wood and bamboo roof and large rattan baskets for lights, as well as sofas with large cushions which are puffed-up daily. During the day you can get light snacks and drinks here, but for dinner you'll have to walk to one of the nearby restaurants or, better, head for Miraflores, a 10-minute drive by taxi.

Rooms at the Beech are spotless like the rest of the *hostal*, but they are also quite small. The singles, which are carpeted but without fans, are just large enough for a narrow bed, a bureau, a desk and one reading chair. Double rooms are slightly larger. Similarly, the tile bathrooms are tiny but clean, with plenty of hot water for the showers. If you're a late sleeper, ask for a room in back, as those facing the street are noisy in the mornings. The hotel is well situated in the heart of San Isidro, the city's most exclusive residential district, with restaurants, the exclusive Camino Real shopping center, parks and the famous Lima Golf Course all a short walk away. Nevertheless, its location can be a drawback if you prefer, like many travelers, to be in the heart of Lima's most active nightlife area, Miraflores. The Miraflores area has a far greater array of upmarket hotels, restaurants and bars and is nearer to the beach than the slightly safer, more tranquil San Isidro quarter.

HOSTAL LA CASTELLANA
Lima-Miraflores
Calle Grimaldo del Solar 222
Phone (14) 44-3530/44-4662
Category: B
B&B, colonial house, 26 rooms, English spoken, restaurant, laundry service, TV room.
Rates: $26/$33 S/D incl. tax & breakfast. All major credit cards.
Directions: 2 blocks south of Cesar's.

One of the most picturesque B&Bs in Lima, the Castellana is an old converted house. Prior to becoming a hotel in the early 1980's, this place was used for many years as a guest house for German priests. The three-story, Spanish colonial-style exterior is white with elaborate molding, a small arched porch and wooden balcony in front and a delightful grassy area in back with tables. On the grass you will find a number of sunning chairs. There are lots of flowers and shrubs and a cedar tree with birds chirping away.

Inside, you'll find a comfortable if plain TV room on your left, with built-in leather sofas and a breakfast room towards the rear overlooking the garden. The dining area has a red tile floor, an exposed-beam ceiling and flowers on all the tables. Continental breakfasts, including orange juice, coffee, bread and ample portions of butter and jam, come free with the room. You can also get sandwiches and drinks here throughout the day.

Most of the rooms are in the newer modern section. They are fairly small, but are comfortable enough, with thin brown carpeting, telephones, plain white walls, built-in closets, firm foam rubber mattresses, reading chairs and tile bathrooms with marble-like sinks, showers (no baths) and plenty of hot water.

When reserving, ask for a room in the older section, as they are slightly nicer and not so plain, plus there's a small sitting area in this section with several sofas, a coffee table, flower arrangements in the corners and a sky light above – perfect for reading.

HOSTAL TORREBLANCA

Lima-Miraflores
Ave. José Pardo 1453
Phone (14) 47-3363/47-9998
Fax (14) 44-4440
Telex 21002
Category: B
3-story B&B, 19 rooms, restaurant, bar, laundry, English-speaking staff.
Rates: $20/$30 S/D incl. tax and breakfast. All major credit cards are accepted.
Directions: On a major avenue 14 small blocks (a 15-minute walk) west of the main plaza in Miraflores.

It's not always clear why some hotels click and others don't, but the Torreblanca seems to have that "je ne sais quoi" that is hugely appealing. The ambience found here makes it a favorite of many travelers. The *hostal's* unique third-floor bell tower, location across from a small flower-filled park, and proximity to the sea, all add a bit more to the feel of this place. The center point of activity in this home-like *hostal* is the main sitting room, which is delightful and well used. On registering, you'll be offered a complementary pisco sour here, which you can sip while viewing the portrait of the owner, Madam Tello, on the wall. There are elegant lamps and always copies of American and local magazines lying about. On a cold August day there may even be a glow from the stone fireplace. The sofas and chairs are plush, comfortable and covered in fine materials. There are throw rugs on the beautiful parquet floors. It's definitely a relaxing place to rest your weary bones and swap tales with other travelers.

Adjoining the sitting area is the dining room, which has a few interesting knick-knacks, including some Peruvian pottery. For short meals it's okay, but as a TV viewing area it's not so comfortable. Next to it is a small courtyard, which has some outdoor chairs and tables (flowers on all) and a grill. This is the best place to have breakfast or a light lunch.

If you reserve a room in advance, ask for one in the main section, as the three rooms in back, all singles, are far inferior to those in the main house. No two rooms are the same, but those in the main building, which are mostly doubles, are carpeted, with floor-length draperies, antique beds, dressing bureaus and small shaded lamps. The rooms in back are add-ons. They seem quite cramped and have inferior bathrooms.

First Alternative: **HOSTAL SENORIAL MIRAFLORES**
Calle José Gonzales 567, Miraflores, phone (14) 45-7306
Rates: $22/$30 incl. 18% tax and breakfast. All major credit cards are accepted.
Directions: A good 10-minute walk southeast of the main plaza in Miraflores.

Like many of Lima's B&Bs, the Senorial is a converted house with a two-story white facade in traditional style and a three-story modern addition in the back. The terrace overlooking the rear garden is a nice place for taking breakfast and listening to the pigeons cooing. There's also an attractive sitting room with carpeting, oil paintings, wrought iron lighting fixtures and ornately carved, antique-style furnishings that are more stylish than comfortable.

Most important, the rooms here are larger than at many B&Bs, with carpets, TVs, built-in closets, desks, and tile baths. The hot-water showers take a while to heat up.

Second Alternative: **PENSION ALEMANA**
Ave. Arequipa 4704, Miraflores, phone (14) 45-6999/46-4045
Rates: $19/$33 S/D incl. tax and a scrumptious buffet breakfast. All major credit cards.
Directions: 7 blocks from the heart of Miraflores on the main street from Lima.

A house converted into a B&B, with 18 rooms, a restaurant, a tiny yard in back and a doorman in front, the Alemana is a good pick if the others are full, especially if you want a single room. Prior reservations are recommended, as this place is frequently booked up. The rooms here are tops among the city's *hostals* – spacious, attractive green carpets, comfortable armchairs for reading, long desks, built-in closets and sizable tile baths.

The public areas, however, do not offer a place to talk or read other than the restaurant. The high-ceiling lobby, for example, has a TV and is functional, but hardly attractive. Similarly, the breakfast area, while sunny and inviting, is open only for breakfast. The staff is English-speaking and usually pleasant, especially with Germans who frequent this place.

Third Alternative: **HOSTAL LA ALAMEDA**
Ave. Pardo 931, Miraflores, phone (14) 47-9806/47-3666
Rates: $18/$26 incl. tax and a good breakfast. No credit cards are accepted.
Directions: On a major avenue 8 blocks west of downtown Miraflores, a 10-minute walk therefrom.

A quiet 15-room B&B, the Alameda is a restored old house near downtown Miraflores. It is unquestionably the best place to stay if you're arriving late at night without a reservation – rooms are almost always available. Also, among the top-quality B&Bs, it's the best deal in terms of value for money. The rooms have small comfortable beds, carpets and large closets. The bathrooms, which have a reliable hot water supply, are not the best, as the shower heads are poor or nonexistent and there are no shelves to put things.

HOTEL ROMA

Lima-downtown, Jirón Ica 326, phone (14) 27-7572/6, fax (14) 34-326684
Category: C. 34 rooms, old style.
Rates: $3.50/$6-$8 S/D. No credit cards.
Directions: In downtown Lima, 4 blocks east of Plaza San Martín.

Highly recommended for years by low-budget travelers and often full, the Roma is one of the safest budget hotels in the heart of Lima – a major consideration for this crime-ridden area.

The uncramped rooms have high ceilings and old style furnishings and the bathrooms, which are shared except for the more expensive doubles, are clean and have hot water. Most important, this place is very secure and well maintained, with a good security gate. There's no restaurant on the premises, but there are lots of cheap places to eat nearby.

First Alternative: **HOSTAL SAN SEBASTIAN**

Jirón Ica 712, Lima, phone 23-2740
Rates: $5/$8 S/D with shared baths.

Some four blocks north of the Roma on the same street, the 23-room San Sebastián has rooms similar in quality and price. It also has a restaurant open for all meals, a sitting room with old style furnishings and a roof with sunning chairs.

Second Alternative: **PENSION JOSE LUIS**

F. Paula Ugarriza 727, Miraflores, phone (14) 44-1015, fax (14) 46-7177
Rates: $8/$12 S/D ($5 dormitory) incl. tax. No credit cards.

José Luis, a small, first-rate B&B in Miraflores with an English-speaking owner, has a family atmosphere. It also offers cooking and laundry facilities and is hard to beat in terms of price and quality in the Miraflores area.

The North

Trujillo

HOTEL DE TURISTAS
Jirón Independencia 485
Phone (44) 23-2741
Fax (44) 23-5641
Lima phone (14) 42-8626
Category: A
65 rooms, pool, travel agency.
Rates: $36/$47 S/D incl. tax.
All major credit cards.
Directions: In heart of town facing the Plaza de Armas.

The Turistas is a grand, old-style hotel and clearly the leading establishment in Trujillo. This three-story majestic beauty faces the main plaza, so to get a feel for the city's life you need only walk across the street, take a seat on a shaded bench and watch the passers-by. Inside, a quiet place to pass time is the attractive and spacious sitting room, which is just beyond the reception area. Recently refurbished, it's completely carpeted, with an array of leather sofas and matching armchairs. Soft music, marble-top coffee tables, brass lighting fixtures, an ornately carved desk and the judicious use of plants all add a touch of elegance.

Through the large arched windows you can view the activity around the eight-sided pool in the central courtyard. Many of the hotel's rooms face this area, which is inviting and full of plants and flowers. Even if there are no sunning chairs, you can at least sit at one of the numerous shaded tables on the stone terrace surrounding the pool and enjoy a drink.

You can also order a cocktail in the hotel's cozy modern bar, which is carpeted and has some comfortable leather armchairs. Try a meal in the Turistas' main restaurant, which has a distinctive brick vaulted ceiling. The Sunday lunch buffet here is outstanding. Even the hotel's less expensive coffee shop is not without charm – carpets, vaulted ceiling, drawings on the walls, attractive tile-top tables and wooden chairs. Rounding out the picture are the hotel's rooms, which are modern, comfortable and carpeted, with color TVs and nightly videos. Ask for one facing the courtyard, as those facing the street can be noisy. Finally, for a guided tour of the fabulous nearby ruins of Chan-Chan, simply consult the hotel's travel agency in the foyer.

***Alternative:* HOTEL EL GOLF**
Urbana El Golf, Manzana J-I, phone (44) 24-2592/23-2741, fax (44) 23-2515
Rates: $26/$35 S/D incl. tax ($45 for a suite). All major credit cards are accepted.
Directions: In Urbana El Golf, 8 km outside Trujillo.

If the Turistas is full, your best bet is the modern Golf Hotel, which is similarly priced, but well out of town.

HOTEL OPT GAR
Grau 595, phone (44) 24-2192
Category: B. 7 stories, modern, 70 rooms, restaurant, bar.
Rates: $8/$13 S/D incl. tax. All major credit cards.
Directions: Near the center, 4 blocks east of the Plaza de Armas.

The best of the category B hotels is the Opt Gar, which is a very friendly and pleasant hotel conveniently located close to the central plaza. The rooms are not cramped and are reasonably attractive, with pale wallpaper, carpeted floors, comfortable armchairs for reading, telephones, and tile bathrooms with modern fixtures and hot-water showers. A TV costs only $1 extra.

The spacious sitting room next to the reception is a pleasant place to sit and read or chat with other guests. It's quite presentable, with blue carpeting, comfortable sofas and a color TV. You can eat at the Opt Gar restaurant which serves good food; the seafood has been rated by some as excellent.

RESIDENCIAL LOS ESCUDOS
Calle Mariscal Orbegoso 676
Phone (44) 25-5691/5961
Category: B
15-room, 2 stories, colonial, restaurant, bar.
Rates: $7/$11 S/D incl. tax. No credit cards.
Directions: In the center, 2 blocks southeast of the Plaza de Armas.

If the Opt Gar is full, try the Escudos. It's a two-story, white colonial building with a small garden and 15 medium size rooms. They have worn red carpeting, phones and old-style tile baths, with showers and fixtures in good working order. The hot water supply, however, is not reliable and the tile-floor sitting room and restaurant both have a cold feel to them. On the positive side, the meals are inexpensive and the rooms are slightly cheaper than those at Opt Gar.

Cajamarca

HOSTAL CAJAMARCA
Jirón Dos de Mayo 311
Phone (44) 92-2532
Lima phone (14) 61-8365/62-3572
Category: A
2-story colonial house, 33 rooms, restaurant, bar, generator.
Rates: $12/$17 S/D incl. tax. All major credit cards.
Directions: In the center, one block from the Plaza de Armas.

If the idea of staying in a traditional colonial town house sounds appealing, book a room at Hostal Cajamarca, which is Cajamarca's finest hotel and well located near the main plaza. The tile roof of this old *casona* (large home) is unexceptional, but the massive stone doorway with a huge wooden door is truly impressive. As you reach the central courtyard, likewise of stone, you'll see the house's original wooden balcony, which is attractive and well maintained like the rest of the hotel. The *hostal's* **El Sitio** restaurant, which serves excellent food, overlooks this courtyard and offers seating inside as well as outside in the courtyard under the balcony. This patio is not just the best place for eating, but also for passing time and, if you're lucky, you may even be treated to some entertainment by local musicians.

The rooms are small to medium size, with spotless white walls, comfortable beds, telephones and modern tile bathrooms and showers. All the rooms are attractive, but the decor varies – the older-looking units have the original wood flooring and old-style beds while the more modern ones have built-in single beds and carpeting. There is also a travel agency here, Cajamarca Tours, which is one of the best in town. Most important, the hotel has a generator, so if the electricity goes off in town (which happens with some frequency) you'll still have light. Moreover, if business is slow and if you ask (the Cajamarca economy has been in the doldrums for years), the *hostal* may offer you a discount. Finally, if you'll be here for more than one night, you might inquire about staying a night or more at

Albergue San Vicente, an old *hacienda* outside town run by the *hostal's* owners.

Alternative: **HOSTAL LAGUNA SECA**
Baños del Inca, phone 05 (ask for the Cajamarca operator), Lima phone (14) 62-3572/46-3270
Rates: $21/$27 S/D incl. tax. Visa and MasterCard accepted.
Directions: In Baños del Inca, 6 km east of Cajamarca and 200 yards beyond the hot springs, a short taxi ride from Cajamarca.

If you're looking for a place to relax for a few days, try the Laguna Seca, located in a wonderful pine grove outside of Cajamarca near some former Inca hot baths. An old *hacienda* that has been converted into a hotel, it's a pleasant, peaceful place with 20 attractive rooms, half of them bungalows, and a restaurant which is open when there's enough demand. The unique feature of this ranch-style hotel is that each room has, in effect, its own private hot spring with a large tile tub in the bathroom, supplied with water from the nearby springs. You can also take a sauna and go horseback riding. The best time to come here is between May and October when the weather is sunny, but don't be surprised if you're the only guest, as business is often slow. This lack of guests gives Laguna Seca a feeling of slow decay.

HOSTAL CASA BLANCA
Jirón Dos de Mayo 446
Phone (44) 92-2141
Category: B/C
2 stories, colonial, 36 rooms, restaurant, tour agency.
Rates: $12/$16 S/D private baths; $6/$8 S/D shared baths. Diners, Visa, & MasterCard
Directions: In the heart of town at the Plaza de Armas.

The Casa Blanca, facing the main plaza, is a marvelous hotel and an excellent choice for travelers preferring old fashioned places. The main sitting area, in the center and lined with plants, has 14-foot ceilings and a two-story skylight, which brightens up the lobby considerably. There's an attractive sunken area here for chatting and watching TV. Adjoining the lobby are a popular, newly-renovated restaurant and a travel agency, Adventuras Cajamarca, which offers a wide range of tours. As you move further inside you'll come to a courtyard with a non-functional stone fountain in the center and a wooden, second-story balcony lined with potted plants. This is a nice spot to relax, as there are several well-worn but comfortable sofas and chairs here.

The rooms offering private baths are by far the nicest, with carpets, old sofas, and comfortable double beds that have firm mattresses and attractive bedspreads. Rooms with shared baths cost half as much and are wonderfully old-style – 14-foot ceilings, meter-wide walls which are freshly painted, and natural wood floors that are a bit creaky upstairs. The beds' mattresses are springy, but comfortable enough, and the shared baths are reasonably clean with a fairly reliable supply of hot water. There's even the luxury of room service.

***Alternative:* HOSTAL PLAZA**
Plaza de Armas 669
Rates: $6/$8 S/D with private bath, less without.
Directions: Faces the Plaza de Armas.

If the Casa Blanca is full, try the nearby Plaza, which likewise overlooks the plaza. It too is a pleasant old building and has wood furnishings, large quiet rooms (some of which have balconies and views of the plaza), and decent private baths with hot-water showers. The water supply, however, is erratic.

Huaraz

HOSTAL ANDINO
Jirón Pedro Cochachin 357
Phone (44) 72-1662
Fax (44) 72-2830
Telex 46529
Lima phone (14) 45-9230
Category: A
40 rooms, Swiss-run, good mountain views, restaurant, bar, parking.
Rates: $26/$29 S/D incl. 21% tax. All major credit cards.
Directions: On the southeastern outskirts, 9 blocks from the Plaza de Armas.

If the idea of a quiet cozy hotel with first-class service, immaculate accommodations and spectacular views sounds appealing, stay at Hostal Andino (the "Chalet Swiss"). Surprisingly, many hotels in Huaraz offer poor views of the mountains; those of Mt. Huascaran, Peru's highest, from the Andino are spectacular, especially from the second and third floors of the new annex. The only rooms with balconies are on those floors, so ask for one when reserving.

The accommodations are medium size and quite comfortable, with new carpets, two large adjoining single beds, telephones, armchairs for relaxing, and top quality bathrooms with combination baths. The Chalet Swiss also has a comfortable living room with a functioning fireplace, a bright Peruvian throw rug, several plants, comfortable chairs and a TV; the atmosphere here is quite comfortable. Meals are served in the adjoining, less atmospheric restaurant, which has small wooden tables, wooden chairs and wrought iron lighting fixtures; fondue is the specialty. For a change, try the **Crèperie Patrick** near the plaza at Ave. Luzuriaga 424; the crèpes, quiche and fish dishes are all recommended. Afterwards, you can go dancing at **Taberna Amadeus** at Parque Ginebra or listen to folk music at **Tambo**, a *peña* (bar) on Calle José de la Mar.

If you're interested in climbing or exploring the Huaraz area, Louis Glauser, the hotel's helpful Swiss administrator, will make all the arrangements, including guides, rental equipment, vehicles, and other necessities. Otherwise, contact Andean Sport Tours (phone 72-1612) or Monttrek (phone 72-1124) at Ave. Luzuriaga 571 and 646, respectively. Call in advance to book a room here, as the Andino, which is clearly the best hotel in town, is very popular with Europeans and often full during the busy season. This is particularly true in July and August, as well as the first week in June during *Semana de Andinismo* (a skiing festival at Pastoruri in the southern Cordillera Blanca). Between January and April when the skies are usually cloudy and the weather is at its worst, getting a room is rarely a problem.

Alternative: HOTEL DE TURISTAS

Avenida Centenario Cuadra 10, phone (44) 72-1640/72-1709, telex 46508, Lima phone (14) 72-1928

Rates: $28/$36 S/D incl. tax. All major credit cards are accepted.

Directions: On the northern outskirts of town, one mile (16 blocks) north of the Plaza de Armas on the main drag (Ave. Luzuriaga, which becomes Ave. Centenario beyond the bridge).

If the Andino is full and having top-quality accommodations is critical, your best bet is the modern, 60-room Turistas. Part of the nationwide Turistas chain, it is well maintained, offering spacious and comfortable accommodations, all of which have carpets. The large public areas are also carpeted and have several fireplaces; they are often devoid of guests, however, giving the Turistas a cold, unfriendly ambience.

HOSTAL COLOMBA
Calle Francisco de Zela 210
Phone (44) 72-1501/72-1241
Category: B
27-room ex-*hacienda*, cabins, German-run, English spoken, restaurant, safe parking.
Rates: $10/$14 S/D incl. tax. No credit cards.
Directions: 9 blocks north of the Plaza de Armas via the main drag, Ave. Luzuriaga. Take the second right after the bridge and go 1 block.

One of the most delightful hotels in Huaraz, the popular Colomba, which is run by a friendly German family, is also one of the best buys in town. Once a *hacienda* for a wealthy family, the Colomba has a picturesque courtyard with a fountain in the middle and flowers everywhere. Don't miss the small ornate chapel facing this area; it was the family's private chapel and has all the original fixtures. The courtyard area is perfect for relaxing and reading a book; one of the porches overlooking it has comfortable cushioned armchairs for this purpose.

All of this gives not a clue of what's in back. There, you'll find a series of attractive wood-like bungalows in a grove of pine trees; most have porches with chairs for relaxing. Inside, the medium-size rooms, which are nothing special, offer comfortable poster beds, closets, and tile baths with reliable hot-water showers. For the low price, the rooms are a steal. To top it all off, the hotel's restaurant serves good food.

First Alternative: **HOSTAL YANETT**
Avenida Centenario 106, phone (44) 72-1466
Rates: $6/$9 S/D incl. tax; MasterCard is accepted.
Directions: 2 blocks before the Colomba and just north of the bridge on the main north-south drag, Ave Luzuriaga, which becomes Ave. Centenario north of the bridge.

If the Colomba is full, try the friendly Yanett, which is just two blocks away. It's a converted old house with original molding on the walls and glass chandeliers in the two-story lobby. The small adjoining restaurant is also attractive, but has a more rustic ambience. Rooms here are fairly plain. They are large, clean and reasonably decent, with hot-water tile baths.

Second Alternative: **LA CASA DE CAMPO YACARINI**
In Urbanización El Bosque-Palmira, 3 km from town.

If you don't mind being a bit out of town, try the highly recommended Campo Yacarini, a comfortable hotel with similarly-priced rooms. Run by some very friendly English-speaking Peruvians, it's a new house with a garden and clean rooms with private baths (those with shared baths are cheaper). It also offers a sauna, hot baths and delicious family-style meals.

EDWARD'S INN
Calle Bolognesi 121
Phone (944) 72-2692
Category: C
3 stories, 30 rooms, family run, restaurant, laundry service, English spoken owners, gear rental.
Rates: $4/$6 S/D incl. tax (25% less with shared baths). No credit cards
Directions: 7 blocks west of the plaza and 3 blocks west of Ave.Tarapaca, on the road to Casma.

The new-looking, three-story Edward's Inn, recommended highly for years by the South American Explorer's Club (SAEC), is clearly the *hostal* of choice among the backpacking crowd. It's the largest and most successful of the cheap hotels in Huaraz, and for good reason. The rooms here are small, clean and freshly painted, with comfortable beds and spotless, tiny bathrooms offering hot water all day long. From the top floor balcony you can get good views of the spectacular Cordillera Blanca range. There's no restaurant, but there is laundry service. The friendly owners, the Figeroa family, are knowledgeable about the area and will assist you in making arrangements for trekking, hiking, and gear rental. Their son, Edward, speaks English. A trip in the Cordillera Blanca is fun and, for the low price, you could hardly hope for more. Tell Edward that my wife Betsy, of SAEC fame, sent you.

Alternative: **HOSTAL ALFREDO**
Avenida Centenario 112 (corner of Jirón Victor Vélez), phone (44) 72-0311
Rates: $4/$6 S/D incl. tax. No credit cards are accepted.
Directions: 7 blocks north of the Plaza de Armas on the main drag, Avenida Luzuriaga, just beyond the bridge (where it becomes Avenida Centenario).

If Edward's is full, try the Alfredo, a reasonably attractive place which opened in 1989. The 10 rooms, formerly part of a college, are large. They feature comfortable beds, two small armchairs, tile floors and large baths with new fixtures and hot water. The *hostal* also has a pleasant sitting area on the ground floor where guests can eat breakfast.

The South

Paracas

HOTEL PARACAS

Reserva del Mar, phone (34) 22-1736, Pisco telex 32533, Lima phone (14) 46-4865/5079, Lima fax (14) 47-6548
Category: A. Resort, 110 rooms/bungalows, ocean views, pool, tennis, fishing, ping-pong, miniature golf, boats to Ballestas Islands, volleyball.
Rates: \$52-\$60/\$70-\$81 S/D incl. 16% tax (\$35/\$45 in winter season). All major credit cards are accepted.
Directions: A 3-hour drive south of Lima and 18 km south of Pisco.

The most popular ocean-front hotel in Peru and within striking distance of Lima, Hotel Paracas is a wonderful weekend retreat, the star attraction being the nearby Ballestas Islands. Often referred to as the "Poor Man's Galapagos," these small islands are only 18 km offshore and are covered with ocean birds. Their droppings literally stain the rocks and for centuries have been used as fertilizer. The species found here include pelicans, boobies, stormy petrels, and various types of cormorants, terns and gulls, plus a few penguins. You're guaranteed to see lots of sealions and seals. Several speed boats holding about 12 passengers each leave the hotel daily at 8 a.m. and 10 a.m. (there's an additional one at noon if demand is high). The cost of the two-hour trip is about \$15 and, as with all excursions here, you stay onboard the entire time.

The hotel itself, which caters primarily to wealthy Peruvian families and secondarily to tourists, offers a wide range of activities including, among other sports, volleyball on the beach, pedal boating and fishing. The beach, unfortunately, is not good here, so the pool is very popular. If you're desperate for a beach, you can head for the nearby Paracas National Reserve where ocean swimming is possible.

The hotel's rooms are not as good as you'd expect at a first-class resort, but they do have one very nice feature, namely porches, which have several lounge chairs each so you can sit and enjoy the ocean breeze. The rooms are small to medium size and simple, with plain white walls, cold tile floors, adequate beds, telephones, and tile baths. There are showers that are somewhat dated but with functional fixtures. At the hotel's large restaurant overlooking the pool and ocean, you'll have lots of dishes to choose from (fish covered with cheese or herbs and green peppers, chicken curry or Aurora style, etc.), but the quality suffers from their having to serve large numbers of guests. The huge and decorative cold Sunday buffet, on the other hand, is excellent, with various types of ceviche. The cost is two or three times that of a normal meal here.

During the day most guests seem to sit around the pool, which has lots of tables and sunning chairs. In the late afternoon and at night, the focal point is the lively **Pelican Bar**, which features a large brick fireplace and a long bar made completely from bamboo. The ceiling is entirely of cane and the walls are decorated with stuffed sea birds and fish. Informality rules here and, if you enjoy Latin music and you're here on a Saturday, don't miss the local guitarist in the bar.

First Alternative: **LA HOSTERIA PARACAS**
Avenida Los Libertadores s/n, no phone, Lima phone (14) 27-6624 (Lima Tours)
Rates: $30-$35 per room ($21 in off-season) incl. tax & breakfast. Major credit cards.
Directions: Next door to Hotel Paracas.

For a less expensive category B hotel, the modern, 12-room Hostería Paracas, which is next door to Hotel Paracas and only 100 yards from the ocean, can be recommended. The beach here is not good for swimming, but the *hostería* has a small, unheated, drop-shaped pool in back with lots of sunning chairs and a bar and restaurant overlooking it. Here and the front screened porch overlooking the ocean are the best places to spend time. For entertainment there's ping-pong and a wide-screen TV. One of the great advantages of staying here is that you have only to walk next door to Hotel Paracas to enjoy its first-rate facilities; buffet lunches, bar, and speed boats to the Ballestas Islands.

The rooms are simple but clean, with red tile floors, bare white walls, double beds and large built-in closets. Only a few of the rooms have private baths; the rest have shared baths with showers and hot water that's fairly brackish – making soap suds is no easy feat.

Second Alternative: **HOSTAL SANTA ELENA**
Paracas National Reserve, Lima phone (14) 71-8222

Located only 100 yards from the ocean in the national reserve, a peninsula where there is no public transport, the Santa Elena is a better place to stay for those interested in swimming. The beach here is clean, accessible and safe, with few or no dangerous fish such as the manta rays that can occur elsewhere. The rooms and restaurant are comparable in quality and price to those at Hostería Paracas. The *hostal* also organizes trips. However, there's no pool and guests here, unlike those at the *hostería,* don't have easy access to the facilities of Hotel Paracas.

Ica

HOTEL LAS DUNAS
Km 300 Panamericana Sur Hwy.
Phone (34) 23-1031
Fax (34) 23-1007
Lima phone (14) 42-3090/4180; fax (14) 42-4180
Category: Deluxe
Desert resort, 80 rooms, pool, tennis, sand gliding, horseback riding, pitch and put, gym, billiards, racketball, sauna, disco, aerobic classes, restaurant.
Rates: $74/$81 S/D incl. tax (about 20% less during the week); $40/$45 S/D off-season). All major credit cards.
Directions: A four-hour's drive south of Lima on the Panamericana Sur Highway at Km 300, just outside Ica.

With gray skies covering Lima for nine to 10 months of the year, it's hardly surprising that for residents of Lima, Las Dunas is a weekend paradise. The area around Ica is total desert with dramatic rolling sand dunes, but there's usually a refreshing breeze and the resort's 40 acres of gardens, palm trees and grass, with sheep and llamas grazing, give it an oasis-like ambience.

There's sun virtually year round here and the number of outdoor activities offered by this family-oriented, Club Med-like hotel is impressive. Some things you'd expect, such as a huge winding swimming pool with palm trees and sunning chairs all around, and racketball and tennis courts in top condition. You can also, however, go horseback riding over the dunes, play golf on a nine-hole, pitch and put golf course or, more adventurous, try your hand at sand gliding on styrofoam boards (rented by the hotel) from the top of a huge dune. And awaiting you at the hotel's airstrip is a small plane to whisk you away for a tour of the world famous Nazca lines, which are not far from here. The price of the plane tour, however, is not cheap – $240 for three people.

Upon entering the hotel and passing the reception area, you'll find a museum-quality collection of Nazca pottery, some dating back to 100 B.C., and centuries-old textiles well preserved by the desert sands. Continuing further back, you'll come to the open-air dining area, which includes an open grill, and three kidney-shaped pools beyond. The cuisine here is both Peruvian and international and there are frequent buffets. The specialty of the house is their *parrillada* (barbecue) of grilled meat served at your table on a bed of hot coals.

The rooms, which are large and attractive, are located in various two-story buildings and separated from the public facilities by a small lagoon. Moorish in inspiration, they have cool, plain white walls both inside and out, curved red tile ceilings that are quite striking, verandas with red tile floors and tables and chairs where you can have breakfast, wide single beds, modern furnishings, carpeted floors, telephones, fans, and thoroughly modern, double-room tile baths. The humidity here is extremely low and the nights are cool, so air conditioning is not really necessary.

HOSTAL EL CARMELO

Km 301 Panamericana Sur Hwy., phone (34) 23-1651/23-2191
Category: B. Hacienda-like, small hotel, pool, restaurant, parking.
Rates: $12/$16 S/D incl. tax. Most major credit cards.
Directions: 1 km south of Las Dunas on the same road.

Just south of Las Dunas, the Carmelo is a far cry from that hotel, but it may be your best bet if you're looking for something substantially less expensive. Catering primarily to Peruvian families, it's a well-maintained and reasonably attractive place which makes great efforts to resemble a *hacienda*. It succeeds to a point. Most of the buildings, which are single story and recently constructed, have old-style porches with wooden railings, tile roofs and floors, and there are numerous shade trees.

In addition to small carpeted rooms with twin beds, fans, and tile baths with hot-water showers, the facilities include a small pool that's often crowded with kids, as well as private parking, and a restaurant/bar. The pool and restaurant are ordinary at best, but since the Carmelo is only a stone's throw from the Dunas, guests have the option of heading over there for meals, drinks and the pool, which is far larger and more inviting than the one here.

Nazca

HOTEL DE LA BORDA

Km 447 Carretera Panamericana Sur
Phone (Nazca Operator) 77
Lima phone (14) 408430
Category: A
Old *hacienda*, family-run, 39 rooms, pool, gardens, paddleball, bar, cockfighting ring.
Rates: $23/$31 S/D incl. tax (more during peak periods). All major credit cards.
Directions: Just south of the airstrip, which is 2 km out of town on the Panamericana Sur Highway, is a sign for the hotel. It's down a dirt road heading in the opposite direction from the airstrip, about 1 km.

If you don't mind being four km outside town in a very peaceful place, you're certain to love La Borda, which is near the Nazca airstrip and surrounded by some irrigated cotton fields. Parts of it date back to the late 18th century, when it was a convent. It was later converted into a *hacienda* by the La Borda family, whose ancestors settled in Nazca in 1776, and who still run this place. Since its conversion into a hotel, some newer sections have been added. The result of these many changes is a marvelous hotel, one of the most restful in Peru. Even though it's in the middle of the desert, you'll hardly feel it as you walk the extensive grounds of this delightful retreat. The area is covered by shade trees, with flowers and chirping birds everywhere, and there's also a vegetable garden, some fruit trees and a cock fighting ring which comes into use on special occasions such as New Year's Day. During the day, after flying over the Nazca lines, most guests relax around the pool; others try their hand at paddleball on one of the two courts here. Children have swings and a soccer field for entertainment.

The rooms, which are standard size, are comfortable and attractive, with tile floors, cushy reading chairs, breakfast tables, beds with firm mattresses, closets, and private baths. The fixtures are old, but in good working order. Most have only showers, but a few have combination baths. The nicest feature of the rooms is their lovely terraces, which are covered with flowering vines and have wicker chairs and good views of the garden. Rooms in the newer section are similar, but smaller, and have showers only.

The restaurant here is excellent and clearly the best in Nazca, and the bar's pisco sours are famous. The menu includes sea bass in mustard sauce, grilled chicken, steak, ceviche and, for desert, pancakes and omelettes with rum. After eating, you can pass time in the attractive bar or one of the two relaxing sitting rooms, which have comfortable furnishings, antique tapestries and paintings on the walls, old lighting fixtures, a few plants and a TV. It's the service, however, that really makes La Borda an outstanding choice; the English-speaking manager couldn't be friendlier. She is also a good source of information.

HOTEL DE TURISTAS
Avenida Bolognesi s/n
Phone (Nazca Operator) 60
Lima phone (14) 72-1928/42-8626
Telex 2393
Category: A
One story, traditional style, 32 rooms, restaurant, pool, bar.
Rates: $38/$52 S/D incl. 16% tax (less with shared bath). All major credit cards.
Directions: In the center of Nazca on the main drag.

For years, one of the major attractions of this traditional-style hotel in the heart of town has been the nightly lectures on the famous Nazca lines by aging Dr. María Reiche (born 1903) and, more recently, her slightly younger sister, Dr. Renate Reiche-Grosse. Both ladies reside permanently at the hotel. Dr. Reiche, a German mathematician, has been studying the lines since 1946, having fled from Germany during WWII. Her theory, now widely disputed, is that these vast lines in the sand, best seen from the air, represent an astronomical calendar constructed by the pre-Inca Paracas and Nazca cultures, before 1000 B.C. Both sisters are now too old to continue these lectures, but hopefully someone else will take over. They truly were an event not to be forgotten.

This small cozy hotel, which dates from 1946, is an appealing one-story structure with an impressive formal lobby and, in back, the guest rooms and a large pool. Flanking the lobby to one side is a large reception area, called the Salon María Reiche, with beautiful tile floors, high ceilings with elaborate molding, attractive wrought iron chandeliers, traditional furnishings, including marble-top tables, high arched windows, numerous plants, and several centuries-old tapestries on the wall. It has a club-like ambience and is a good place to talk, read a book, or watch TV; it's also where the Reiches held their lectures.

Further back is the formal dining area, where very good Peruvian and international specialties are served. Offerings include fish soup, various types of *anticuchos* (grilled meats), fettucini marinara, scallops parmesan, and peach melba for dessert. They also serve dynamite pisco sours in the adjoining bar, which is both formal, with high ceilings and chandeliers, and clubby, with captain's chairs and leather-top tables. At night, temperatures are usually cooler outside, so most guests prefer having their drinks brought to them on the adjoining terrace overlooking the pool.

The rooms are attractive and almost standard size, with comfortable beds, polished brick floors, vanity tables, minibars, telephones, small closets, and fine tile bathrooms with lots of counter space and hot-water showers. Each unit also has a terrace with built-in seats facing the pool. All in all, the Turistas is a very peaceful place and, even if you don't stay here, you can come to enjoy the pool, which has lots of sunning chairs and costs just $3 for non-guests.

***First Alternative:* HOSTAL LA MAISON SUISSE**
Km 446 Carretera Panamericana Sur

If the above two are full, don't despair; the Maison Suisse, which also has a shady garden feel about it, is a good alternative and similarly priced. It's near La Borda, directly across from the airport, and has attractive bungalows, a pool, and tennis courts and jai alai. Those interested in camping should inquire here as they reportedly accept campers.

***Second Alternative:* HOTEL MONTECARLO**
Jirón Callao, phone (34) 234456, Lima phone (14) 623056
Rates: $13/$17 S/D bungalows incl. tax (about 30% less for a room).
Directions: In the heart of town across from Ormeño bus station.

Among the less expensive category B and C hotels, the only one with a swimming pool is the 34-room Montecarlo. If you arrive in Nazca by midday, this can be a significant advantage; you will be able to relax around the pool that afternoon while waiting to see the Nazca lines the following day. Otherwise, you may be twiddling your thumbs here as there's little to do in this hot desert town. The lines can be seen only during the morning. The ambience and management here could stand some improvement but, for those traveling on a tight budget, the Montecarlo can be especially appealing. If you book a flight over the lines through the Montecarlo, they'll offer you a free night at the hotel (the night preceding the flight).

The bungalows are the only accommodations that can be recommended; they are in back and cost slightly more. They have no telephones, but you'll have a quiet sleep and a hot-water shower. The regular rooms, on the other hand, are noisy (especially those on the street side) and plain, with narrow twin beds, bare wooden floors, and no telephones or chairs. And while they do have private baths, the water supply is unreliable and some of them don't receive hot water at all. There's also a good inexpensive restaurant, **Mister Tiburón II**, next door and an excellent reliable guide, Jesús Erazo, across the street (next door to the Ormeño bus station). The major attraction here, besides the lines, is Chaucilla (30 km), where you can see many ancient, well-preserved cemeteries in this area.

Arequipa

HOTEL DE TURISTAS
Plaza Bolívar s/n
Phone (54) 21-5110
Telex 51040
Lima phone (14) 72-1928
Category: A
80 rooms, estate-like hotel, unheated pool, tennis.
Rates: $36/$47 S/D incl. tax. All major credit cards.
Directions: 1½ km north of the Plaza de Armas in Selva Alegre, a quiet residential neighborhood.

Part of the government-run Enturperu hotel chain, the Turistas, which was built around 1940 and remodeled in 1982, has for years been the city's top hotel. It still maintains its charm despite its aging fixtures. In a comfortable, cushioned chair on the front terrace, with the hotel's elegant pink facade in white trim to your back, you can view and enjoy the peaceful shady surroundings.

Inside, you'll find a huge and impressive sitting area: high ceilings with exposed beams, attractive black stone flooring, old brass chandeliers, large ornate mirrors with gold trim, a magnificent fireplace, panelled windows to the floor and a long mural with scenes of old Arequipa. Relax and enjoy it from one of the ubiquitous leather sofas. Then step into the red-carpeted, wood-panelled bar, which has some fine leather-top tables with matching chairs, ceiling lights with Tiffany-like glass shades, a fireplace and an upright piano. The decor of the dining room is similar and the exposed-beam ceilings are identical.

The Turistas is not just for travelers, but also serves as a meeting place for the locals, especially those with children. In back there's a large garden with tall trees, flowers, a play area for kids, a tennis court that doubles as a soccer field, and a kidney-shaped unheated pool that's popular on weekends, particularly between November and April when the water is fairly warm. And don't miss Juanito, the huge jungle turtle that has entertained children here for over 30 years. Parents can view all of this from the covered terrace restaurant, where lunch and a Sunday buffet are served. The awning is more for protection from the sun than from the rain, as the weather in Arequipa is extremely dry.

The nicest feature of the rooms is that most of them overlook this garden. Their furnishings are a bit old, especially the showers and fixtures in the old style white-tile bathrooms, but everything is basically in good order. The rooms have carpets, stylish draperies to the floor and at least one comfortable sitting chair per unit. All in all, Arequipa's grande dame seems to be aging quite gracefully, which is why the clients keep coming and the ambience remains lively.

***Best Alternative:* PORTAL HOTEL**

Box 119, Portal de Flores 116 at the Plaza de Armas, phone (54) 21-5530, fax (54) 21-5046, telex 51062, Lima phone (14) 40-6447

Rates: $33/$47 S/D incl. tax ($49/$65 for more deluxe rooms with views of the plaza). All major credit cards are accepted.

Directions: On the eastern side of the Plaza de Armas.

From the exterior, which is part of the Plaza de Armas, the five-story Portal is barely noticeable. It's surprisingly large and modern inside, with 58 carpeted rooms; the more expensive ones have small tile terraces and views of the plaza. The nicest features are the small pool and bar on the roof; the views of the plaza from here are wonderful, as they are from the restaurant. There's also a sauna.

For business people, the central location and efficient management are the main attractions, and some tourists may prefer it for these reasons as well. If you'll be staying a week or more, check the **PORTAL CAYMA**, a modern three-story aparthotel run by the same people.

HOSTAL EL CONQUISTADOR
Calle Mercaderes 409
Phone (54) 21-2916/21-8987
Telex 51263
Category: B
3-story colonial, 28 rooms, owner speaks English, restaurant, bar.
Rates: $13/$20 S/D incl. tax. All major credit cards.
Directions: Near the center, 3½ blocks east of the Plaza de Armas.

If you have a soft spot for old colonial hotels, you'll probably prefer the Conquistador to La Casa de Mi Abuela. It is the best alternative. The Conquistador's rooms, most of which are in the new three-story section out back, are small with plain white walls, thin carpeting, built-in closets and tiny tile baths with hot-water showers – nothing to write home about. Try to get a room facing the rear yard as it will seem less spartan. The yard is large, sunny and attractive, with potted plants hanging from the walls. You may want to plan on taking a noon-time break to lie on the grass, read a book and soak up some rays.

Otherwise, the nicest place to unwind is the main lobby. The high vaulted brick ceilings, gold framed mirrors and oil paintings, the large wrought iron and glass chandelier and a small altar give this area an elegant Old World feeling. The comfortable leather sofas and matching chairs, rugs and fancy shaded lamps add warmth. For drinks, sandwiches and light snacks, the small adjoining restaurant is perfectly adequate, but for full meals you'll do better eating out. The owner speaks English and a travel agency flanks the main entrance, so you shouldn't have any problem developing a travel itinerary. In short, the Conquistador, which has the added feature of being centrally located, is one of the nicer rest stops in southern Peru.

First Alternative: **LA CASA DE MI ABUELA**
Calle Jerúsalem 606, phone (54) 24-1206/22-3194
Rates: $8/$12 S/D incl. tax; $20 for a 4-bedroom apartment.
Directions: 6½ blocks north of the Plaza de Armas.

If service, friendliness and cost are more important than a colonial ambience, try this ever-popular B&B instead of the Conquistador. The hostel is clean, friendly and well prepared for travelers, with its own travel agency and a small library of American and European books. It's in an old house with a lawn and a hedge in front; in back you can stay in an apartment with a small fully-equipped kitchenette stocked with bottled water and sodas. In the mornings or evenings, you can have a hot-water bath and ask for your laundry to be done, then have breakfast or drinks on the patio or in the garden. English is spoken and the baths are private.

Second Alternative: **HOSTAL NUNEZ**
Calle Jerúsalem 528, phone (54) 21-8648
Rates: $5/$7 S/D incl. tax.
Directions: 5 blocks north of the Plaza de Armas, before La Casa de Mi Abuela.

For the money, it's hard to beat the Nuñez, which is one of the most popular category C hostels. It's a friendly, safe and pleasant place to stay, the nicest feature being the roof-top terrace and courtyard where delicious full breakfasts are served for $1.50. The rooms are nothing special, but they are clean, comfortable and have the essentials – private baths with hot water. There's laundry service as well. If you plan to take the night train to Puno, for a small service charge the management will handle getting you a ticket, which can be quite difficult. Otherwise, try Misti Tours (phone 21-7191) at Calle Santa Catalina 312, which runs along the eastern side of the Plaza de Armas; they seem to have connections.

The East

Cuzco

HOTEL LIBERTADOR
Calle San Agustín 400
Phone (84) 23-1961/2601
Fax (84) 23-3152
Telex 52043
Lima phone (14) 41-6492
Lima fax (14) 42-3011
Category: Deluxe
Pizarro's palace with modern wing, 131 rooms, gift shop, travel agency.
Rates: $60/$72 S/D plus 28% tax. All major credit cards.
Directions: 4 blocks east of the Plaza de Armas.

Who would have guessed that visitors to Cuzco can stay at the former residence of Francisco Pizarro, the Spanish Conquistador of Peru. The 16th century "House of the Four Busts," restored in 1973, was his palace;

Inca laborers built the foundations and meter-thick walls, which you'll see from the street. If you reserve well in advance, you may get one of the 18 rooms in the original two-story section. The furnishings are not old, but the beds and tables are colonial style and ornately carved. Mini-bars, carpets, music and, in a few rooms, TVs add a modern touch, as do the marbled bathrooms. Most important, the rooms are heated.

After a long day of walking around Cuzco, you'll probably want to sit in one of the comfortable antique chairs or benches outside your door and view the hotel's most attractive feature – a stone courtyard with pigeons drinking from the fountain. It is surrounded by an arched stone portico lined with potted plants. Two of the pots are so large you could hide in them.

Most guests, however, stay in the new four-story section. The rooms are unexceptional but comfortable, with carpets and colonial-style furnishings, and overlook a small flowered courtyard.

For meals, guests have a choice between the brick vaulted **La Cholita** in the modern section and the more formal **Inti-Raymi** overlooking the old courtyard. The latter's pisco sours are outstanding; the food and the service are not. You can also have a drink in the adjoining **Bar Marqués**, with stone floors and antique Cuzco paintings. My favorite place for passing time, however, is either of the two front sitting rooms. Both have antique furnishings, wrought iron chandeliers and meter-thick walls – a pleasant place to read up on tomorrow's adventure.

HOTEL ROYAL INKA I

Plaza Regocijo 299
Phone (84) 22-2284/23-1067
Telex 50060
Category: A
3-story colonial, 37 rooms, restaurant, bar.
Rates: $43/$57 plus 19% tax; price includes breakfast. All major credit cards.
Directions: Overlooks Plaza Regocijo, 2 blocks west of the Plaza de Armas.

Dating from the early 19th century, the Royal Inka is the former residence of one of Cuzco's early governors and overlooks a pleasant shaded plaza. If exterior looks count, you won't be disappointed. The ground level incorporates an older Incan wall and has an ornately carved door; the upper two levels have balconies enclosed in wood and glass, giant potted plants hanging from the wall, and flags flapping in the breeze.

As you enter you'll find a small brick-floor lobby with an assortment of wall decorations, including a conquistador helmet and swords, colonial paintings, an ornate gold leaf mirror, and pottery. The adjoining restaurant is cafeteria-like and good for breakfast. For lunch and dinner, most guests go out on the town. For drinks, a favorite of many is the legendary **Cross Keys Pub**, just around the corner – watering hole for legions of expeditionaries, scientists and adventurers. Barry Walker, co-owner along with his wife, Margot, is an amateur ornithologist and jungle guide and one of a small group who make a living leading people into Peru's remote mountain and jungle regions. If you're lucky enough to meet him, you'll have any interesting evening indeed!

What's special about the Royal Inka I is the second-floor stone courtyard, now a glass-roofed lounge resembling a greenhouse – perfect for drinks or reading. Instead of music, there are serenading macaws and parakeets flying about unrestrained, plus a slowly dripping fountain in the center. White cane-like chairs with colorful material and plants everywhere add to the tropical ambience. In separate corners are a huge antique ceramic jar and a fabulous ceramic piece from Ayacucho of the type for which the city is famous – a stylized meter-high model church. Upstairs on the wooden balcony, overlooking this courtyard, you'll find some interesting color photographs of Cuzco and surrounding areas. There are also colonial furnishings and paintings.

Rooms here have carpets, wall heaters, telephones and are large enough to include two cushioned chairs for relaxing. The bathrooms are tiled and small, with modern fixtures and combination baths (showers only in the small single rooms). The best accommodations, however, are the unusual two-floor, three-bedroom suites, with arched wood-beam ceilings. What's special is that each has an enclosed balcony, great for people-watching.

First Alternative: **HOTEL ROYAL INCA II**

Calle Santa Teresa 399, phone (84) 22-2284/23-1067, telex 50060

If the Royal Inca I is full or you want nicer accommodations, try its newer sister hotel, the Royal Inca II, which is 1½ blocks away and has the same phone and telex. In operation since 1988, it's also in a former magnificent Cuzco mansion and has central heating and accommodations that are slightly larger and in the same price range as its sister hotel.

***Second Alternative:* HOTEL CUZCO**
Calle Heladeros 150, phone (84) 22-4821/22-1811, telex 52049, Lima phone (14) 28-3320
Rates: $36/$49 S/D incl. tax, children under 12 free. All major credit cards.
Directions: One block south of the Plaza de Armas and one block east of Hotel Royal Inka I.

This imposing three-story grande dame of Cuzco was the first major hotel in the city. It is aging, but retains much of its old-fashioned charm, despite its state-run management. It has impressive high-ceiling public rooms with royal red carpeting, brass chandeliers, exposed wood-beam ceilings and lighted fireplaces. Reinforcing the grand theme are the high arched windows which afford views of the lovely inner garden. A favorite hangout for guests is the hotel's magnificent bar, the Emperador, which has 18-foot ceilings, fancy wood panelling, a huge wrought iron chandelier in the center, high-back wooden chairs and an ornately carved, 20-foot-long bar. The 107 rooms are fairly large, with old carved beds, walk-in closets and space heaters, but otherwise they are fairly simple and showing their age. There's also a large popular restaurant where, at night, you'll be serenaded by local musicians while you dine; the food here is quite good and relatively inexpensive.

PENSION LORETO
Calle Loreto 115
Phone (84) 23-6331/22-6252
Category: B
2-story colonial with Inca walls, 9 rooms, laundry service.
Rates: $12/$15 S/D incl. tax high season (June-August); $7/$9 S/D low season. No credit cards.
Directions: 20 yards east of the Plaza de Armas.

Would you like to sleep in a room with original Inca walls? You can do just that at the friendly Loreto, which is literally a stone's throw from the Plaza de Armas and on Calle Loreto, one of the best streets in Cuzco for viewing Inca stonework. An old wooden door painted blue marks the obscure entrance. Upon entering you'll find a small stone courtyard, onto which all nine rooms face. Only those on the lower floor next to the street have the Inca walls. Those on the second floor open onto a wooden balcony lined with potted plants, adding to the colonial ambience.

Rooms vary in size, some being quite large, with three beds; all are carpeted, and have high ceilings, comfortable beds, space heaters upon request, and small but clean private baths. There's also a small bright lobby on the ground floor with five comfortable chairs and carpeting; about the only thing it's good for, however, is watching TV. Breakfast isn't available here, but that's no problem because the most popular breakfast and afternoon tea spot in Cuzco, **Café Ayllu**, is next to the cathedral, a block away. It is open from 6 a.m. and offers classical music, wonderful apple pastries, a wide variety of milk products, and quick service.

One big drawback is that it's difficult to reserve a room in advance here; they will normally accept telephone reservations, but almost never more than a week in advance. You'll find that prices vary considerably, depending on the season.

RESIDENCIAL LOS MARQUESES
Calle Garcilaso 256
Phone (84) 23-2512
Category: B
Colonial-era house with bar.
Rates: $8/$12 S/D incl. 11% tax high season (June-Aug); $5/$7 S/D low season. No credit cards.
Directions: 2½ blocks southwest of the Plaza de Armas, beyond Plaza Regocijo.

If a charming 400-year-old residence sounds like your cup of tea, check Los Marquéses, one of the most picturesque hotels in Cuzco. Like most traditional South American homes, this stone structure, the family home of the Marquéses for years, has a central courtyard with a fountain in the middle (not working) and a wooden second-floor balcony lined with potted plants. There are 15 large rooms, mostly upstairs, each with a unique ornately carved doorway and old style furnishings, including wrought iron lanterns and brass beds. As you're walking up the stone stairwell to the balcony, you'll see a huge mirror that is truly magnificent. Most surprising, however, is the old horse-drawn coach in the courtyard.

In other respects, this old residence suffers a bit. The staff seems lackadaisical, the carpets are thin and frayed, and the private tile baths are functional at best. Don't expect much in the way of service – it's practically non-existent. And count on eating and drinking out; there's no restaurant and the tiny bar doesn't open before 6 p.m. You should, however, sleep well. The mattresses are in fairly good condition and the only noise you're likely to hear is that of creaking planks as guests walk along the balcony. Also, if business is slow, which is often the case, you should be able to bargain down the price a bit.

***Alternative:* CASA SUECIA II**
Calle Tecsecocha. To get to Calle Tecsecocha from the Plaza de Armas, walk one block up Procuradores, then take your first left on Tecsecocha.

If you're looking for a cheaper category C hotel, but one with a little character, try the Suecia II. It's a beautiful colonial house and the rooms have comfortable beds, although not all have private baths. This friendly place is two blocks northwest of the plaza, opposite the Inca World Hostel. Look for the blue door; there's no sign. If it's full, try the sister hostel, **CASA SUECIA I**, several blocks to the east at Calle Suecia 332.

The Sacred Valley Of The Incas

(El Valle Sagrado de los Incas)

HOSTAL ALHAMBRA III
Km 65, Yucay
Phone (84) 22-0204
Cuzco phone (84) 22-4322/2122
Cuzco telex 52218
Lima phone (14) 47-8776; ***fax*** (14) 46-6767
Category: A
Restored 19th-century monastery, 53 rooms.
Rates: $38/$50 S/D incl. 16% tax. All major credit cards.
Directions: In the center of Yucay, northwest of Cuzco (65 km via Pisac) and four km before Urubamba on the paved Cuzco-Pisac-Urubamba Highway.

The finest hotel in the Sacred Valley, the Alhambra III, sister of Hostal Alhambra II in Cuzco, is a wonderful place to pass a few days while visiting the nearby markets and Inca ruins. It dates back to the early 19th century when it was constructed as a monastery, but since 1977 it has operated as a hotel. The management here is very friendly and professional, so the chances are that you'll be pleased with the service.

If you're more interested in having a unique experience than in sleeping comfort, reserve one of the rooms in the old section where the monks slept. Their beds are still there; the only difference is that the beds have comfortable mattresses now. As you might expect, the rooms are cell-like and dark, some without windows. Just outside your door on the second floor, however, is a covered balcony lined with potted plants and with comfortable wicker chairs and sofas. At night it is lit by small wrought iron lamps hanging from the ceiling and, during the day, the views of the nearby mountains are splendid from here. You can also visit a small textile museum on this floor.

On the ground level you'll find two rooms that have been converted into a wonderful bar; it often hops on weekends during the evening. One section has numerous sofas with colorful cushions. Stained-glass windows fill the room with color at night. Somewhat more rustic is the adjoining bar. It has an attractive brick floor, an old upright piano and, most unusual, 90 old stirrups hanging from the exposed beams. During the chillier months, you'll want to head here after sundown, as the small fireplace in this room really heats the place up.

This original section, with its stone courtyard wooden arches, is clearly the most attractive part of the hotel, but for sleeping most guests prefer the new section in back. The architecture is similar, but the rooms are far more comfortable and are not so small or spartan – exposed-beam ceilings, floor-length draperies, tile floors and, most important, comfortable reading chairs and beds as well as space heaters. The tile bathrooms with combination baths are also entirely modern. If you want real luxury, ask for a room in the newest section; quite sizeable, they have sofas, desks, large closets and baths.

In this new section you'll also find a simple old chapel and a cockfighting ring; for a price, they'll arrange a fight. The hostel's major restaurant is also here. On Thursdays and especially Sundays, when there is a lunch buffet served on the patio to the strains of local music, it is a very popular attraction for tourists coming from the Indian market at Pisac. (While in Pisac, stop by **Frank's Café** at Avenida Pardo 619; all the proceeds go to the Emergency Care for Children program.) That's about the only time that your stay at this charming and exceedingly tranquil place will be the least bit disturbed.

HOSTAL TURKESA
Urubamba
No phone
Mail: Box 606, Cuzco
Wire: Turkesa Urubamba
Category: A
Old *hacienda* with 21 rooms. Unheated pool, water only during summer months.
Rates: $27/$35 incl. 16% tax. No credit cards, but some travelers checks are accepted.
Directions: About 53 km from Cuzco via the new road to Urubamba (65 km via Pisac), at the eastern entrance to Urubamba on the Urubamba-Yucay-Pisac Highway. It's about 3 km beyond Hostal Alhambra III, which is on the same road, and a 15-minute walk from the heart of Urubamba.

A lovely old *hacienda* on the outskirts of Urubamba, the Turkesa, previously called the Naranjachayoc, is a popular lunch stop for tourist buses on the Sacred Valley circuit, but it's also a great place to stay for the evening. The main horseshoe-shaped building, owned for years by the Figeroa family, is quite old and a typical *hacienda* of its era – white walls, paned windows, a red tile roof and a dark wooden balcony. Inside, the rooms are fairly small and spartan, but attractive nonetheless, with wooden floors painted red, exposed beam ceilings, wrought iron lighting fixtures, wooden chairs, plus colorful curtains and flowered bedspreads, which add a bit of warmth. Adjoining each room is a small tile bath with hot-water showers.

A good place to unwind is the upstairs living room. It has a view of the garden below and the mountains in the distance. There are numerous comfortable chairs and a sofa, all attractively upholstered; the numerous plants and the fireplace give this room a decidedly warm ambience. Nevertheless, during the day the temperature is often warmer outside, so many guests prefer the garden. It is full of flowers and is a good place for relaxing, reading or sunning. Lying on the grass or sitting at a wooden picnic table on one of the sawed-off tree trunks that serve as seats, you will hear the soothing sounds of a nearby stream. Part of this area is shaded and, if you look hard, you'll see a scarlet red macaw in one of the trees; watching one of these jungle creatures can be fascinating. This particular bird loves to say "hola," so say it once and chances are he'll respond in like fashion.

Most people who stop at the Turkesa come just to eat; the restaurant and bar, which often have roaring fires, are in a new section completely separate from the *hacienda*, with walls of glass overlooking the garden. The Sunday lunch buffet is very popular. Up to 80 people can be seated at a time. King fish (*pejerrey*), fried or à la meunière, is the specialty of the house; the trout (*trucha*) here is also fabulous, but it comes from Lake Titicaca and is frequently not available.

If you come for a meal, don't fail to check out the *hacienda* because a night or two here could be quite memorable, especially when combined with some sightseeing of the ruins and markets in the Sacred Valley. If you do stay here, for a change of scenery you might walk into town and have an excellent and plentiful $3 lunch at **Quinta Los Geranios**, a partially open-air restaurant 150 meters before the main intersection.

EL ALBERGUE

Ollantaytambo, Cuzco phone (84) 22-6671 (Expediciones Manu at Procuradores 50, Cuzco); Cuzco fax (84) 23-6706 (Expediciones Manu).
Category: B
Rates: $15 per person, full board. No credit cards, but will change money.
Directions: One km south of downtown Ollantaytambo, very near the Río Urubamba and just before the railway station.

The Albergue is hardly plush, but if you're looking for an interesting experience and don't mind roughing it a little, this charming place is highly recommended. It's a rustic lodge run by a delightfully friendly North American, Wendy Weeks. With her husband (now deceased), she has been guiding adventure seekers on some true wilderness experiences in the Inca heartland since the mid-1970's. As a result, the clientele, mostly from the US, has tended to be quite adventuresome, taking week-long trips into the hinterland. More recently,travelers from across the world have been arriving. The Albergue is clean, the meals (full board is the norm) are wholesome, the sounds of the nearby Urubamba river are wonderful, and the management is tops. Otherwise, don't expect too much. For a shower you'll have to use a bucket of cold water. There is, however, one luxury – a sauna – which is free and may be used at any time.

Alternative: **HOSTAL URPIHUASI**

Urubamba, no phone

If the Albergue is full, your best bet among the less expensive hostels in the Sacred Valley is Hostal Urpihuasi in Urubamba, which is about 20 km away and comparably priced, with full board rates. The owner, Rae Pieraccini, is a very friendly man, and you'll have the satisfaction of knowing that the profits he makes from your stay will go mainly toward financing a project for street children. This quiet and relaxing place is quite clean, with modern rooms, a pool and even a sauna!

Machu Picchu

HOTEL DE TURISTAS

Ruinas de Machu Picchu
Cuzco phone (84) 22-3339 (Emp. Turistica Regional Inka)
Cuzco fax (84) 22-3239
Cuzco telex 52008
Lima phone (14) 42-8696/72-1929 (Entur Peru)
Category: A
Modern, 31-room hotel just outside the ruins.
Rates: $60/$75 S/D plus 18% tax. No credit cards, but accepts AmEx Traveler's Checks.
Directions: At the entrance to the ruins.

At the entrance to Machu Picchu, far above the Urubamba River, sits the Turistas. It is the only hotel at the site of the ruins. Tourists swarm to them daily between 10 a.m. (when the tourist train arrives from Cuzco) and 2 p.m. (when they must start heading down the hill to catch the train back). For many travelers, the opportunity of seeing the ruins without hoards of people around is well worth the price of staying here overnight. This will allow you to view the ruins from 7:30 a.m., when the gates open, to 10 a.m., and from 2:30 p.m. to dusk, in relative tranquillity.

One wonders whether the hotel's architect ever visited the ruins because, except for being constructed of the local rock, this modern structure is totally lacking in inspiration from the surroundings. Even the location, which the architect probably could not control, is far from ideal. The hotel is alongside and slightly below the ruins, so you can't even see them very well. However, this is more than made up for by the inspirational views of the steep surrounding mountains, which are often shrouded, almost mystically, in clouds or mist.

The hotel's rooms, which have carpets, wood and leather chairs, iron beds, clean baths and space heaters upon request, are unexceptional, but some have good views, in particular rooms 10, 16, 18, 20 and 22. When guests are not visiting the ruins, they generally can be found at the cafeteria, which is commodious and offers fine views, but unexceptional food at outrageously high prices – $13 for an American breakfast. There is also an interior sitting area, which has large windows for viewing the mountains. This is where you're most likely to meet other travelers, as the ambience here is warm and the setting, with a fireplace, carpets, wood ceilings and local arts and crafts, is fairly intimate.

The hotel is always heavily booked during the tourist season, June through August and around Christmas time, and is often full at other times as well, so reserve as far in advance as possible. Often, however, you can arrive at the hotel even when it's theoretically full and find a room available due to a late cancellation.

***Alternative:* MACHU PICCHU PUEBLO HOTEL**
Aguas Calientes, phone (84) 22-0803, Cuzco phone (84) 23-2161 (Calle Procuradores 48), Lima phone (14) 46-1915, Lima fax (14) 45-5598 (Calle Andalucía 174, Miraflores)

This new upmarket hotel in Aguas Calientes has nicer and similarly-priced rooms with private hot-water showers, but the views are not the same. The hotel consists of 25 white-stucco bungalows set in a garden, plus a comfortable lounge and an expensive restaurant, all overlooking the Urubamba River.

GRINGO BILL'S (Hostal Qoñi Unu)
Aguas Calientes. No phone.
Category: C
15 rooms/35 single beds, English spoken, restaurant, laundry, no reservations.
Rates: $5/person, cash only.
Directions: One short block behind, and up the hill from, the train depot in Aguas Calientes, the third house to the left of the church. Only the local train stops at Aguas Calientes, a village 1½ km before the Machu Picchu stop. Those taking the tourist train must walk back alongside the tracks towards Cuzco for 20-25 minutes to reach Aguas Calientes. From Gringo Bill's to the ruins is a 1½-hour hike, mostly uphill.

If hotels were rated on a fun scale, Gringo Bill's, which is near the bottom on the luxury scale, would be right at the top of hotels in South America. Owned by American William Kaiser and his Peruvian wife Margarita, who left Peru in the late 1980's, the mountain-side "Hostal Qoñi Unu," better known as Gringo Bill's, is unquestionably the place to stay in Aguas Calientes. It has a lot more character than the Hotel de Turistas at the ruins, which is tops in terms of accommodations and location.

The managers here, who change every so often, are almost invariably young foreigners and very friendly. They're also trusting – help yourself to drinks from the refrigerator, just remember what you take. So it's hardly surprising that this laid-back *hostal* has become a meeting place for travelers on the cheap from all over the world and especially for Americans, Brits, Germans and the French.

The stone wall rooms, many with psychedelic murals, are just big enough for the beds to fit into. The mattresses are reasonably comfortable and the units are clean, as are the common bathrooms, which now have showers with electric heating attachments. Try to get one of the newer rooms upstairs. All the others are quite cramped (like all other quarters in this crowded mountain-side village, whose occupants service Machu Picchu) and not as good value. Most guests unwind in the open-air dining area, where there's a good view of the steep verdant mountains surrounding the area.

For breakfast, there are a number of choices, including orange juice, pancakes with honey, and oatmeal with bananas. The dinner menu, on the other hand, tends to be – quite sensibly – more limited, typically pizza and spaghetti; both dishes are excellent. Their preparation can sometimes take up to an hour, but guests are usually so wound up talking to one another that no one seems to mind. For $2, they'll also pack you a lunch to take to the ruins. When guests aren't eating, drinking or chatting here or visiting Machu Picchu, they're usually at the warm springs the other end of town. Soaking there costs only 50¢. Gringo Bill's also offers a place to store your luggage.

All in all, this is a delightful surprise and, while Machu Picchu hardly needs anything else to make a trip there memorable, staying at Gringo Bill's will almost certainly add to your adventure. Let's hope the Kaisers never let go of this gem; if they do, the good vibes may go as well. There's no phone, but if you meet someone heading that way before you, you could give them some money to pre-pay a room. Otherwise, you'll have to take your chances; just make sure you make a bee-line for the hotel when you get off the local train, which leaves early in the morning and, unlike the tourist train, stops in Aguas Calientes.

***First Alternative:* HOSTAL MACHU PICCHU**
Aguas Calientes, no phone

If Gringo Bill's is full, which is often the case, and an occasionally noisy, state-run youth hostel isn't your cup of tea, try the Hostal Machu Picchu, which is in the same price range and by the railway station, with a balcony over the Urubamba grocery store. The place is clean and quiet, with hot-water showers, and the people are very friendly, especially Wilber, the owner's son, who is a good source of travel information.

Second Alternative: **ALBERGUE JUVENIL**
Aguas Calientes, no phone. You'll find it on the main road through town, about half way up the hill from the railway station towards the hot springs.

Who would ever guess that a 64-room, 210-bed youth hostel, one of the largest in South America, would be located in such a small village as Aguas Calientes. The rooms, both dormitories and private rooms, are modern, fairly large, comfortable and presentable. The bathrooms, however, are often dirty and noise can be a problem when there are lots of Peruvian students on vacation. Filling this hostel is almost impossible, so even during the high season you won't need to worry about finding a place to stay. The price of a bed is about the same as Gringo Bill's and Hostal Machu Picchu.

Puno

HOTEL ISLA ESTEVES
Isla Esteves, Puno
Phone (54) 35-2271/3870
Telex 54785
Lima phone (14) 42-8626
(Entur Peru)
Category: A
126 rooms, modern, restaurant, bar.
Rates: \$46/\$64 S/D incl. 16% tax.
All major credit cards.
Directions: 5 km northeast of downtown Puno by paved road.

If having a view of Lake Titicaca is of primary importance, you may prefer the modern Esteves, which is part of the Hotel de Turistas chain. Built in 1979 and well maintained, it is on an island just outside Puno, set magnificently on a cliff overlooking Lake Titicaca. The hotel's public areas, which are quite comfortable, have huge windows, so the views of the lake are wonderful.

The facilities of this massive four-story hotel are tops in Puno. The lobby, for instance, is spacious and impressive, extending four floors upwards, with shiny brick floors and an elevator. The main sitting room is huge, with three levels and no less than 14 sitting areas – all carpeted, with numerous plush sofas and matching armchairs covered in a stylish modern fabric. Several large local tapestries adorn the walls. One of the hotel's two restaurants adjoins this area; the views are great, as they are from the adjoining bar/TV room, but neither area is particularly inviting. They lack carpets and have a distinctively cold feel to them.

The stylish rooms, which are medium size, offer carpeting and small electric space heaters. Each has a telephone, piped-in music, reading lights over the beds, reading chairs, a breakfast table, built-in closets, and modern combination baths.

The Isla Esteves suffers from three major drawbacks – high prices, an isolated location, and a cold ambience – which is why the less expensive Sillustani is more popular despite the Esteves' superior facilities. The latter is well away from the city and you must take a taxi to go anywhere – going out at night to a restaurant or *peña* (bar), for example, is problematic, if not impossible. There is a sterile and austere ambience in the public areas, which are often exceedingly quiet. They are also so large, with usually so few guests, that you'll feel you're the only one staying here. Even the one fireplace in the main sitting room appears to be rarely used.

HOSTAL SILLUSTANI
Jirón Lambayeque 195
Phone (54) 35-2641
Fax (54) 35-1431
Telex 54792
Lima phone (14) 27-6720
Category: A
4 stories, modern, 25 rooms, restaurant, bar.
Rates: $26/$31 S/D incl. 16% tax. All major credit cards.
Directions: 4 blocks south of the railway station in the direction of the Plaza de Armas.

The best managed hotel in Puno, with the friendliest, most helpful staff, is the Sillustani. The ambience here is also tops.

Upon entering the hotel, you'll be struck by the four-story atrium, onto which all the rooms face. As a result, the hotel is very bright inside. There's a sitting area at the bottom, with plants and several vinyl-covered sofas, but the best places to spend your spare time are the cozier sitting areas on each landing. They are carpeted and offer more comfortable sofas and chairs, TVs and, for decoration, plants and large colorful murals by local artists.

The rooms here are quite modern and comfortable. There are attractively covered beds with reading lights, IDD phones, built-in closets, piped-in music, carpets, and modern tile baths with hot-water showers. If your room is a bit cold, ask for an electric space heater.

For meals, you can't do better in Puno than the Sillustani, which has a very popular restaurant. The menu includes lots of choices, but the best ones are invariably fish – *trucha* (trout) fried or, better, *al ajo* (broiled with garlic), and *perjerry* (king fish) in various styles, including steamed with onions and tomatoes. Other selections include chicken *al vino*, filet mignon and steak cordon bleu, all very reasonably priced and served with warm bread. It also offers a variety of desserts, including crèpes. Breakfast is served starting at 6 a.m. and they'll pack you a lunch if you're going on a day trip.

For a change of scenery and/or live music with your meal, you might try **Peña Hostería** nearby at Calle Lima 453; they serve only pizza, but it's good, as is the music. Finally, Turpuno, one of the city's best travel agencies, is located next door to the Sillustani, so you can get all the travel information you need, from trips to Taquile Island, to tickets for the train to Cuzco.

HOTEL ITALIA
Calle Valcarcel 122
Phone (54) 35-2521
Category: B/C
30 rooms, modern facade.
Rates: $10/$16 S/D incl. tax. No credit cards.
Directions: 1½ blocks southwest of the railway station.

Among the cheaper hotels in Puno, the pickings are pretty slim. One possibility is the Italia, which has a helpful staff, a convenient location and is reasonably presentable, although the decor is totally uninspired. The small lobby has several plants, sofas and a bulletin board with information on tours. Adjoining it you'll find a restaurant and TV room. The former has wooden floors, wall decorations, tables with white tablecloths, and serves meals, reportedly good ones, three times a day. The TV room is quite comfortable, if somewhat stark, with a sofa, chairs and a locally-made rug.

The rooms are clean and the two single beds in each are reasonably comfortable, with bedspreads and overhead reading lights. The rooms overall are somewhat barren. There are no decorations on the walls or carpets. They do, however, have space heaters – very important in this frigid town – and the tile baths, though small and cheap with dated fixtures and showers, have hot water 24 hours a day. That is more than many hotels in Puno can claim. Avoid rooms on the first floor, however, as they have no hot water.

Alternative: **EL BUHO**
Jirón Lambayeque 142, phone (54) 35-1409

You could also check out the Buho, which is similarly priced and on the same street as the Sillustani. It too has a friendly staff, rooms with heaters, and baths with a fairly reliable supply of hot water.

Tambopata Wildlife Reserve & Manu National Park

EXPLORER'S INN
Lima: Peruvian Safaris SA, Ave., Garcilaso de la Vega 1334. Lima phone (14) 31-3047/6330; fax (14) 32-8866; telex 20416. Cuzco: Plaza San Francisco 122. Cuzco phone (84) 23-5342
Category: A. 30-room jungle lodge at Tambopata Reserve.
Rates: $150 per person for 2 nights, all-inclusive from Pto. Maldonado; $45 for each night extra (10% discount 12/14-4/14, 10% discount for SAEC members, 7-17% for groups of 5 or more, 35% for children 6-12). All major credit cards.
Directions: The lodge is on the edge of Tambopata Wildlife Nature Reserve, which is about 45 km as the crow flies southwest of Puerto Maldonado. By motorized canoe, it is 58 km (3 hours) up the Tambopata River from Puerto Maldonado, which is a 25-minute flight from Cuzco. Guests are met at the airport in Puerto Maldonado. The flight arrives around 10 or 11 a.m., so you get to the lodge mid-afternoon. Coming back, you leave the lodge around 5 a.m. to catch the 9 a.m. plane to Cuzco and Lima.

The Tambopata Reserve, east of Cuzco in the Amazon Basin and in 1990 enlarged to include the Candamo Wildlife Reserve, is famous worldwide for having, in an area of its size, the greatest diversity of wildlife yet discovered anywhere on the globe! So if you have the time and money and you're a bird watcher or interested in rainforests, a trip here (or to nearby Manu National Park) is likely to be the trip of a lifetime. The Tambopata section of the reserve has more species of birds (over 570), butterflies (over 1,200) and many other animals than any other location of its size (13,600 acres) on earth. Pumas, jaguars, tapir, capybara, monkeys, otters, black caiman, giant anteaters and other mammals are all sighted from time to time. However, mammals in general are not easily spotted in the rainforests, so don't expect to see large numbers of them on a short trip here. But it's the bird life – above all, the macaws – that stands out for most visitors. Macaws are the largest of the parrots and there are seven species here, including the incomparable scarlet macaw. There are also 11 other species of parrots in Tambopata. You're guaranteed to see lots of macaws, as they often flock together with other parrots and toucans. Such riotous faunal diversity is due to the reserve's privileged location at the meeting point of lowland Amazonia with three other ecosystems, including Andean foothills, dry forest, and pampas grassland. For the same reason, at least seven major forest types are found here.

The Tambopata section was set aside as a reserve by the Peruvian Government in 1977, which is when Max Gunther, a German, founded the Explorer's Inn. Since then, this lodge, also one of the main research centers for scientific work in the Amazon Basin, has become a favorite destination for ornithologists the world over. It also attracts photographers, researchers, biology students, adventurers and just people who enjoy nature – mostly Americans and Germans, plus a few Brits, French and, occasionally, Peruvians.

The lodge is several hundred yards from the river, so the views from this spacious place are restricted. Seven separate thatched-roof bungalows surround a central, octagonal, two-story building where guests and resident naturalists dine and socialize. Meals here are family style and quite good, with lots of fresh produce provided by a nearby farmer. There is also a small reference library so guests can learn more about what they see. Like many jungle lodges in Peru, the inn, though modern and comfortable, is made from local materials – wood and palm thatch – to the traditional design, with the worthwhile addition of screens. In all, there are 30 rooms with twin beds and private bathrooms, all lit by candlelight to maintain a natural atmosphere. There's no hot water, but in the jungle who needs it! Also, the beds do not have mosquito nets, but the rooms are screened.

A number of pet animals wander freely around the lodge, including several macaws, a tapir and two miniature wild boars. If you don't close your door, one of the macaws may try to get into your room! Near the lodge, you'll find an interesting small garden containing medicinal plants used in traditional medicine, such as quinine and ayahuasca, an important hallucinogenic vine. During the day, when you're not out on a guided tour, you can go swimming in the murky red waters of the river – the crocs are asleep then and the piranha are only found near the shore!

A trail network 30 km long stretches through the reserve and to several oxbow-shaped lakes. The trails are sufficiently well marked that you can go out alone, but without a guide you'll miss a lot. Indeed, one of the best features of the lodge is the outstanding staff, which includes English-speaking resident naturalists who study at the reserve in return for acting as guides. In short, you're assured of having a very enlightening trip, even more so when there are other guests, as they are often researchers or nature specialists. The reserve and this lodge, which plays a critical role in the ongoing research, offer travelers ecotourism at its best – a unique opportunity to see and experience scientific research, tourism and rainforest conservation combined for mutual benefit.

MANU LODGE

Manu Nature Tours, Avenida Sol 528, Cuzco
Cuzco phone (84) 22-4384
Cuzco fax (84) 23-4793
Cuzco telex 52003
In the US (800) 327-0080
Category: A
Jungle lodge at Manu Park.
Rates: $674 (groups of 6) to $1719 (groups of 2) per person for a 4-day/3-night package tour incl. roundtrip charter flights from Cuzco. $1988 per person package tour incl. airfare from Miami on Faucett Airlines. All major credit cards.

Directions: The lodge is on the edge of Manu Park, which is northeast of Cuzco and west of Puerto Maldonado. Most visitors arrive by chartered plane from Cuzco, but Manu Nature Tours offers the choice of traveling overland from Cuzco (a 2-day trip), incl. the option of going one way overland and the other way by air.

Declared a Biosphere Reserve by UNESCO in 1977, Manu National Park, which covers 4.5 million acres, is the largest tropical park in South America and one of the most pristine in the world. There's nothing like it in all of South America except for Tambopata, which is smaller and to the southeast. Like Tambopata, the park encompasses a wide variety of habitats, ranging from high altitude grassland to the Amazon rainforest. Thanks to this protection and its larger area, one can find in Manu an even greater diversity of flora and fauna, indeed the greatest diversity in the world. The wildlife here includes many of the same species found in Tambopata, but also includes pumas, jaguars, giant otters, black caimans, tapir, capybara, and 11 species of monkeys. The superlatives sound like a repeat of those of Tambopata which, remember, is smaller. There are more species of birds (over 1,000) and plants (over 15,000) here than in any other area of comparable size in the world.

The star attraction of Manu is the macaw; indeed, the park has one of the most spectacular colpas (macaw mineral licks) in South America, attracting 70 or more wild macaws at a time. There are seven species of macaws (the largest of which are blue and yellow, scarlet, and red and green). They begin mating in December, and fierce battles between rival males, sometimes lasting for several days, often occur. If you see some that look a little scruffy during that period, it's probably because of this. You'll learn many more interesting facts about macaws – one of the most intelligent birds on earth.

Manu Lodge is the only hotel in the section of Manu that is reserved for ecotourism. All other hotels are in the "cultural" section, where the locals live. On the edge of the park, the lodge overlooks a tranquil, two-km-long lake, which is 180 yards wide and surrounded by huge vine-festooned tropical trees. Herons, kingfishers, hoatzins, monkeys and giant otters may be seen from the canoes that visitors must take to reach the lodge. On the edge of the lake is a colpa (a mineral lick) were you can occasionally see rare game birds, such as razor-billed curassows and piping guans, in addition to macaws.

The hotel's facilities are of traditional design and are comparable to those of the Explorer's Inn. The rooms have private baths and bunk beds with mosquito nets. One difference is that the views from the lodge here are much better. From the upstairs bar, visitors can get a panoramic view of the lake and surroundings; then they can walk out on a short pier leading from the hotel for a closer look. The trade-off is that guests cannot intermingle as closely with researchers as they do at the Explorer's Inn. Manu Nature Tours' guides, however, are top notch, and if you come here overland from Cuzco (a two-day trip) and return by air, you're sure to have an even more interesting trip. The scenery along the way is magnificent and diverse.

***Alternative:* EXPEDICIONES MANU**
Procuradores 50, Cuzco, phone (84) 22-6671, fax (84) 23-6706

Owned by ornithologist Barry Walker, this small personalized expedition company offers camping trips into the same protected section of Manu Park where Manu Lodge is situated. Camping with Barry, you are sure to experience the rainforests much more in-depth, if less comfortably, and you will see a greater variety of wildlife. For the truly adventurous, this is the only way to go.

Iquitos

EXPLORAMA INN, LODGE & CAMP
Office: Ave Col Portillo block 3
Phone (94) 23-5471
Fax (94) 23-4968
Telex 91014
Lima office: Jirón Camaná 851; ***phone*** (14) 24-4764
USA phone (800) 223-6764 (SHR)
Category: Deluxe & A
Three separate jungle lodges.
Rates: $230 all-inclusive package for 3 days/2 nights incl. airport shuttle and river transport. All major credit cards.
Directions: The Explorama Inn is 40 km (1½ hours by boat) downstream of Iquitos on the Amazon River, and the Explorama Lodge is 40 km further downstream (2½ hours from Iquitos) at Yanamono, near where the Napo River flows into the Amazon. There is also a more rustic Explorama Camp, which is up the Napo and on a tributary, the Sucusari, 160 km from Iquitos (5 hours). Guests with reservations are met at Iquitos airport and transferred to a riverboat for the trip downstream to one of the lodges.

The areas along the Amazon River are much more civilized than those in Manu or Tambopata; therefore travelers going to Iquitos for a jungle experience should not expect to see as much wildlife or pristine rainforests as in those places. However, with a few exceptions, the many lodges along the river tend to be more accessible and travelers here get the added advantage of boating on the mighty Amazon, which from Iquitos on down becomes very wide indeed.

There are lots of jungle tour operators based in Iquitos that have lodges along the Amazon River. However, considering the cost of getting here, you might as well pay a little more and go with the best one, Explorama Tours, which is also the oldest, largest and most reliable of the operators. In operation since the mid-1960's when two enterprising American anthropologists set up the Explorama Lodge at Yanamono, it now has three separate jungle lodges. The newest, Explorama Inn, inaugurated in 1985, is the closest to Iquitos and the most luxurious of the three, with electric lights and running water. Guests also enjoy the comfort and privacy of their own separate cottage. Each is quite attractive and of traditional jungle-style design, with a steep palm-thatched roof, split-palm floors and walls, and a small porch with a view of the river. All are screened and have fans, twin single beds with mosquito nets, private baths, running water and lights. A large dining room, bar and patio for lounging are all housed in a screened, 160-foot central pavilion. You can get excellent food at the restaurant and the bar has a folkloric show every night. There's less fauna in this area than at the Lodge and Camp, but you're guaranteed to see monkeys and lots of birds. A variety of guided excursions are available, including jungle hikes and canoe trips to neighboring villages.

The Lodge, the original of Explorama's lodges, is further downriver and a much better place for viewing fauna and birds. Larger and more rustic, it has eight separate buildings, including a hammock house, and can sleep well over 100 guests at a time. Five of the *casas* are long thatched-roof structures with 10-17 bedrooms each, 72 altogether. Kerosene lamps light the rooms, which are screened with mosquito nets over the beds, and walkways lead to the shared toilets and showers nearby, as well as to the central dining room and adjoining bar.

The best of all, and even more remote, is Explorama Camp, which is located on the Sucusari, a small tributary of the Napo. It's now the most popular of the three, especially with bird watchers and visitors staying for a week or more. It offers the chance of seeing the elusive hoatzin, the horned screamer, the great potoo and the wood stork, as well as jungle birds more commonly seen, such as macaws, hawks and toucans. In all, close to 600 species of birds have been spotted by guests in the area of the lodges.

The facilities here, which are the most primitive of the three establishments, consist of thatched open houses with dormitory sleeping, kerosene lighting and open-hearth cooking. There are excellent shared bathroom and shower facilities. The best recent innovation is a fantastic canopy walkway some 35 feet above the forest floor and 450 yards long; visitors can walk along it for a much closer view of the birds and other tree wildlife.

With a reservation, you'll be met at the airport and whisked away to the river, but if you're willing to take a slight risk and arrive without booking ahead, you may be able to save money. The reason is competition – at the airport, all of the jungle lodges have representatives fighting for business, and independent travelers who are willing to bargain can usually get better deals.

***First Alternative:* AMAZON CAMP TOURIST SERVICE**
Requena 336, phone (94) 23-3931, fax (94) 23-1265, USA phone (800) 423-2791

This slightly less expensive, American-owned company has one lodge, Amazon Camp, which is far too close to Iquitos to be of any interest, but it also has a more rustic Camp Amazonia, which is further away and better located. This outfit offers a greater variety of excursions, including cruises on the Amazon and rugged expeditions to various jungle campsites.

***Second Alternative:* HOTEL ACOSTA 2**
Calle Ricardo Palma 252, phone (94) 23-2904

For a category A hotel in Iquitos, try the Acosta 2. It's a modern 40-room hotel two blocks from the Plaza de Armas and near the river. It's nothing special, but it has what's necessary – air-conditioned rooms, carpeting and TVs, hot showers, a pool and a good restaurant – and it's a better buy ($38/$45 S/D) than the city's top hotel, the **AMAZONAS** ($50/$55 S/D, phone/fax 94-23-1091/23-5811), which is inconveniently located three miles out of town.

Before booking a room, you might check the new **EL DORADO** on Napo Street, half a block from the Plaza de Armas. It is similarly priced and has comparable facilities to Acosta 2, including a pool and cable TVs, but it's newer and preferred by some travelers. Those on a tight budget should try the much less expensive sister hotel, **HOSTAL ACOSTA 1** (phone 94-23-1761), which is five blocks north of the Plaza de Armas on Calvo de Araujo; it has no pool but the quality of the rooms is similar.

***Third Alternative:* HOSTAL LA PASCANA**
Calle Pevas 133

For a much less expensive category B hotel in Iquitos, your best bet is the Pascana, a very popular B&B that has rooms with fans and cold showers, a breakfast area, a TV lounge and a garden. It's eight blocks north of the Plaza de Armas and near the river, with rooms priced between $10 and $15.